Geopolitics and Energy Transition 1

Geopolitics and Energy Transition 1

The Basics

Jean-Pierre Favennec
with the collaboration of
Matthew Van der Beeuren

iSTE

WILEY

First published 2024 in Great Britain and the United States by ISTE Ltd and John Wiley & Sons, Inc.

ISTE Ltd
27-37 St George's Road
London SW19 4EU
UK

www.iste.co.uk

John Wiley & Sons, Inc.
111 River Street
Hoboken, NJ 07030
USA

www.wiley.com

Library of Congress Control Number: 2024937859

British Library Cataloguing-in-Publication Data
A CIP record for this book is available from the British Library
ISBN 978-1-78630-970-9

Contents

Foreword to *Géopolitique de l'énergie* Published in 2008 – A Tribute to Jean-Marie Chevalier

This book arrives just in time: energy has been in the headlines for several years. The sharp increase in the barrel price in the first six months of 2008, followed by its drop, the growing energy demand followed by its recent decline, the supply threats (due to tensions and attacks in some producer countries, accidents, etc.), the debates on reserves and, above all, the climate change threat are all in the news.

The energy range is broad (oil, gas, coal, nuclear, hydroelectricity, wind, solar), but these energies are often replaceable, and from now on all these energies will be needed. There is a rich literature dealing with oil and geopolitics. This book focuses on the geopolitical aspects of energy, in which oil obviously plays an important role.

This book presents a clear overview of various stakes of the energy sector: how various energies are generated, what their future is, who the players in the energy sector are, what the supply constraints are and what the significant characteristics of the various world regions are.

This book is organized into two volumes: Volume 1 presents the most important characteristics of the energy sector; Volume 2 includes a region-by-region analysis of the stakes and a detailed presentation of the political aspects.

Volume 1[1] is composed of four chapters.

---

1 *Geopolitics and Energy Transition 1: The Basics*.

The first chapter describes the major sources of energy, indicates the production and processing techniques, and provides a certain number of economic elements.

The second chapter covers the various aspects of the energy transition.

The third chapter focuses on an analysis of prices, demand and resources: while many geopolitical and financial factors (the role of pension fund investments, for example) influence prices, offer and demand remain fundamental elements. This chapter ends with an analysis of constraints related to environmental protection at the local, regional and global levels: climate change will heavily impact the global energy consumption and the structure of the future "energy mix".

The fourth chapter is dedicated to the structures of the companies and organizations involved in the energy sector. There have been many spectacular evolutions. The oil sector was developed by a limited group of large private companies – the Majors – until 1960. The situation changed as result of the creation of OPEC, and of the nationalizations in the 1970s. The size of the large national companies in producing countries, which often have a quasi-monopoly over the resources on their territory, is equivalent to and even greater than the size of large international companies. The companies operating in the gas and electrical sectors have also been subjected to many structural evolutions. After World War II, small private companies operating on a limited territory were replaced by powerful national companies operating over large spaces in order to benefit from the advantages of natural monopoly. For over 40 years, Americans and Europeans, followed by many emerging economies, have been involved in policies aimed at establishing active competition, leading to the end of monopolies, the appearance of new players and a proactive deregulation policy.

The fourth chapter also deals with supply security and the means to ensure it. While in the 1990s, the best way to ensure stable energy supplies seemed to be the improvement of market operations, current tensions justify the active intervention of the national states. The Americans and the Chinese, for example, have developed a strong oil diplomacy, and Moscow makes no secret of its willingness to use energy as a weapon in its relations with European and Asian neighbors.

Volume 2[2] deals with the situation of each large part of the globe, continent or region (such as the Commonwealth of Independent States (CIS)/Russia or the Middle East) that plays a particularly important role in the world energy scene.

---

2 *Geopolitics and Energy Transition 2: From One Continent to Another, Contrasting Situations.*

North America stands out for its very significant energy consumption, high and increasing oil imports, significant gas consumption, high coal consumption for power generation, and significant needs for production facility renewal in the electrical sector. Due to its needs and power, North America is a key zone.

The energy sector in South America is dominated by several countries: with a barrel at over $100, Venezuela has recovered a power that was recently deeply altered. Brazil, the geographical and economic giant, is a key player in the oil and gas game. The nationalizations of the gas industry in 2006 in Bolivia did not cause significant stirs, as the wave that brought to power left-wing leaders (of very different orientations) in various countries banned too violent conflicts. However, the tensions between the ambitions of Venezuela, whose aim is to become the leader of South America, at least in the energy sector, and those of other countries are latent.

Europe consumes and imports a lot of energy, and its dependence will increase. The Middle East will eventually become once again a major oil supplier, which the European diplomacy will have to take into account. The very important role of Russia in the European gas imports is a concern for the governments. Europe, the major partner in the Kyoto protocol, must also address its increasing needs by limiting CO_2 emissions, while some countries have decided to reduce their nuclear energy production.

The CIS – in which Russia plays an essential role – is once again a major player on the energy scene. Having extremely abundant reserves of oil, gas and coal, Russia is a massive exporter of oil and gas, and can arbitrate its supplies between Americans, Europeans and Asians, sometimes threatening one or the other to change the destination of exportations. The relations with the Europeans, the main gas purchasers, are especially critical. The Europeans expect the monopoly of Gazprom to be transformed – which the Russians refuse – while Gazprom would like to achieve participation in some European companies, which is opposed by European governments. Coal is still very widely used, and this does not allow the exportation of the maximum amount of oil and gas, which are more profitable.

Africa's weight in terms of energy consumption is very low. Only South Africa and, to a lesser extent, the North African countries are significant consumers. However, most sub-Saharan African countries have very low energy demands, with the exception perhaps of Nigeria, due to its huge population. In contrast, North Africa and West Africa are important producers of oil and gas. West Africa, which is undoubtedly the most open zone to foreign companies, has attracted many interests: Americans and Chinese are playing a wide poker game in that region, where most companies are present.

Asia, which has over half of the world population, is the region with the greatest increase in energy demand due to the extraordinary economic growth in China and, to a lesser extent, in India and in neighboring countries. This increase is at the core of the energy issue: the needs of Asia weigh on the demand and on the production capacities and, consequently, on prices. However, it would be absurd to hold this region responsible for the current difficulties, as the consumption per inhabitant remains low there. It is consumption by Western countries that is incompatible with reserves and productions. Tensions are, however, high between the large consumers to secure their future supply.

The Middle East remains the key area for oil supplies and it covers the fuel needs of many countries, especially Asian ones. There are many geopolitical tensions in the region. The Israeli–Palestinian conflict is certainly at the core of these tensions: the Israeli intervention in Lebanon and the war with Hezbollah in 2006, as well as the events in Gaza in 2009, testify to the intensity of the conflict. In the short and medium term, the oil and gas of the Middle East will become increasingly important, as this region is the only one that can cope with the increasing needs of the planet.

The conclusion of this book is that energy will continue to be in the spotlight. While for several dozen years, there have been few significant transformations in this sector, revolutionary changes and even breakthroughs will be needed to meet, in particular, the needs of emerging countries and the climate change constraints.

Jean-Marie CHEVALIER
Director of the Centre de géopolitique
de l'énergie et des matières premières
2008

Introduction

Why energy?

The main uses of energy are heating and transportation. Energy can be generated from oil, natural gas, coal, nuclear energy, hydroelectricity, biomass and renewable sources (wind, solar, etc.). The total global energy consumption (including firewood) reached 15 billion tons of oil equivalent (France consumes around 260 million tons of oil equivalent). Roughly speaking, nearly 20% of the energy is used for transportation, and nearly 80% of it, in various forms, is used for heat generation (for residential uses – heating, cooking, air conditioning – and for industrial uses, as well as for electric power generation).

To a large extent, the needs of the transportation sector are still met by oil products, but the energy transition is leading to a rapid development of electrical vehicles. Oil products have two advantages: they are liquid, and therefore easily accessible, and they have a high energy density. Filling a tank with gasoline or diesel fuel at the gas station takes two or three minutes, and provides autonomy for several hundred kilometers. Charging the batteries of an electric vehicle or filling the tanks with compressed gas takes a longer time. However, because of the necessity to reduce greenhouse gas emissions, searching for alternatives to fuel petroleum products is essential.

Heat can be generated from all the types of energy. In some cases, in order to limit the emissions of polluting products, less polluting fuels are chosen, such as gas or light petroleum products. In many cases, the choice will be dictated by practical and economic reasons (e.g. coal is no longer used as fuel for residential heating because it is much easier to use heating oil and natural gas).

Brief historical review of energy uses

Due to scarce resources, energy consumption was at a low level until the 18th century. Energy was essentially generated by human force, animal force, watermills and windmills, and the energy released by wood combustion. Industrial development, whose needs exceeded the limited wood resources, led to the invention of the steam engine fueled with coal. Oil was discovered around 1860, but it had no significant use prior to the first decades of the 20th century (invention of heat engines, gasoline or diesel fuel engines, massive use of fuel oil after 1945). Nuclear energy came next. Wind and solar energy became significant in the 21st century.

Starting in 1945, there was a huge increase in energy consumption. Until 2000, this increase was concentrated in industrialized countries – members of the Organization for Economic Cooperation and Development (OECD), which included until 1990 the United States, Canada, Japan, Australia, New Zealand and Western European countries (Germany, Austria, Belgium, Spain, Finland, France, Greece, Ireland, Island, Italy, Luxembourg, Norway, the Netherlands, Portugal, the United Kingdom, Sweden, Switzerland, Turkey). At the end of the 20th century, the population of these countries counted 1 billion (the global population being 6 billion) people, but accounted for half of the global energy consumption. This trend was reversed by the rapid development of China and the progress of other emerging countries. Countries outside OECD now account for 70% of the global energy demand.

Energy and climate change

Global warming and the resulting climate change have been a major concern for several years. Already mentioned in the preface to the book *Géopolitique de l'énergie* published in 2007, of which this book is a continuation, climate change has become an undeniable reality. Most of the past few years have been the hottest ever observed since the beginning of meteorological records. In the summer of 2021, temperatures exceeded 50°C in Eastern Canada. California and Australia experienced extremely long periods of drought that led to rarely seen fires.

Global warming has now been accepted as a reality by all scientists, and only some conspiracy theorists are denying this reality. The works of the Intergovernmental Panel on Climate Change (IPCC) are no longer disputed. Only the magnitude of the consequences of climate change is still under debate.

Rising temperatures are obviously due to increasing greenhouse gas emissions that retain the heat which is normally reemitted to the space (in the absence of greenhouse gases, Earth's temperature would be –18°C). Also, energy is to a large extent responsible for these emissions. We use various sources of energy: wind energy, solar energy, hydraulic energy, nuclear energy, etc., but the main part of our energy consumption relies on fossil fuels – oil, coal and natural gas – representing about 80% of our total consumption. However, these energies are obtained from carbon-based fuels whose combustion generates heat, and carbon is then transformed into carbon dioxide (CO_2), the most important greenhouse gas. Methane (natural gas consists mainly of methane), another significant greenhouse gas, results essentially from gas leakages during the production or transportation of the natural gas we use.

The capacity of some gases to retain heat, and to possibly cause an increase in the Earth's temperature, had been identified since the 19th century by some scientists. However, it was only at the end of the 20th century that this phenomenon was effectively acknowledged and its effects were measured. The first Earth Summit was held in Stockholm in 1972, and resulted in the creation of the United Nations Environment Programme. It touched on climate. But the third Summit, which was held in Rio in 1992 (also known as the United Nations Conference on Environment and Development), led to the creation of the United Nations Framework Convention on Climate Change (UNFCCC). The signatory countries of this convention have been meeting annually ever since. The Kyoto Protocol, which established the policies for reducing greenhouse gas emissions, was signed in 1997. The Johannesburg Summit was held in 1992, and on this occasion the French president declared: "Our house is burning, but we are looking the other way". These various conferences have been important steps in the attempt to limit the effects of climate change.

Abundant energy?

Throughout history, energy has in fact been abundant, despite persistent fears of shortages. In the 1920s, the United States feared oil shortages. Significant discoveries on the American territory, then in the Middle East, put these fears to rest. Concerns were revived in 1970, when oil reserves were assumed to cover only 30 years of consumption. This prognosis undoubtedly inspired the Club of Rome to elaborate the famous report entitled "The limits to growth", the first warning of a possible shortage of energy, mining and even food resources. Without embracing an overly optimistic perspective, it is important to mention that at that moment oil reserves were estimated at about 75 billion tons, while in 2022 they were estimated at 250 billion tons.

The situation changed at the beginning of this century.

Energy is now scarce and expensive

At the end of the 20th century, energy seemed still abundant and was therefore cheap. Oil, gas and coal reserves seemed significant. Oil price dropped to $10 per barrel by the end of 1998.

From 2000 to 2008 (the year of a major financial crisis), global economic growth was very strong (especially due to China's economic boom) and the prices of widely dominant fossil energies increased significantly. Oil prices reached $147 per barrel in 2008, then dropped and rapidly reached high levels after 2010.

The shale oil and gas revolution in the United States was a game changer. Started a little before 2010, this revolution produced its full effects by 2014 (virtually nonexistent before 2010, shale oil production represented over 5% of global oil production in 2014). Prices remained relatively low, especially because of the Covid-19 pandemic, but increased sharply in 2021 due to the economic recovery.

What about the future?

There is a proven link between economic growth and increasing energy demand. For a long time, and especially during the "thirty glorious years" (1945–1975), the rate of energy consumption followed that of wealth (measured by the GNP). The current rate of energy consumption is lower than that of wealth. At the beginning of the 1980s, the tenfold increase in oil price was followed by a significant drop in oil demand and a reduction in the global demand for energy, while wealth increased.

The population growth (which should pass from 7.5 to 9 and even 10 billion people by 2050) and the increase in average living standards (recently reaching spectacular levels in Asia) should lead to an increase in energy demand. According to the most conservative scenarios, which rely on reduced economic growth to limit polluting emissions, there will be about a 30% increase by 2050.

According to other scenarios, in which the current tendencies will continue, there will be a twofold increase in demand. Two recognized organizations, the International Energy Agency (IEA) and the US Department of Energy (DOE), expect a strong increase in energy demand by 2030. This can be readily explained: economic growth is needed to reduce unemployment in developed countries and poverty in emerging countries. Also, economic growth requires energy.

Two constraints should lead us to modify our policies:

– by 2050, an inevitable depletion of gas and oil reserves;

above all, the necessity to cope with climate change.

Therefore, the objective should be to reduce our consumption as much as possible and to make the best use of all the energies, while respecting environmental constraints (and especially by taking climate change into account). It is a challenging objective. Since 1945, energy consumption has increased tenfold and our needs have been met by increasing production of oil and gas in particular.

Our future will be very different. The measures proposed by many specialists are technically feasible, but difficult to accept in terms of policies. The educational effort to be undertaken is huge. Let us hope that education will be sufficient, and no coercive measures will be needed.

Acknowledgments

There is a long history behind this book and its predecessors. It is an old project that started to materialize in the summer of 2002 when, encouraged and supported by Nadine Rouzaut, we made a detailed plan.

Many people contributed to the elaboration of this book. Many students, such as Julien Bassaler, Thibault Servan and Yann Balaÿ, took part in the 2007 edition of this book.

My former colleague Robin Baker contributed to the elaboration of the first English version in 2011.

Amit Garg, former student at IFP School, helped me write a new English version in 2017.

Finally, Aishwarya Dar, Juliette Guilbaud and Matthew Van der Beeuren brought their contributions to a more recent version (2021).

The present book was written in close cooperation with Matthew Van der Beeuren.

I am taking this opportunity to thank them all.

And of course, according to the usual disclaimer, all remaining errors are my own.

Tribute

I preserved in this edition the foreword written for the first version of the book *Géopolitique de l'énergie* by Jean-Marie Chevalier, a prominent energy specialist, who sadly passed away in October 2021.

This foreword is quite prescient, even though the expressed perspective has changed in the past 15 years.

1

Different Forms of Energy

1.1. Energy at the heart of the development of civilization

The term "energy" is taken from the Greek *energon*, which means "force in action". Energy is the capacity to perform work, impart movement or raise temperature (heat a building, cook food, etc.). It is produced via the use of natural forces like wind or solar energy, from the combustion of fuels or combustible materials (oil, gasoline, diesel fuel, fuel oil, natural gas, coal, wood, etc.) or from electricity.

Energy has always been vital for humankind. Living organisms use a large quantity of energy, for which the main natural source is the sun. Human beings obtain their energy from food, which is transformed in the cells of their bodies during a multitude of biochemical reactions allowing them to maintain their body temperature, grow, multiply and move about.

Although the rest of the animal kingdom has always been content with what nature provides for it, humankind has been able to free itself from the weather variations and random food resources that threatened the demographic growth of its species. Through the discovery of fire, humans were able to cook food – leading to the development of agriculture and breeding – and produce heat, thereby promoting their longevity. In addition, this allowed them to forge tools and weapons to ensure their survival.

Much later, various energy innovations helped to shape society as we know it today. Energy is present at every moment of our lives. These innovations such as motors operate with petroleum products, gas or electricity.

In the same fashion, light has become indispensable to us. Light that once came from a candle, then from oil lamps and street lamps powered by town gas, today is mainly produced by electricity.

Therefore, energy, now essential to our well-being (reduction of physical effort, heating and lighting of premises, etc.) and economic development, has become a key element of progress.

However, energy needs continue to increase, although today nearly 2 billion people still do not benefit from even the simplest of modern energy resources.

Access to abundant and inexpensive energy sources and an increasing worldwide population are leading to an explosion in the demand for energy at the same time as humankind is becoming aware of the impact of its lifestyle on the environment. The survival of the human species now depends on its intelligence and creativity.

1.2. Energy: major stages and innovations in its history

In antiquity, the only resources available were manpower (it is estimated that one-third of the population of Rome was composed of slaves), animal traction (for transport) and biomass, in particular wood for cooking and heating. In Europe during the Middle Ages, the use of windmills was imported from the Orient, providing efficient energy, particularly for the industries of food (nuts and olives) and textiles (fabric milling). More powerful watermills allowed for the development of paper mills and iron mills.

Modern forms of energy did not make their appearance until just over 200 years ago, starting with coal. In the 18th century, England had exhausted its forestry resources and started to use its coal resources to develop the use of the steam engine, thereby paving the way for the advent of the industrial age.

The next step was the discovery of electricity. The principle was known quite early on, but it was only at the end of the 19th century that electricity really became a source of energy.

Another step was the "discovery" of oil. In fact, it was used (because its existence had been known for a long time) from 1860 onwards to make paraffin, which was used in oil lamps, then for motor transport with the invention of the petrol engine and the diesel engine at the end of the 19th century and finally as fuel for ships, particularly warships, around 1910.

In the 20th century, electricity consumption grew first from coal-fired plants, then from heavy fuel oil, later from nuclear reactors and combined cycle gas turbines and at last from renewables.

Finally, the 21st century will undoubtedly see a shift in the share of different energy sources in total production (the energy mix) to reduce CO_2 emissions and limit climate change, with a reduction in the consumption of fossil fuels and an increase in the share of hydroelectricity, wind power, solar energy, geothermal energy, biomass, etc.

1.3. Energy demand

After World War II and throughout the second half of the 20th century and the beginning of this century, global consumption of primary commercial energy exploded, rising from 2 Gtoe (gigatons or billions of tons of oil equivalent) in 1945 to around 15 Gtoe or 600 exajoules in 2023. This increase is the result of strong economic growth after World War II until 1973 and again after 2000, combined with the discovery of major oil, natural gas and coal deposits, particularly at the end of the 20th century.

Commercial energy is energy that can be bought or sold. It includes oil, natural gas, coal, electricity from nuclear and hydro sources and new renewable energies.

Non-commercial energy corresponds to traditional biomass (wood and charcoal) which, particularly in developing countries, is directly harvested and used by the consumer.

Box 1.1. *Commercial and non-commercial energy*

To illustrate commercial energy consumption in 2023, imagine a cube measuring 2.4 kilometers on each side (about three times the height of the Burj Khalifa tower in Dubai) filled with oil: this is equivalent to the total amount of energy consumed in the world each year.

Oil as such accounts for only 32% of this quantity, i.e. consumption of 150 m^3 per second, equivalent to the flow of the Seine in Paris. The rest is consumed in the form of natural gas (24%), coal (26%), nuclear power (4%), hydroelectric power (6%) and new renewable energies (8%) (Figure 1.1).

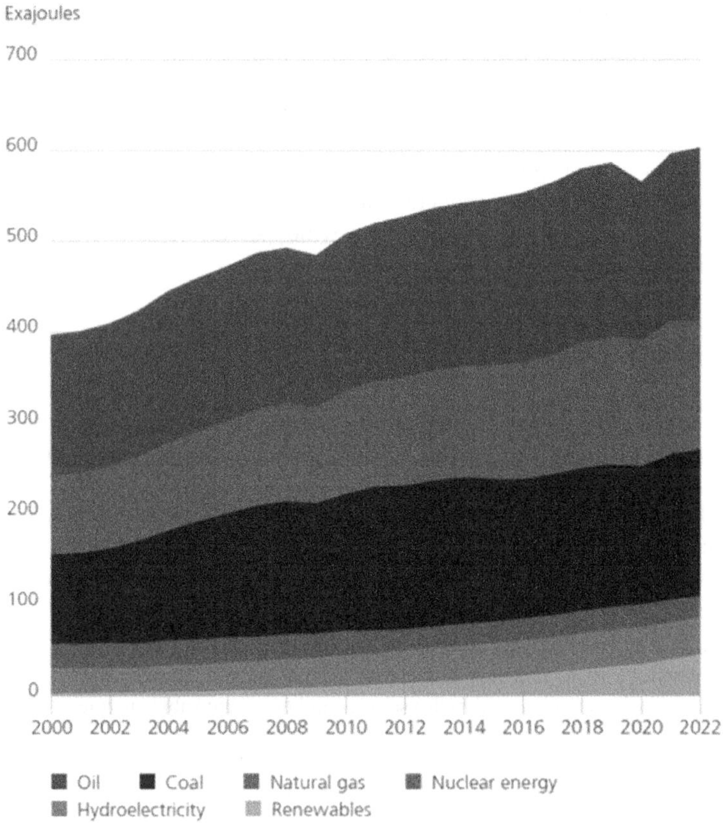

Figure 1.1. *World energy consumption by energy source (source: EI Statistical Review of World Energy 2023). For a color version of this figure, see www.iste.co.uk/favennec/geopolitics1.zip*

In addition to the consumption of so-called "commercial" energy, we need to add the consumption of non-commercial energy. This is mainly biomass (especially firewood for cooking, particularly in Africa, where access to "modern" energy is difficult), which represents between 1.5 and 2 Gtoe.

The world can be divided into several groups, each using one of the three energy systems that have succeeded one another throughout history: wood and human or animal power in much of sub-Saharan Africa and the Amazon; coal in China and India; and oil in the Organization for Economic Cooperation and Development

(OECD) and producer countries. The development of renewable energies is gradually changing this situation.

After a period of moderate growth in the 1990s, energy consumption grew much more rapidly between 2000 and 2010. Global economic expansion, extremely strong growth in China and, to a lesser extent, India, and sustained demand in the United States (until 2008) all contributed to this increase. For many years, China commissioned a new coal-fired power plant every week, and each plant had a capacity of around 1 GW (equivalent to a conventional nuclear power plant). China's total electricity generation was 8,850 Twh in 2022, up from 3,287 Twh in 2007, an annual increase equivalent to the UK's annual electricity consumption.

Global energy consumption continues to rise, but at a slower rate (1.5–2% per year) since 2010, significantly slower than global GDP, which is increasing by 3% per year. Oil consumption is growing by around 1.5% a year, gas by 3%, while coal consumption remains stable. Hydroelectricity consumption is growing at a slow pace, while consumption of new renewable energies (wind, solar, etc.) is increasing by more than 10% a year, although they still account for only a small proportion of the energy mix.

1.4. 2020: Covid-19's impact on energy demand

In 2020, global energy consumption and production fell by around 5% as a result of the Covid-19 pandemic, which paralyzed the world economy. Oil consumption fell by 9% compared with 2019, while gas consumption fell by 2% and coal by 4%. Oil prices collapsed to historically low levels at the start of the year.

Conversely, renewable energy production continued to grow at a rate of 10%, slightly slower than in previous years. The Covid-19 crisis highlighted the resilience of renewable energy production. The pandemic may have provided a glimpse of a cleaner, low-carbon world thanks to the reduction in CO_2 emissions and air pollution. However, by 2022, energy consumption had exceeded its 2019 level and pollutant emissions were back on the rise.

1.5. Drivers of energy demand: wealth

Wealth is the determining factor in energy consumption. On average, each citizen of the United States has an annual income of around 66,000 dollars (GDP per capita 2022). This income is 40 times higher than that of a West African citizen (around 1,000–2,000 dollars a year). The annual energy consumption of an American (just over 7 tons of oil equivalent) is also around 20–30 times higher than that of an African citizen (consumption can vary from 100 to 700 kg of oil equivalent, excluding biomass, depending on the country, Figure 1.2).

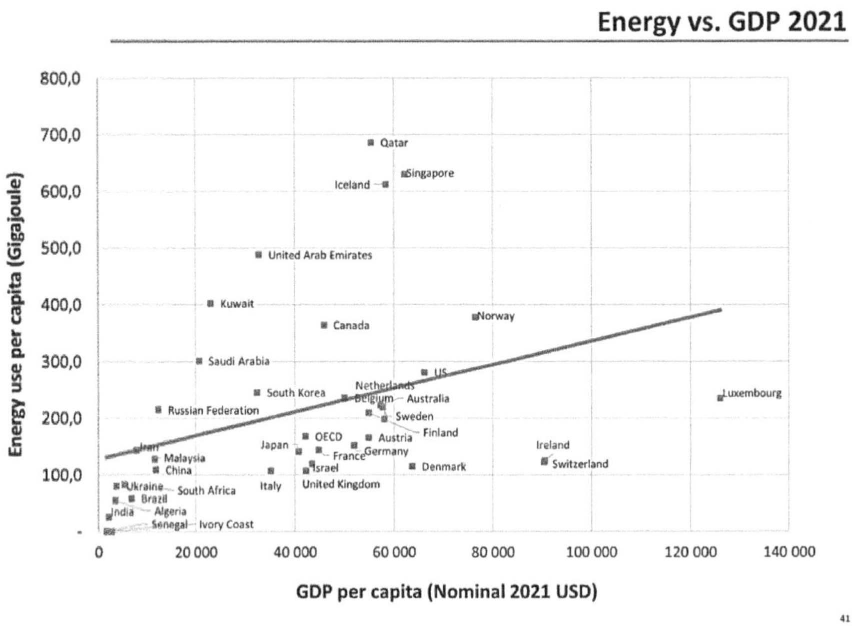

Figure 1.2. *Commercial energy consumption and income (source: World Bank and BP Statistical Review 2022)*

Energy consumption rises very rapidly with income, particularly when income is low and countries are in the process of industrialization. Then, when services play a more important role in the economy, energy consumption rises more slowly than income. In developed countries, for example, the ratio between growth in electricity demand and economic growth is around 0.6, while in developing countries, the ratio is over 1.

At higher income levels, energy consumption rises very slowly, as household appliance use nears saturation.

Therefore, the number of automobiles stabilizes, and the number of heating appliances and household appliances per household no longer increases in the wealthiest countries. Energy consumption is simply keeping pace with demographic growth (Figure 1.3).

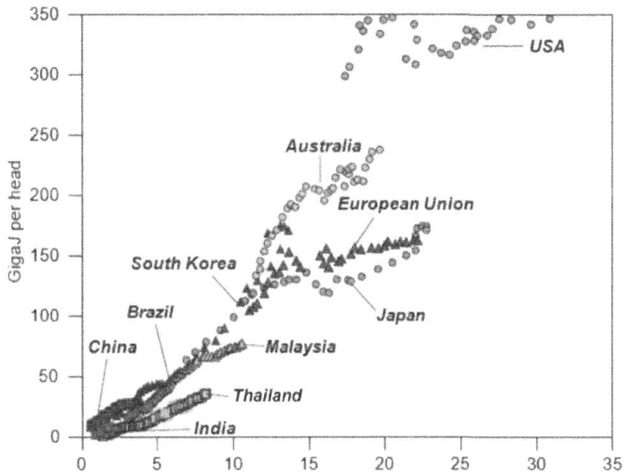

Figure 1.3. *Evolution of energy consumption (in gigajoules per capita) as a function of wealth (GDP in thousand dollars per capita). For a color version of this figure, see www.iste.co.uk/favennec/geopolitics1.zip*

If we analyze the relationship between energy consumption and wealth, we can identify several groups of countries:

– First, there are the major non-OECD oil-producing countries (the Middle East and Russia), whose energy consumption is very high in relation to their income. They consume a lot because energy is made available to consumers at a low price, since energy is abundant.

– Second, the energy-rich OECD countries (USA, Canada, Norway, Australia), whose per capita income is much higher than that of the previous group and whose per capita consumption is relatively high. Their consumption has risen partly because their oil, gas, coal and hydroelectricity resources are abundant, and there is no need for them to seek to optimize their energy consumption.

– The third group includes the major European countries and Japan, most of which have no energy reserves and which, despite high per capita incomes, limit their energy consumption in order to reduce imports.

– Finally, as already mentioned, there are the world's poorest countries, where per capita commercial energy consumption (excluding wood) is low, both as a consequence and a cause of still-limited economic development.

Other factors influence a country's energy consumption:

– Climate has a direct effect on the use of lighting, heating and air-conditioning.

– Geography influences the transmission network.

– Industrial facilities such as mining, shipbuilding, chemicals, glass and metallurgy consume large quantities of energy.

– Cultural factors influence energy consumption, as shown by the differences in consumption between Northern Europe and the United States or Australia.

1.6. Different forms of energy

1.6.1. *Main forms of energy*

The main forms of energy are as follows:

– Mechanical: the cause or result of a change in potential energy (e.g. waterfall) or kinetic energy (movement).

– Thermal: expressed in the form of heat.

– Chemical: liberated via a chemical reaction that can be explosive.

– Electrical: produced by a difference in electrical charge between two points; can result in a direct electrical current.

– Nuclear: can be created by fission (splitting atomic nuclei) according to the principle of nuclear reactors currently in use or by the fusion of atomic nuclei (two nuclei combine to form a new, single nucleus with the release of energy). Nuclear fission has been widely used since World War II. First, there was the development of the atomic bomb and then the start of the use of nuclear energy for electricity generation in the United States in the 1950s. However, electricity generation by nuclear fusion is still in the research phase.

Over 30 countries produce nuclear electricity. However, various accidents (Chernobyl, Fukushima) have limited or halted the development of nuclear power in many countries.

1.6.2. *Fossil fuels and renewable energies*

1.6.2.1. *Fossil fuels*

Oil, gas and coal still account for over 80% of energy consumption. A detailed description of these energies is given below. Nuclear energy can be considered a fossil fuel, since the uranium needed to produce it is a fossil resource.

1.6.2.2. *Renewable energies*

In the International System (SI), the unit of energy is the joule, which represents the work done by a force of one Newton (N) traveling a distance of one meter. Another definition comes from energy's use to heat water. Therefore, a calorie is the quantity of energy required to raise the temperature of one gram of water by one degree Celsius. Physicists have shown that this energy, referred to as calorific or thermal, is equivalent to mechanical energy (or work). Another important type of energy is electrical energy: the joule is also the energy produced by a direct current of one ampere at a voltage of one volt for one second.

Another important concept is power, which is measured in watts (W), and is the energy consumed or generated per unit of time, i.e. one second: 1 watt is equivalent to 1 joule/second. For large facilities, power is expressed in kilowatts (1 kW = 1,000 W) or megawatts (1 MW = 1,000 kW) and energy in kWh, i.e. 1 kW (produced by a generator or consumed by a machine) for one hour.

Oil companies use the metric ton of oil equivalent (toe), which is the energy that can be produced by one metric ton of oil, or the barrel of oil equivalent (boe), which is the energy that can be produced by one barrel of oil. Gas can be measured in cubic feet or cubic meters and its calorific value in kWh or British Thermal Units (BTUs).

International statistics are now increasingly provided in joules or exajoules.

One fundamental property of energy is that it can be converted from one form to another, with the following equivalents:

1 calorie = 4.18 J.

1 toe = 42 billion J (approximately).

1 toe = 42 million BTU (approximatively).

1 kWh = 36 million J.

Box 1.2. *Units*

Renewable energies include the following:

– Biomass: a versatile source of energy which can provide heat and electricity. It includes wood, which is used as a cooking fuel. It consists also of gas and liquid fuels produced from all organic matter derived from living organisms.

– Hydraulic: produced by the movement of water.

– Wind: which powers windmills.

– Solar: produced by solar radiation. There are several forms of solar energy:

- solar thermal energy used to produce hot water in a dwelling;

- concentrated solar power which uses a parabolic system to concentrate solar rays onto a heat transfer fluid, often water or melted salt, in a pipe or another vessel, thereby generating steam and ultimately producing electricity;

- solar photovoltaic energy which directly transforms some of the sun's rays into electricity via panels made up of cells;

- tidal energy.

– Marine energy: produced from marine currents or from swells and waves.

– Geothermal: heat generated in the Earth's core.

Fossil energy resources (coal, oil, natural gas, uranium) are by definition limited. The time needed to replenish them is on a planetary scale (tens of millions of years) not a human one. Conversely, renewable energies are permanently created by nature, but the resources available depend on natural conditions:

– solar energy (day/night);

– wind energy (strong wind/dead calm);

– hydraulic energy (large river/absence of precipitation).

Prefixes	Symbols	Values	Examples
Kilo	K	10^3 (thousand)	Kilowatt (kW)
Mega	M	10^6 (million)	Megawatt (MW)
Giga	G	10^9 (billion)	Gigawatt (GW)
Tera	T	10^{12} (trillion)	Terawatt (TW)
Exa	E	10^{18}	Exajoules (EJ)

Table 1.1. *Commonly used multiples*

1.7. The laws of energy

Different forms of energy change continuously from one to another: light energy to thermal energy, chemical energy (from fuels or food) to mechanical energy, nuclear energy to heat, mechanical energy to electrical energy, etc. Yet these conversions are subject to two principles of thermodynamics:

– The principle of the conservation of energy: the quantity of energy subjected to a transformation process is equal to the energy output in other forms once the process is finished.

– The principle of degradation of energy: in a closed system, the quantity of energy that is available for use must diminish. Therefore, an electric motor transforms electrical energy into mechanical energy and operates by releasing heat (the motor heats up). This heat generally goes unused.

Nonetheless, there are limits to the energy conversions possible: a car's brakes slow it by transforming kinetic energy into heat, but we cannot move a car forward by heating the brakes.

Different energy sources may be used for the same purpose. For example, heat can be produced by burning wood, coal, gas or petroleum products or by using nuclear energy. In the same way, electricity can be generated from many forms of primary energy (e.g. natural gas, oil or coal in a thermal power plant). For the time being, transport still relies heavily on oil-based products: petrol, diesel, heavy fuel oil (for ships) and jet fuel. Of course, electric vehicles are becoming increasingly important.

There is a further distinction between three types of energy sources:

– energy sources such as fossil fuels which can be stored;

– flux energies, which are characterized by random availability and cannot be stored (wind and solar energy);

– semi-renewable energies such as biomass (depends on replacement planting) or hydroelectricity (depends on precipitation).

Primary energy is energy directly resulting from the exploitation of a resource available in nature: wood, coal, oil, natural gas, wind, solar radiation, hydraulic or geothermal energy. However, these energies cannot always be used directly, they must first be converted (e.g. oil refining to obtain gasoline).

Secondary energy results from the transformation of a primary energy by the use of a conversion system: for example, electricity (secondary energy) is produced via the use of coal (primary energy) or gas (primary energy) in a thermal power plant or uranium (primary energy) in a nuclear power plant. It can also be produced by water, wind or sun.

Changing primary energy into secondary energy involves transformation or conversion losses.

Box 1.3. *Primary and secondary energy*

In order to analyze global energy consumption, we must add up – and therefore compare – the consumption of oil, coal, gas, etc. A common unit is used for these comparisons: the joule is increasingly used, but the ton of coal equivalent and then the metric ton of oil equivalent (toe) have long been the main units of measurement. The ton of oil equivalent – which we will use extensively in this book – is the quantity of energy contained in one ton of crude oil.

Why do we refer particularly to the "oil equivalent"? Simply because oil is the most widely used energy source. Fifty years ago, the ton of coal equivalent was used. To generate the same quantity of heat as that contained in one ton of oil, we must burn roughly 1.5 metric tons of high-quality coal (anthracite); for lignite (a low quality form of coal), a larger quantity is required. Likewise, 1,100 cubic meters of "gaseous" natural gas are needed to obtain the energy contained in one ton of oil equivalent. The energy content of liquefied natural gas (LNG) is greater than that of oil: one ton of LNG is equivalent to 1.23 toe.

The case of electricity, which is a secondary energy, is more complex.

The quantity of heat provided by 1 kWh is equivalent to that provided by 0.083 kg of oil. Therefore, 1,000 kWh = 0.083 toe.

However, the average efficiency of a power plant is of the order of 38%. Therefore, approximately 0.083/0.38, i.e. 0.22 kg of oil equivalent, is needed to generate 1 kWh. Using this input assumption, 1,000 kWh = 0.22 toe. This is the equivalence that is generally used to convert kWh into toe, particularly for nuclear energy.

Quantities	Calorific equivalents
1,000 m^3 of natural gas	0.9 toe
1 metric ton of LNG	1.23 toe
1 metric ton of coal (anthracite)	0.67 toe
1 metric ton of coal (lignite)	0.33 toe
1 megawatt-hour (MWh)	0.22 toe (production) or 0.083 toe (consumption)

Table 1.2. *Calorific equivalents*

It should be remembered that primary energy (coal, oil, gas, renewables) is directly burned or transformed into secondary energy for use.

"Final energy" is the energy that is delivered to consumers (in the form of electricity, gasoline, etc.) and then transformed by them into useful energy (lighting, heating, transport, etc.). At every stage of the process, however, losses are incurred. Between the secondary energy (after transformation of primary energy) and the final energy (received by the consumer) losses resulting from transformation are incurred.

Useful energy is the energy available to the consumer after losses in the equipment which is used. For instance, in a car, only a fraction of the energy contained in the gasoline or the diesel is effectively used to drive the car.

Considering all energies together, energy losses between primary energy and useful energy can be broken down as follows:

– 25% during conversion;

– 5% during transport;

– 35% during end-use.

The result is that useful energy only represents one-third of the primary energy used in the process.

Box 1.4. *From primary energy to useful energy*

1.8. Electricity

Worldwide electricity production reached some 29,165 TWh in 2022. Had this electricity been entirely of thermal origin, it would have required the use of 6 billion tons of oil equivalent, equivalent to one and a half times total world oil production for that year. Electricity use is growing more quickly than that of any other form of energy: its production was less than 1,000 TWh in 1950.

However, several hundred million people on the planet still do not have access to it, and one of the major challenges in the years to come will be to reduce this number. Those without electricity are mainly concentrated in Africa.

Projects to increase electricity supplies have been met with variable rates of success. China and India's achievements in this domain have been spectacular: 100% of Chinese households and 95% of Indian households now have electricity, although only 30 years ago the proportion was very low.

– Voltage (V): analogous to pressure.

– Current (I): analogous to flow – measured in amperes.

– Power (P) = V × I measured in watts. A watt is 1 joule per second.

– Impedance (Z) = V/I measured in Ohms.

– Electrical energy = power x time, is measured in watt hours (Wh) or multiples of that such as kilowatt hours (kWh, 10^3 Wh), megawatt hours (MWh = 10^6 Wh), gigawatt hours (GWh = 10^9 Wh), terawatt hours (TWh = 10^{12} Wh), etc.

Frequency of alternating current is measured in hertz.

Box 1.5. *Units for electricity*

Electricity has several particular characteristics:

– It is very difficult and costly to store. Of course, dams can be considered as stores of electricity. Traditional dams are good storages of energy. Another system can be used: pumped-storage energy transfer stations where surplus electricity produced during off-peak hours (times of low demand) can be used in mountainous regions to pump water from one dam to another at a higher location. This water can be released during times of high electricity demand and can help to smooth out differences between supply and demand. Batteries are valuable, but they are costly and do not allow very large storage. Production must therefore be in real time; it must continuously adapt to demand.

It is the consumer who controls demand, and this demand fluctuates continuously. Electricity is supplied from the producer to the consumer instantaneously, and so users never have to wait for their supplies.

Electricity can travel through all links in the network, so according to the law of physics, it is difficult for the producer to determine the supply route the energy will take.

A distinction must be made between production during off-peak hours and production during peak hours. The former is base-load production. Base-load generating plants operate continuously to meet that portion of electricity demand that is constant, i.e. the level below which demand does not fall. In contrast, plants used for peak-load generation are only used as needed to respond to peaks in consumption, the timing of which is not always predictable. However, it is essential that production capacity is adequate for peak demand.

These physical characteristics result in the following specific characteristics of the electricity market:

– Limited storage is possible, making it continuously necessary to balance supply and demand.

– No substitution is possible over the short term.

– Demand is highly dependent on time and very sensitive to temperature variations.

– Significant losses occur during distribution (e.g. average losses in Europe are in the order of 5% throughout the high-voltage network). The location of generating plants is therefore determined by two considerations. The first is the advantage of proximity to areas of consumption. The second is the benefit of optimizing the site's position with regard to the fuel supply (coal-fired power plants close to coal mines or ports) or in consideration of technical and environmental constraints (nuclear power plants close to a source of cold water such as rivers or oceans).

– However, despite the above, it is possible to transport electricity over large distances For instance, the distance is 1,200 km (720 miles) between Canadian hydroelectric power plants and major centers of consumption. Transportation is made via very-high-voltage lines (735 kilovolts). Therefore, it is possible to trade electricity between neighboring countries when production costs are far lower in a given country. Thus, Canada and Norway are very large producers of hydraulic energy, and this energy is exported (in the case of Canada, to the USA; in the case of Norway, to countries of Northern Europe through interconnected lines).

1.8.1. *Electricity generation*

The sources of electricity supply vary considerably (Figure 1.4):

– Thermal processes operate by producing steam from water or hot gases by combustion and passing them into a turbine to make it rotate. This rotation drives an alternator that generates electricity. The steam is produced by the combustion of wood, coal, gas, oil or petroleum products (diesel, heavy fuel oil or even crude oil), or by splitting atoms, or even by concentrating sunrays on a heat transfer fluid.

– Electricity can also be generated hydraulically by water flowing through turbines or by wind-driven turbines.

– Electricity can be produced by photovoltaic cells that transform solar radiation into electricity without the use of turbines.

– Electricity can also be generated using geothermal energy, ocean energy, etc.

Most electricity produced throughout the world comes from fossil fuels. The main source remains coal (38% of electricity is produced from coal, and roughly 75% of coal is used to produce electricity), particularly in major coal-producing countries like the USA, China, India, South Africa and even Germany. The use of oil is decreasing because of competition from both coal, which is cheaper, and natural gas, which is not only cheaper but also less polluting.

Natural gas is being used more frequently, thanks to the efficiency of combined cycle gas turbine (CCGT) power plants. Here, electricity is generated first by expanding the gas burnt in a turbine, then by expanding the steam recovered by using the heat from the burnt gas in a second turbine. This process is favored by the low cost of power plant construction and the significant reduction in pollutant emissions (no dust or sulfur oxides, and lower CO_2 emissions than coal or oil). However, the use of gas plants very much depends on the price of gas.

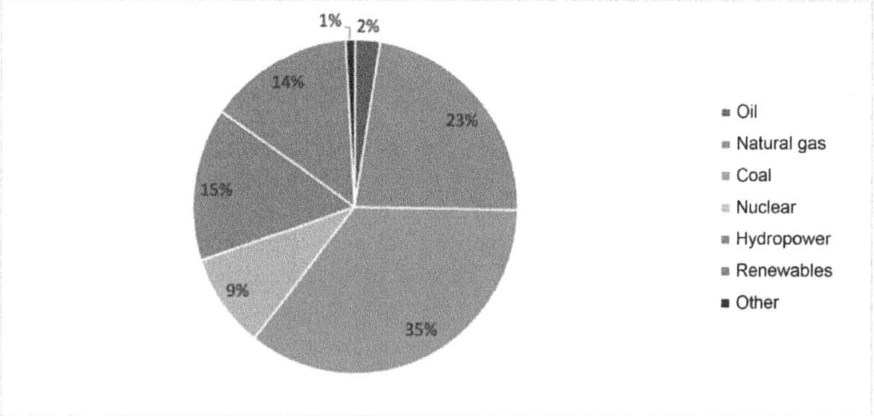

Figure 1.4. *World electricity generation by origin (source: IE Statistical Review of World Energy 2023). For a color version of this figure, see www.iste.co.uk/favennec/geopolitics1.zip*

Nuclear energy went through a strong development phase in the USA during the 1950s, then in France, Japan and several European countries during the oil shocks of the 1970s. However, its development was halted by incidents such as that of Three Mile Island in the USA in 1979 and particularly by the accident at Chernobyl in 1986, and finally by the Fukushima accident in March 2011. In many countries, large proportions of the population are opposed to nuclear energy because of the risk of accidents and fears associated with nuclear waste storage, and this opposition has been strengthened by the damage at Fukushima in March 2011 (a tsunami submerged the cooling systems of several power plants, resulting in several explosions that neutralized part of the Japanese territory). For several years now, nuclear power generation has been more or less stable worldwide.

The development of hydraulic energy, which was significant in Latin America and Europe following the war, seems to have reached a saturation level with the construction of the Three Gorges Dam in China. That was inaugurated in May 2006 and has a capacity of roughly 22 GW, 20 times that of the typical nuclear plants built in the 1980s. Other very large dams already exist (Chapter 2) or will be built in the future.

Electricity is generally produced in large plants to permit production at a low average cost to benefit from the economy of scale. Some countries (Figure 1.5) still rely on diesel power plants operating with heavy fuel oil or even diesel fuel. Production costs are extremely high, due to the high price of fuel oil and even more so of diesel. Nigeria is an interesting case in point: the country has 13 GW of power generation capacity, but only 5.5 GW is available (for a population of over 200 million; in France, the capacity is 120 GW for 67 million inhabitants). Also, despite the widespread availability of gas, these power plants are not always operational, for both political and technical reasons. Access to electricity for the population connected to the grid does not exceed a few hours a day. There is therefore a huge market for small diesel-powered generators.

The share of renewables in electricity generation is increasing very fast, reaching 14% in 2022. In addition, renewables accounted for over 40% of global primary energy growth in the last years. This increase is mainly due to Europe, Brazil, the United States and China.

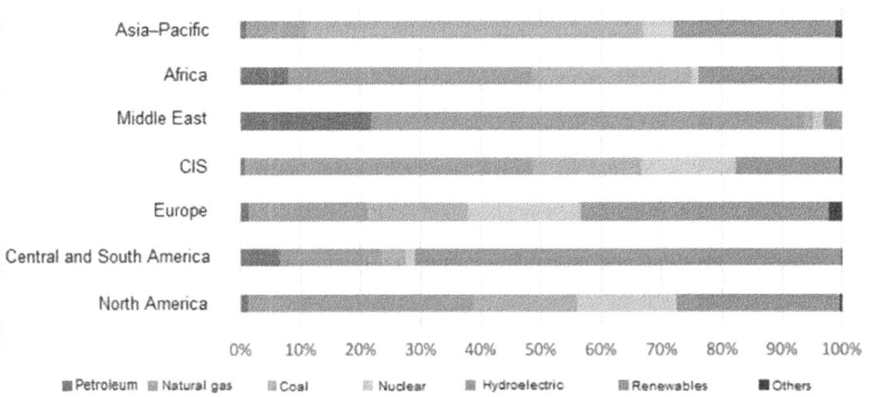

Figure 1.5. *Electricity generation by source, by region (in %) (source: EI Statistical Review of World Energy 2023). For a color version of this figure, see www.iste.co.uk/favennec/geopolitics1.zip*

Electronuclear energy is based on the use of uranium as a fuel to produce electricity. Uranium is a highly concentrated source of energy and is available throughout the world in what are considered to be sufficient quantities. In most reactors operating today, one ton of uranium can produce roughly as much electricity as 15,000–20,000 tons of coal. Today, there are some 440 nuclear reactors in operation in 30 countries, with a combined capacity of 400 GW. In addition, 56 new reactors are under construction in 15 countries, including China, India and Russia.

When an additional neutron is added to the nucleus of a uranium atom, it splits and releases thermal energy. When the nucleus splits, several neutrons are released, which will in turn collide with other nuclei and result in new fission reactions in other uranium atoms. This leads to a chain reaction. The heat produced during fission transforms a heat transfer fluid (often water) into steam, which then powers a turbine and produces electricity.

There are various types of nuclear power plants based on different types of heat transfer fluids and coolants (the term "moderator" is preferred for the element that slows – or cools – the neutrons): graphite-gas, ordinary water (light water reactors (LWRs)), heavy water, boiling water, fast neutrons (breeder reactors), etc. Ordinary water (or LWR) nuclear plants are most widely used throughout the world, particularly those which use pressurized water (abbreviated to PWR: pressurized water reactors, which represent 60% of worldwide nuclear power plants).

During the primary combustion of uranium, plutonium is released as a byproduct. This plutonium can be partially reprocessed and then used as a new fuel source. Pure plutonium is only used in fast reactors, often for research purposes (Japan, the United States and Phoenix in France), but the Superphoenix reactor was intended for the commercial production of energy. Most of the time, the plutonium is mixed with uranium: the fuel produced in this manner is called MOX (mixed oxide) and can be used either in adapted LWRs or in fast neutron reactors. In France, 20 of the 58 PWRs are equipped to operate with this type of fuel. Its use is also authorized in Japan, Germany, Belgium and Switzerland.

Currently, the first generation III reactors are being built, such as the European Pressurized Reactor (EPR). These reactors have higher capacity and a longer operating life. However, research is now underway into generation IV reactors, which will have far higher efficiencies and so be able to produce up to 50 times more electricity from uranium than today's plants. An international collective known as the *Generation IV International Forum* was created by the United States in 2000. It represents 13 countries committed to jointly developing this new generation of nuclear reactors by sharing research and development.

Box 1.6. *Nuclear electricity today*

The advantage of nuclear energy is that it does not produce greenhouse gases. However, it does give rise to radioactive waste and the storage and disposal of this must be managed with care to minimize the risk to people and to the environment. Although its radioactivity decreases over time, the handling of this waste remains a very important concern over the long term as radiation can continue for many decades.

1.8.2. *The atom: will it lead to the third energy revolution?*

Known uranium resources, accessible at a cost of less than 130 $/kg, are sufficient for existing nuclear power plants to operate for at least 100 years. The cost of natural uranium represents only a small percentage of this nuclear electricity cost. Uranium deposits, which are relatively abundant, have been little explored to date. Uranium reserves could therefore be considerable.

Prior to the Fukushima accident in March 2011, despite the waste problem, there was talk of a nuclear renaissance. From North America to the Middle East and Southeast Asia, the vast majority of nations seemed ready to revive nuclear power.

Figure 1.6. *Nuclear power plant*

After the Fukushima accident, which led to the shutdown of almost all nuclear power plants in Japan, the situation changed. The challenges that the nuclear industry now faces are considerable: public reluctance to accept the risks of accidents and the problem of waste disposal, the complexity of the political processes involved in setting up or developing the industry, the small number of players with the necessary construction know-how and extremely high barriers to entry. The development of nuclear power is therefore uncertain.

Nuclear power capacity is growing rapidly in Asia, where there are currently 130 nuclear reactors in operation, 35 under construction and plans to build 70 to 80 more. China is set to see the biggest increase in nuclear power generation. Between 2007 and 2023, it increased its nuclear power generation by 500%, with a capacity of 54 GW (51 reactors) and an output of around 420 Twh in 2022. A total of 24 reactors are currently under construction, and the aim is to reach a capacity of 400 GW by 2060. India is also committed to increasing its nuclear power generation capacity to 22.5 GW by 2031 (from around 8 GW at present). India has developed power plants using thorium as fuel (instead of uranium) and has several advanced facilities for this purpose.

Studies are underway to try to reproduce the atomic fusion reactions that take place within the sun's core. Proposed in the mid-1990s, the International Thermonuclear Experimental Reactor (ITER) project was launched in 2010 with the experimental reactor built in France, at the Cadarache site. The ITER project is a collaboration of 35 nations around the world. The seven core members – China, the EU, India, Japan, South Korea, Russia and the USA – signed the ITER Agreement in 2006, agreeing to share the costs of construction, operation and decommissioning of the project. The sums involved are more than 10 billion dollars.

The production of helium from the fusion of heavy isotopes of hydrogen (deuterium and tritium) has still only been achieved on an experimental scale because the conditions for fusion are extremely difficult to produce. A temperature of 100 million degrees Celsius is needed for the fusion reaction to take place. Although deuterium is available naturally in large quantities from the oceans (but requires a very complex extraction process), tritium must be prepared artificially, since it is only found in very small quantities in the natural world.

In November 2017, the ITER project passed the halfway point to the first plasma. By May 2020, the project's progress to the first plasma was at 70%. The first plasma is scheduled for December 2025. This will be the first time the machine is powered up.

Nuclear fusion is interesting because it can potentially produce much more energy than fission for the same mass of fuel. However, even though the results are conclusive, it will not be possible to exploit them industrially before the second half of the 21st century.

Box 1.7. *Prospects for nuclear fusion: the International Thermonuclear Experimental Reactor (ITER) project*

1.8.3. *Distribution and commercialization of electricity*

Distribution is a very important part of the electrical system.

At production site outlets, transformers change the voltage of alternating current – generally used in modern electrical networks – into high, medium or low voltage. The electrical distribution network consists of five main elements:

– the outlet station of the power plant with the transformers that increase the electrical voltage for transport over high-voltage lines to minimize the loss of power;

– the high-voltage lines themselves;

– substations in which the voltage is lowered for medium-voltage transmission;

– the medium-voltage distribution lines;

– transformers, which then decrease the voltage to the level used by the consumers' equipment.

Therefore, each phase of the network can operate at the appropriate voltage.

To transport electrical current over long distances, high-voltage lines are used to limit losses. Power is the product of voltage and intensity ($P = U \times I$), so the higher the voltage, the lower the intensity needed for the same power. Losses are reduced because they are proportional to the square of the intensity (power dissipation = $R \times I^2$, R being the resistance). This also means that fewer lines have to be used and, since the size of the network is smaller, its environmental footprint is reduced.

Alternating current is easier to use for:	Direct current is required for:
– Electricity generation even in high-capacity power plants – Voltage change in transformers – Prevention of short circuits	– Submarine transmission over long distances (around 30 km at 400 kV) – Transmission over very long distances (over 600–800 km for 1,000 MW power) to limit losses associated with AC transmission – Asynchronous links between networks of different frequencies (e.g. the interconnection between Great Britain and France where, although the two countries operate at 50 Hz, the networks are not synchronized) – Limiting the number of conductors (two wires instead of three)

Table 1.3. *Alternating current and direct current*

In the French electricity distribution network, the lines used have the following voltages:

– The domestic power network is supplied at a low voltage of 230 V.

– At the neighborhood level, the network is supplied at 20 kV. Small and medium industries, shopping centers, commercial superstores, major local authorities, hospitals and schools are connected to the medium voltage network. These institutions and businesses have access to power of several hundreds or thousands of kW and account for nearly one-third of national consumption.

– Regional transport is powered by lines whose voltage varies from 63 to 90 kV.

– Finally, transport at the national level is powered by lines of 225 or 400 kV. The major industrial consumers, for example chemical industries, steelmaking and metallurgical plants, railways and the RATP (Paris Transport Authority), which account for nearly one-third of the country's electricity consumption, are connected to this network.

The 400 kV lines that connect the distribution networks of different countries are known as international interconnection lines. They serve a dual function: providing mutual backup between countries and providing a means for international trade in electricity which favors the operation of power plants with the lowest cost at the expense of those with the highest cost.

The interconnected networks are complex and large: they include parts controlled by different operators and enable significant savings to be made. To protect against electricity blackouts, hospitals, public buildings and other facilities for which continuous electricity supply is crucial all have backup generators (blackouts are most often caused by distribution networks or even regional transport networks).

1.8.4. *Electricity: end-use*

Electricity serves a very wide range of needs. At present, only non-rail transport is still a captive customer for petroleum products (a major part of rail transport is now powered by electricity).

In the automotive transport sector, hybrid cars (combining internal combustion engines and electric motors) and 100% electric vehicles are rapidly gaining ground. Hybrid cars run either on petroleum-based fuel or on electricity generated when the vehicle changes speed. Some hybrid vehicles are also rechargeable. The worldwide fleet of electric vehicles (hybrids and fully electric vehicles) has grown from 112,000 in 2012 to 26 million in 2022. The main users of electric vehicles are

China, the United States, Norway, Germany and Japan. China is both the biggest manufacturer of electric vehicles and the biggest buyer. Government initiatives, such as subsidies for new electric vehicles (NEVs) and tax relief policies, are encouraging Chinese automakers to rapidly ramp up electric vehicle production.

Electricity consumers can be classified according to the type of energy that results from the different uses of electricity:

– Mechanical use: motors and machines;

– Thermal use: heating buildings or water;

– Household appliance use: alarm clocks, vacuum cleaners, computers, refrigeration and air conditioning;

– Radiant use: lighting (residential, industrial or public spaces), lasers, radar and radio-frequency emissions like radio, television, telephones, etc.;

A single device may use several forms of electrical energy simultaneously: a computer uses mechanical energy to operate the hard disc and cooling fan, as well as radiant energy for the monitor.

End-uses of electricity can also be classified by categories of consumers; i.e. the industrial, commercial and institutional, residential and transport sectors.

Thermal electricity generating plants have low efficiencies: roughly 40% for coal-fired or fuel oil power plants and 60% at best for gas-fired combined cycle power plants. The rest of the energy is lost in the form of heat. This has led to the idea of so-called cogeneration power plants, which simultaneously produce heat and electricity. The heat must of course be used nearby.

Combined heat and power or cogeneration units allow for optimal management of natural resources, since they can result in efficiency of the order of 80–90%. A gas turbine equipped with a recovery boiler can produce roughly 35 megajoules (MJ) of electricity and 50 MJ of heat from 100 MJ of fuel. If the same quantities of heat and electricity were produced separately, consumption would be roughly 90 MJ of fuel for the generator set and 55 MJ for the boiler or a total of 145 MJ. In this simplified example, cogeneration results in a fuel savings of more than 30%.

Box 1.8. *Cogeneration*

1.9. Renewable energy

Renewable energy is derived from the major forces that operate on our planet, i.e. sun, water, wind, etc. It also includes wood. Such energy is inexhaustible, at least over a very long timescale. Historically, renewable energy was the first energy source used by humankind; until the end of the 17th century wood was the most widely used energy source.

We discuss the different types of renewable energies in greater detail in Chapter 2, which is devoted more specifically to the energy transition.

1.10. Oil: the reference energy

Oil remains the reference energy because it presents several essential characteristics. It is a liquid, concentrated form of energy that is easy to produce, transport and distribute.

1.10.1. *The characteristics of oil*

Oil has several essential characteristics.

1.10.1.1. *A strategic raw material*

Much of our civilization is based on the transport of individuals or goods. In addition, passenger cars operate mainly with gasoline or diesel fuel, trucks with diesel fuel and planes with jet fuel. Oil is therefore indispensable in the transport sector, even though the development of electric vehicles is rapid and the use of other fuels (gas) is possible.

Oil is a major source of fuel in a war. The importance of oil became apparent before and during World War I. In 1914, Winston Churchill, British First Lord of the Admiralty, committed the Royal Navy to the use of heavy fuel oil rather than continuing with coal as its fuel. This was an important decision, as the UK is rich in coal but has no oil. However, the use of oil conferred an irrefutable advantage in terms of speed and ease of use, which was essential for maritime conflicts. During World War I, tanks and motorized vehicles, few in number in 1914 (horses were still used to pull heavy weapons), played an essential role in the final months of the conflict. Fighter planes also made their appearance in the final months of the conflict.

1.10.1.2. *"Oil is liquid"*

This famous sentence spoken by the economist Paul Frankel may seem trivial, but this characteristic makes oil an energy that is easy to produce, transport and use. In addition, oil is a concentrated energy source: gas is much more costly to transport and distribute, coal is a solid which is more difficult to handle and electricity is also an energy that is costly to produce and very difficult to store. This ease of production means that oil trading dominates world trade in terms of both volume and value: depending on the price of crude oil, oil transactions can represent 2–4 trillion dollars per year. The oil market is global since oil can be easily transported from one part of the world to another.

1.10.1.3. *Oil, a raw material whose price can be much higher than the cost of production*

Oil only costs a few dollars per barrel to produce in the Middle East, and a few tens of dollars at most in more difficult conditions, but the price of oil at the start of the 21st century often exceeds the highest cost of its production. Is this a consequence of its strategic nature? The effect of actual or planned scarcity? Whatever the case, oil is what is referred to as a rent industry: the rent is the difference between the price (which is supposed to represent a fair value for the consumer) and the cost of production.

> Economists call the difference between the selling price and the production cost of a raw material a "rent" and often distinguish between differential and absolute rents.
>
> Take wheat for example. If it costs producers with good land $100 to produce a ton of wheat, and producers with less good land $300 to produce a ton of wheat, and if wheat costing $300 to produce is needed to meet consumer demand, the price should rise to $300. A producer able to produce at a cost of 100 dollars will benefit from a differential rent of 200 dollars (300 – 100). If, for reasons linked to market pressure, the price reaches 400 dollars, all producers will benefit from an additional absolute rent of 100 dollars (400 – 300).
>
> Currently, in the case of oil, the cost of production (depending on the zone) is approximately between 5 dollars (Saudi Arabia, some even claim a lower cost) and 40 dollars per barrel (in rare cases it may be slightly higher) for a selling price of around 80 dollars. The absolute rent for all producers is therefore 40 dollars (80 – 40), with Saudi Arabia receiving an additional differential rent of 35 dollars (40 – 5).
>
> In most oil-producing countries, and in particular in OPEC, the sale of oil is the main source of government revenue. The price needed to balance the budget (equilibrium price) is high. This explains why the price of oil often remains well above the cost of production.

Box 1.9. *Oil income and rent*

In Saudi Arabia the cost of production (excluding capital) is roughly $5 per barrel (some sources cite higher figures), whereas the price of oil has always been higher, even much higher, since 2000. This rent goes to the state, which returns a portion of it to the national company, Saudi Aramco, which holds the monopoly on exploitation of the kingdom's hydrocarbon resources, to finance exploration, production and processing operations. Except in the USA, in countries where private international companies (international oil companies (IOCs): ExxonMobil, BP, Shell, Total Energies, Chevron, etc.) operate alone or in association with a state-owned company (as is the case for Nigeria, Angola, and in numerous producing countries) the rent is shared between the state and the *joint venture* that produces the oil, which involves the national company and the foreign company(ies).

1.10.2. *The origins of oil*

According to the most widely recognized theory, "rock oil" (petroleum or petrol) is formed from microorganisms. Tens of millions of years ago, these microorganisms accumulated in sediments and were then gradually buried in the soil. Under the effect of temperature and pressure, they were transformed into kerogen – immature crude oil – composed of a mixture of large hydrocarbon molecules (Figure 1.7).

When the transformation of kerogen into oil is completed, this oil rises to the surface. There are then two possibilities. In the first stage, the "oil" rises to the surface without encountering an obstacle. The light fractions then either evaporate or are destroyed by bacteria and a residue remains, natural bitumen, whose traces and uses have been recorded in many periods of history (caulking for Noah's Ark and Moses' cradle, bitumen found by Marco Polo in today's Iraq, sources of pitch from the Massif Central in France, and the oil sands deposits of Canada). Alternatively, the oil may encounter a reservoir rock – carbonates, sandstone, compacted sand and corals – and creep into the pores and interstitial spaces of these rocks. Provided the reservoir has an impermeable overburden or cap rock, the oil remains trapped in this rock until the bit from a drilling device allows it to escape.

Quite often, above the layer which contains the crude oil, there is a sedimentary layer whose pores are filled with gas, natural gas mainly composed of methane, which is called associated gas (associated with the crude oil). Other deposits – similar in many points – will only contain what is known as "dry" gas, i.e. there will be no liquid hydrocarbons in the reservoir. This results from different conditions from those giving rise to the formation of heavier hydrocarbons, for example a higher temperature. Under the sedimentary layer(s) containing the crude oil and/or gas, there is another sedimentary layer that is water-saturated.

Crude oil and natural gas are mixtures of hydrocarbon molecules. As the word hydrocarbon implies, each molecule is composed of atoms of carbon and hydrogen.. Crude oil includes molecules that range from the simplest, methane, with just one carbon atom, to very heavy molecules that contain 20 to 30 or more carbon atoms. Natural gas – whether associated or dry – mainly consists of methane and also contains variable proportions of heavier molecules.

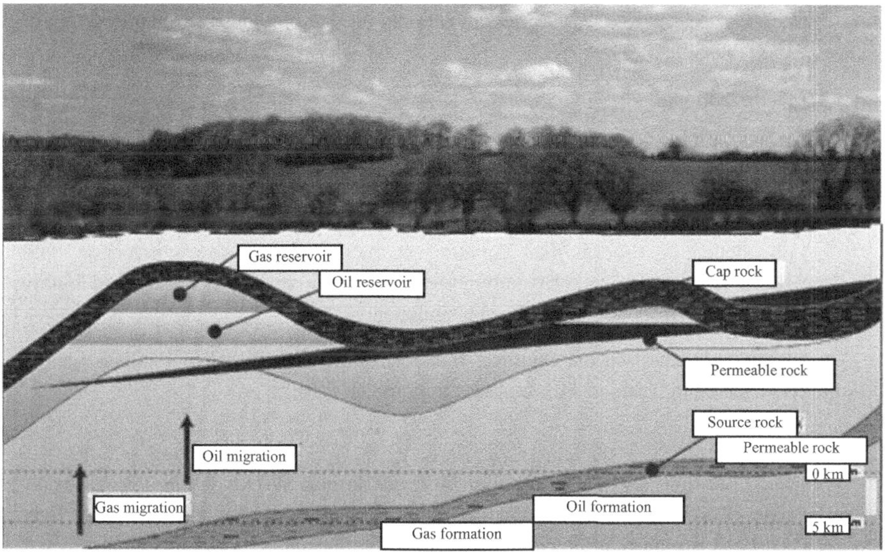

Figure 1.7. *Formation of oil. For a color version of this figure, see www.iste.co.uk/favennec/geopolitics1.zip*

To simplify, there are three types of hydrocarbon deposits: oil deposits covered by associated gas, oil deposits without associated gas and "dry" gas deposits with no liquid in the reservoir.

When natural gas emerges from underground, the decrease in temperature and pressure causes the heavier molecules present in the gaseous state in the reservoir to condense. These heavy fractions are called condensates or natural gas liquids (NGLs). A condensate is therefore a very light petroleum which, on distillation, will provide a high proportion of gasoline and diesel fuel.

The nomenclature has not been fully established, but for users – who are above all interested in the gasoline and diesel they buy at the pump – these distinctions are not very important. All of these "liquids" can be transformed into fuel or combustible material.

Different categories of oil

1) Conventional oil: each deposit or field contains a different crude oil, meaning that there are in fact 400–500 different qualities of crude oil, whose specific gravity – density – varies from roughly 0.8 to 1. A conventional crude oil can be produced with traditional processes. When they are refined, the lightest, i.e. those with a density close to 0.8, mainly provide gasoline and diesel fuel (the highest value products) while the others will mainly provide heavy fuel oil. The condensates (light liquids associated with natural gas

production) correspond to a very light conventional oil that provides a large proportion of gasoline and diesel fuel.

2) Unconventional oils:

- very heavy or extra-heavy oils and oil sands, which are mainly concentrated in Canada and Venezuela. They require specific production and transformation processes in order to be transformed into synthetic crude oils that can be used in refineries;

- oil shale, i.e. rocks that contain organic matter whose conversion into hydrocarbons is not complete. Extracting this oil is both extremely costly and highly damaging to the environment. It has been abandoned;

- liquids obtained via the chemical transformation of coal, gas or biomass (gas to liquid (GTL), coal to liquid (CTL), biomass to liquid (BTL));

- biofuels;

- shale oil, light oil in very low-porosity rock produced by hydraulic fracturing. A similar type of oil is found in low-porosity deposits. These are now known as light tight oil (LTO). LTO is mainly produced in the United States and accounts for around 5% of total world production.

Box 1.10. *Different categories of oil*

1.11. From oil exploration to oil marketing

1.11.1. *Oil exploration*

Initially, geologists search for clues that might indicate the presence of hydrocarbons. Next, geophysicists proceed with seismic techniques that send sound waves from the surface to the depths of the soil. These waves will be reflected by the interface between ground layers which, after processing of the raw data, enables maps and cross-sections of the subsoil to be prepared. These diagrams, previously in two dimensions, can now be produced in three dimensions (seismic 3D). Seismic 4D has even been proposed, by adding in the time dimension (e.g. seismic projects done on exactly the same zone, but at intervals of several months).

Once the possibility of the presence of hydrocarbons has been assessed with reasonable certainty, exploration drilling takes place. This drilling will be referred to as "dry" if it does not uncover a deposit of hydrocarbons (gas or oil). In case of success, where indications of oil or gas are found, in many cases, more extensive drilling must take place to assess the volume of reserves and whether the deposit has commercial potential.

1.11.2. *Oil production*

Production from oil (or gas) deposits is developed by drilling several producer wells (Figure 1.8). The flows from the various wells are collected by a network of pipes and directed to processing facilities where the crude oil is "stabilized". Stabilization means separating the gaseous and liquid fractions to permit transport of the oil safely. If the crude oil were not degassed, it would give rise to a high risk of explosion.

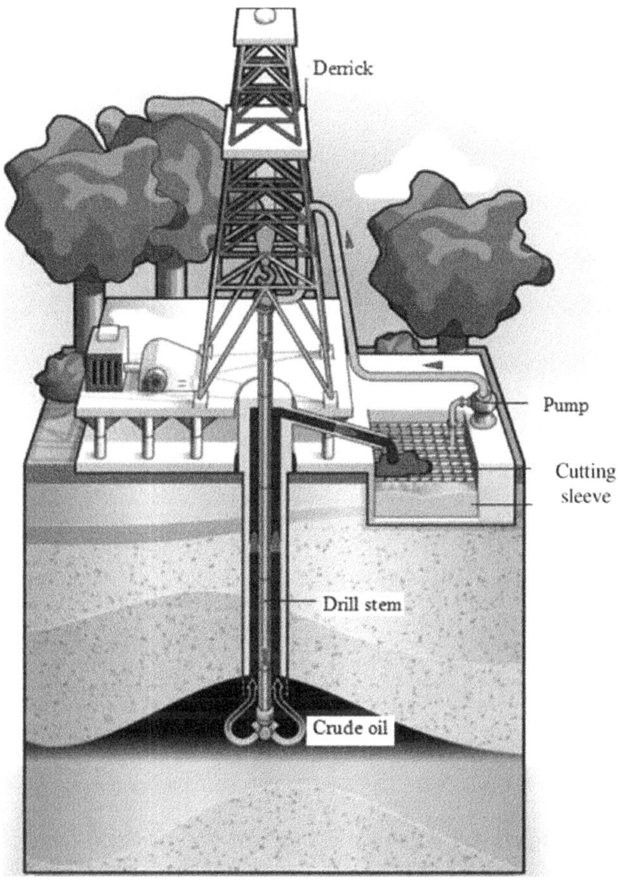

Figure 1.8. *Drilling*

If production is onshore, the liquid crude oil will then be routed either directly to a refinery that may be either close or some distance from the oil field[1] or to a marine terminal where it will be loaded onto tankers to be shipped to consuming regions.

Figure 1.9. *Example of offshore oil production*

1 The crude oil produced in some inland American states is routed over several miles via pipes (or by truck in the case of stripper wells or marginal wells) to nearby refineries where it is processed. In Russia, crude oil from Western Siberia can be routed over thousands of miles to refineries in the region of Moscow or the Ukraine. Within the framework of the "socialist division of labour" and to avoid concentrating production and processing activities in the same region – which would give it major strategic power – Stalin ordered the construction of very large refineries in regions lacking in crude oil.

If production is offshore the crude oil may be processed above the oil field on platforms carrying separation facilities, then sent to the coast via pipelines (in the North Sea, this is the case for Brent crude oil which is stored and loaded on ships at Sullom Voe, the Shetlands Islands Port). It can also be stored on a platform which includes production, storage and shipping facilities. This type of platform is referred to as floating production, storage and offloading (FPSO). This involves an extremely large barge (usually made of steel, but sometimes made of concrete) connected to pipes that bring up the crude oil from undersea deposits. This is where the oil is stored, and where the ship will dock to take delivery of the crude oil (Figure 1.9).

1.11.3. *Oil transport*

Crude oil may be transported entirely via pipelines (this may be necessary if imposed by the location of the production fields and the refinery) or by ships. Over long distances – greater than several thousand miles – transport by large ships is generally more economic.

The size of ships used to transport crude oil varies from several thousands to several hundreds of thousands of tons. The capacity of oil tankers has significantly increased over time. It especially increased between 1945 – when it did not exceed 15,000–20,000 tons – and the start of the 1970s, when several tankers of more than 500,000 deadweight tons (dwt) were built. This increase was made possible by progress in construction techniques, which resulted in economies of scale and met the needs of a significant increase in consumption in the 1950s and 1960s.

By decreasing the demand for oil and favoring production in zones close to consuming countries, the oil shocks reduced the advantages of very large tankers, which also required special and costly facilities to accommodate them.

Currently, the main types of tankers used are as follows:

– Ultra-large crude carriers (ULCCs), which are larger than 320,000 dwt (deadweight tons), with 1 dwt being roughly 1 ton of cargo;

– Very large crude carriers (VLCCs), which are tankers from 160,000 to 320,000 dwt, used to transport large quantities of crude oil over long distances, particularly from the Middle East to the United States, Europe and the major consumers of Asia;

– Suezmax tankers for transport via the Suez canal, which are 120,000–160,000 dwt;

– Aframax (80,000–120,000 dwt) and Panamax (60,000–80,000 dwt), etc.

Another classification, used by specialists, is as follows:

– general purpose: 16,500–24,900 dwt;

– medium range: 25,000–44,900 dwt;

– large range 1: 45,000–79,900 dwt;

– large range 2: 80,000–159,900 dwt;

– VLCC: over 160,000 dwt.

Petroleum products are generally transported in smaller ships, simply because the quantities to be transported are lower. However, the development of export refineries capable of producing hundreds of thousands of tons of gasoline or diesel has led to the transport of products by large vessels.

Typically, the barges that ship end-products manufactured in Rotterdam down the Rhine to Germany, Switzerland or France have a capacity of 1,000–3,000 tons.

While a large proportion of oil is transported by ship, other means obviously exist.

Oil and gas pipelines have been particularly developed in North America and Europe but traverse all continents and, on a worldwide scale, total roughly 1.2 million miles in length. Although sometimes located offshore, pipelines are mainly ground-based, built either on the ground or buried at a depth of several yards for safety reasons. Depending on the zones crossed, they will include varying degrees of insulation, protection or even heating. Highly capital-intensive, it is essential for pipelines that the zones they cross be secure. They create relationships of economic dependence between countries, as reflected by throughput tariffs that may equate to several percentage points of the value of the oil transported.

Rail transport is rather important. Therefore, between China and Russia, several hundred thousand barrels are transported daily by rail. In Iraq, although most crude oil is exported via pipelines, recent years have seen the transport of nearly 200,000 barrels daily by road tank wagons heading for Turkey, Syria or Jordan .

As an indication, the following figures were recorded for the Indian market in 2011: 52% of oil was transported by pipeline, 18% by boat, 14% by road and 16% by rail (Ganguly 2011). In terms of average cost, transporting one ton of oil over 1,000 kilometers (620 miles) in India costs \$17 using a newly built pipeline, \$13 if the pipeline is fully depreciated, \$37 by road tank wagon and \$30 by rail tank car.

Box 1.11. *Different methods for transporting hydrocarbons*

1.11.4. *Oil processing: refining principles and end-uses for products*

It is better to speak of the consumption of petroleum products rather than oil, since all oil is consumed in the form of gasolines, diesel fuels, heavy fuel oils, etc. Crude oil is transformed into these end products in refineries, made up of groups of processing units.

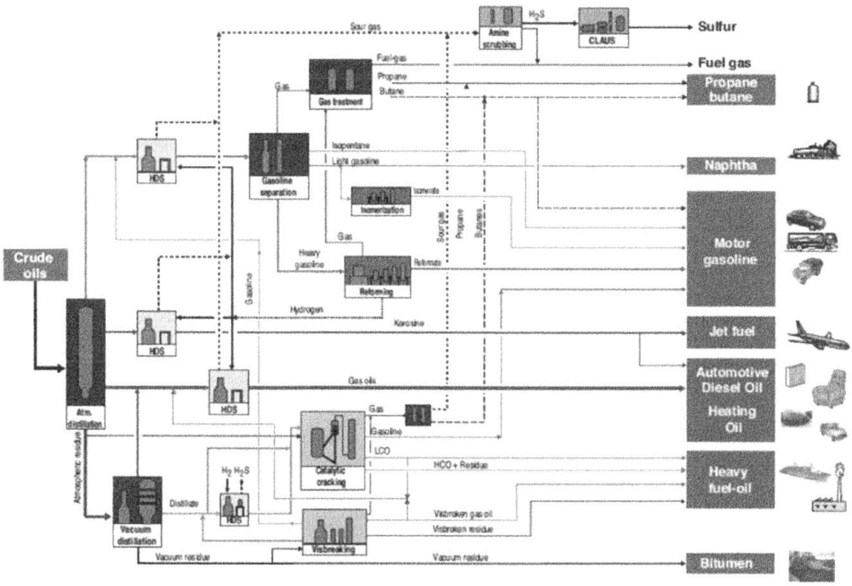

Figure 1.10. *Refinery flow chart*

The first of these is the atmospheric distillation unit, which separates the crude oil into various cuts (light, medium or heavy) which, after upgrading, will result in commercial products (Figure 1.10):

– Light cuts include liquefied petroleum gas (LPG; propane and butane), automotive gasolines and naphtha, a raw material needed for the manufacture of basic petrochemical products.

– Medium cuts include jet fuel, diesel fuel and domestic heating oil.

– Heavy cuts include heavy fuel oil, bitumen and lubricating oils.

– Other process units make it possible to improve product quality and to reduce the production of heavy fuel oil, the demand for which is declining, through conversion or cracking into light products.

1.11.4.1. *Automotive fuels: gasoline and diesel fuel*

The internal combustion engines that powered most automobiles (up to recently) have either been spark ignition engines (which use gasoline) or diesel engines (which use diesel fuel). In Europe and many other countries, diesel fuel has long been in high demand, as diesel engines are more efficient than petrol engines and consume less fuel. The affair called "Dieselgate" refers to the actual pollutant emissions of vehicles, which often turn out to be much higher than the figures announced by carmakers. This has reduced demand for diesel vehicles, which could soon be banned in many cities. In the United States, most cars and a significant number of small transport vehicles operate with gasoline.

Land vehicle fleet and operating modes

The world's vehicle fleet stands at around 1.5 billion units and is growing by almost 100 million units a year.

The majority of the world's motor vehicles are still powered by petroleum products such as gasoline or diesel.

However, the progress of electric vehicles is impressive. There are almost 40 million electric vehicles in the world, and growth is running at over 10 million a year, with more on the way. Two types of electric vehicles have been developed. First, hybrid vehicles are equipped with a combustion engine (petrol or diesel) and a small electric motor. Electricity is generated during certain periods of vehicle operation and can power the small electric motor. Then there are the "all-electric vehicles", equipped with high-capacity batteries. Vehicle range, limited at first, is improving and can now reach several hundred kilometers. However, the size, weight and cost of the batteries remain a handicap. The very high consumption of metals in the construction of these vehicles is a further constraint. Specialists hope to improve battery capacity and reduce costs. Electricity enables motor vehicles to reduce pollution, and several cities around the world are strongly encouraging their use because of growing health concerns about air pollution:

Other energies can be used to power motor vehicles. The use of alternative fuels is on the increase worldwide, particularly in Europe.

For cars, the following alternative fuels can be considered:

– LPG, or liquefied petroleum gas, contains mainly butane, sometimes mixed with propane. Replacing petrol with LPG requires very little adaptation. LPG is an excellent fuel and less polluting than petrol (or diesel). However, LPG availability is limited.

– CNG or compressed natural gas (also known as "vehicle natural gas"). Natural gas, or methane, is an excellent fuel but, even when compressed, range is limited and, in most cases, it will be used in combination with gasoline (in fuel-powered vehicles, gasoline is used when the natural gas has run out). However, given the very large reserves of natural gas, the use of CNG as a fuel has the potential to develop in many countries.

– Biofuels: ethanol or vegetable oil, see Chapter 2.

– LNG: liquefied natural gas can – since it is methane – be an excellent fuel. The problem is the product's very low liquefaction point (–162°C). However, new regulations concerning the sulfur content of fuels used by ships (enacted in 2020 by the International Maritime Organization) stipulate that sulfur content must be less than 0.5%, a specification that is very difficult for traditional fuels to achieve. This will encourage the development of LNG as a fuel for large ships. This would also help to contain the very significant pollution associated with cruise ships when they are in port.

– Hydrogen: any vehicle can use a fuel cell, a device that combines hydrogen and oxygen to produce electricity and extremely pure water. The electricity powers an electric motor. The key problem is hydrogen production and storage. Production is still mainly achieved by so-called steam reforming of hydrocarbons, releasing CO_2. The electrolysis of water using electricity from solar panels or wind turbines could be a solution. Storage also remains a major concern, given the number of explosive accidents. However, some countries are investing large sums of money in the development of hydrogen as an automotive fuel.

A number of alternatives, some of them very costly, exist that could replace petroleum products as fuels for most mobile engines, with the exception of aircraft. An electric aircraft capable of carrying 100 or 200 passengers will remain a dream for many years to come.

Box 1.12. *Transportation alternatives*

With 5% of the global population, the USA consumes nearly 50% of the automotive gasoline used throughout the world. Automotive gasoline also represents nearly 50% of the total demand for petroleum products in the USA. Why such a demand? First, because the development of the petroleum industry started in the USA. Next, this is also the country where the development of the automobile industry has been greatest, and transport needs are particularly important in this very large country. In contrast to the situation in Europe, diesel use has always been limited to big trucks. Most of the light duty vehicles (traditional cars) use gasoline.

1.11.4.2. *Jet fuel*

An intermediate product (by density) between gasoline and diesel fuel, jet fuel is definitely the product for which consumption is increasing the fastest, due to the strong growth in air transport. Jet fuel must of course remain liquid at temperatures in the order of 50°C, close to those encountered in the upper atmosphere.

1.11.4.3. *Heating fuel oils*

A significant quantity of oil continues to be consumed in the form of fuel oils: domestic heating oil (also called home heating oil or light fuel oil) and heavy fuel oil.

Domestic heating oil is mainly used to heat residential homes and commercial buildings, but it is also used in agriculture and by fishing boats. The high consumption of domestic heating oil in the major industrialized countries significantly decreased after the oil shocks and remains low. This product has largely been replaced by natural gas.

The consumption of heavy fuel oil has developed similarly: in the 1960s, it was rapidly substituted for coal in many industrial applications, including the production of electricity. However, in the 1980s, the strong increase in its price along with the oil shocks resulted in its replacement by gas and coal in industry, and by the same products plus nuclear energy for the production of electricity. In most countries, consumption of heavy fuel oil is decreasing relentlessly, with the market being increasingly limited to that of bunker fuel oil. Heavy fuel oil remains the fuel for the large diesel motors that power major transport ships. However, new regulations concerning sulfur content are likely to further reduce outlets.

1.11.4.4. *Liquefied petroleum gas (LPG)*

LPG is propane and/or butane. The name comes from the fact that, at ordinary temperatures, they are in a gaseous state, but they can be maintained in a liquid state under moderate pressure. They are therefore sold in the well-known bottles (12 kg, 6 kg or even less).

There are two sources of LPG: the propane and butane recovered during the production of crude oil or natural gas and the propane and butane recovered at the refinery. Altogether, roughly 60% of LPG available in the world comes from the production sector and 40% from refining.

World production of LPG is roughly 300 million tons p.a. With similar characteristics, natural gas and liquefied petroleum gas also have similar markets. LPG is mainly used for cooking and heating, either alone or as a complement to natural gas. It is also used as an industrial fuel in sectors that require a very clean type of fuel. LPG is also used in transport as a replacement for gasoline, thereby reducing pollutant emissions.

1.11.4.5. *Condensates*

Condensates are liquid fractions produced in association with natural gas by condensation during production. They are also known as natural gas liquids (NGLs).

The production of condensates is increasing strongly with the rapid development of natural gas production. Light condensates can be directly used as feedstock in the petrochemical industry, but heavy condensates must be treated in refineries in order to extract gasoline, diesel fuel and other products. Due to their characteristics, a condensate cannot be processed in a traditional refinery. Several specialized refineries have been or will be constructed, but the majority of production is mixed with other crude oils for transport and subsequent processing.

1.11.4.6. *Naphtha and petrochemicals*

Petrochemicals are omnipresent in our lives. They are used to produce plastic materials, synthetic fibers, drugs, solvents, perfumes, fertilizer, insecticides, etc.

The petrochemical industry is based on two basic processes. Steam cracking brings naphtha (or in some cases LPG or middle distillates) to temperatures that are far higher than those used in other refining processes, of the order of 900°C. Steam cracking mainly produces olefins, particularly ethylene and propylene, as well as heavier streams (e.g. steam-cracked gasoline) which contain aromatics including benzene. Another process – catalytic reforming – provides aromatics, which are base molecules that along with ethylene and propylene undergo polymerization (the molecules become linked) to produce plastics, synthetic fibers and synthetic rubbers, which we are all familiar with.

The proportion of oil used as a raw material for petrochemicals only represents some 12% of world oil production. However, the added value is high.

1.11.5. *Marketing and distribution of petroleum products*

Depending on the type of products and the users, delivery and storage will vary significantly. Large users (industry, airports, etc.) are often directly supplied by refineries using pipelines, inland waterways or rail. Road transport fuels sold in service stations follow a more complex route. They are transported as above from the refinery to a storage depot and from there by road tank wagon to the service stations. The latter requires very good logistics and has proven to be costly (two-thirds of jobs in the oil sector are in this last stage).

For the past 20 years, in Europe, companies have been streamlining their distribution network by reducing the number of their service stations, concentrating them on major traffic routes and expanding the services they offer, to fight competition from new entrants, particularly the hypermarkets, which have won a large market share in many countries. In developing countries, there is still a fair increase in the consumption of motor fuels and in the construction of service stations.

1.12. Natural gas

Natural gas, like oil, consists of hydrocarbons, but contains a higher proportion of hydrogen and a lower proportion of carbon. Therefore, using natural gas to generate electricity means emitting 50% less CO_2 than using coal and roughly 30% less CO_2 than using oil. The electricity yield is 60% in CCGTs versus barely 40% for other thermal fuels such as coal, heavy fuel oil, etc. Natural gas is the main source of electricity generation in North America, the CIS, the Middle East and Africa.

The geography of gas production is very different from the geography of oil production. While the cost of transporting oil represents only a small part of its price, the cost of gas transport and distribution is very high. Natural gas can be transported by gas pipeline or by ship following liquefaction (LNG chain). The vessels are called methane tankers or LNG carriers. In the case of a pipeline, the same pipeline can transport five to ten times more energy in liquid form (oil) than in the form of gas. Trade is therefore subject to the constraint of proximity, and it is harder to speak of a worldwide price for this product. Furthermore, the nature of the supply, via gas pipeline or LNG, greatly affects prices. Hence, for example, Japan pays more for its gas, since it must be imported in methane tankers.

Therefore, for a long period, the gas market remained mainly regional and several trade zones developed relatively independently from one another (North America; Europe with suppliers coming mainly from Russia – before the invasion of Ukraine – Norway and North Africa; Asia with supplies from Qatar, Malaysia, Indonesia, Australia, more central Asian countries and Russia). The main gas producers are therefore either consumers (United States, China, Russia) or countries that are close to major consumers (Canada for the United States; Norway and Algeria for Europe; Malaysia, Indonesia, Australia and Qatar for Asia). Demand for natural gas has grown considerably in the United States and China in recent years.

1.12.1. *Natural gas: exploration and production*

The formation of natural gas is analogous to that of oil. The evolution of microorganisms into either liquid (crude oil) or gas (natural gas) mainly depends on temperature and pressure conditions.

The cost of producing gas is generally lower than that of oil: once wells have been drilled, gas rises spontaneously from the reservoir. Furthermore, when it is "associated" with oil production, its production cost may be considered to be zero

– or nearly so – since both the capital and operating costs are primarily incurred to produce the oil.

1.12.2. *Natural gas processing*

Raw gas from reservoirs is processed to remove the major impurities and heavy fractions. Natural gas is mainly composed of methane, but it also contains varying proportions of ethane, propane, butane, etc. It can contain significant proportions of CO_2 and nitrogen, which must be eliminated as they reduce the calorific value. Lacq gas, discovered in France in 1951, contained high proportions of H_2S (hydrogen sulfide), which had to be eliminated for reasons of pollution and corrosion.

Processing consists of recovering most of the propane and butane, as well as the heavier fractions.

1.12.3. *Natural gas transport*

Natural gas can be transported by pipeline or in liquid form on ships specialized in the transport of LNG or in methane tankers.

Transport by pipeline remains the preferred method, particularly over short distances. It is more economical than the LNG chain, which only becomes competitive beyond several thousand miles (Figure 1.11). Used to transport gas over long distances, a gas pipeline must be resistant to the high pressure (exceeding 150 bars) provided by compressor plants located throughout the route (every 30–120 miles), permitting the gas to be transported at speeds of tens of miles per hour (mph).

The number of compressor plants and their power depends on the resistance of the gas pipeline and that depends on its diameter, which may reach 120 cm (50 inches).

Transport by ship requires that the natural gas be liquefied. To do this, the temperature of the gas must be lowered to –162°C, the liquefaction temperature of methane. This operation is extremely expensive. A liquefaction plant generally includes several parallel units (trains), and each train can process up to several billion cubic meters of gas per year. Therefore, Qatar now has LNG trains with a unit capacity of 8 Mt/year.

The liquid gas is then loaded onto a specialized ship, called a methane tanker. For a long time the capacity of a methane tanker was of the order of 100–150,000 cubic meters, but today, it may reach 260,000 cubic meters. Of course, the liquid gas must be regasified upon arrival in the consuming country, to be introduced into the mass transport network.

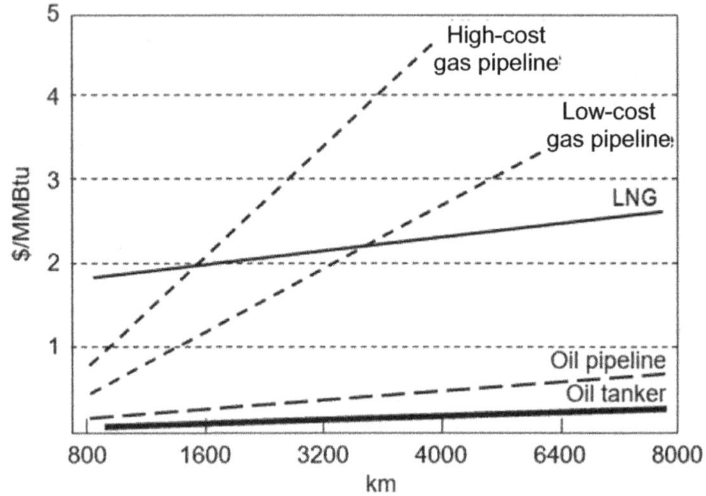

Figure 1.11. *Gas transportation costs: pipelines versus LNG (source: IFP énergies nouvelles)*

1.12.4. *Use of natural gas*

The first gas used on a large scale was town gas, simultaneously discovered at the end of the 18th century by the Frenchman Philippe Lebon and the Englishman William Murdoch. This gas is produced by pyrolysis of hard coal or wood, i.e. heating it to a high temperature in the absence of air. Up to the mid-19th century, it was mainly used to light streets and buildings; then other uses, such as heating, were developed.

After 1880, the development of electricity slowed growth in the use of town gas, which came to a halt around 1929 with the Great Depression.

Natural gas then took over from town gas, principally in the USA, from the start of the 20th century. Its use would remain marginal in the rest of the world until World War II. In France, town gas manufacturing plants still existed in the 1960s (the last one at Belfort closed in 1971). However, the discovery of the natural gas deposit in Lacq in 1951 encouraged rapid development of natural gas. The same situation occurred in Italy with the reserves of the Po Plain and, in the Netherlands, with the Groningen deposit (discovered in 1960, it allowed the Netherlands to export natural gas throughout Europe).

Natural gas is a fuel that can be used in most sectors where the production of heat is needed, the so-called residential and commercial sector for cooking and the heating of buildings, the industrial sector and the electricity generation sector.

Compressed natural gas (CNG) is used to power internal combustion engine vehicles in the Asia–Pacific region (Singapore, Malaysia, China, Pakistan, India), in Iran and Egypt and in some South American nations such as Brazil and Argentina. CNG is increasingly used to power buses, trains, cabs, tuk-tuks and vans in developing countries. In Delhi, India, all commercial passenger vehicles must now run on CNG, by government decree, in a bid to reduce air pollution.

Finally, natural gas can be used to produce methanol, a basic raw material used in the manufacture of many chemical compounds. Currently, its main use nevertheless remains the generation of electricity.

GTL is a process used in the chemical conversion of natural gas, for the production of high-quality liquid petroleum products (naphtha, diesel and lubricants). It is based on the same principle as CTL, which starts by gasifying coal. Then – in both cases – the gas is partially burned, resulting in a mixture of carbon monoxide and hydrogen which is used to synthesize heavy molecules, leading finally to the production of fuels.

In 1923, German chemists Fischer and Tropsch developed a process for producing liquid fuels (gasoline, diesel) from coal (CTL process). This process was used by Germany during World War II to manufacture fuels, as Germany had no oil deposits.

In the 1950s, South Africa built a coal liquefaction plant (the SASOL plant at Secunda) in response to the international community's embargo on oil deliveries to combat apartheid. In the same context, South Africa also built a GTL plant: the PetroSA plant in Mossel Bay, in the south of the country.

Due to the abundance of gas, a few new plants have been built, mainly in Qatar and Nigeria.

However, GTL fuels are more expensive to produce than conventional fuels and development of this technology is likely to be limited.

Box 1.13. *CTL, GTL: coal to liquids, gas to liquids*

1.13. Coal

Coal is a mixture of mineral elements, sulfur and nearly pure carbon. Its combustion therefore releases large amounts of CO_2 (and also SO_2 and NO_x). Major efforts are currently underway to make coal "cleaner", both for old and new power plants.

The steam engine was the key factor in the industrial revolution and its use depended on coal. This use of coal marked a dual break: first, the switch from renewable energies (mainly wood) to fossil energies; second, the switch to a system in which energy distribution became a structured industry. It was only by 1800 that coal replaced wood as the main source of energy, and it was in turn replaced by oil as the main source of energy at the start of the 1950s.

Coal is available throughout the world. The main consumers of coal are also major producers (China, the United States, India, etc.), since transport costs are relatively high. More than 85% of coal extracted throughout the world is currently consumed in the country of production.

A clean coal plant has the following characteristics:

– It eliminates sulfur oxides (SO_2) and nitrogen oxides (NO_x) upstream via a circulating fluidized bed and downstream via the processing of exhaust gases.

– It shows improved efficiency: the average efficiency of coal-fired power plants is only 38%. The switch to supercritical cycles can achieve 40–45%, while ultra-supercritical cycles (700°C) can achieve 50%.

– It can operate using co-combustion with biomass.

In summary, the majority of traditional pollution is eliminated and CO_2 emissions are reduced.

Box 1.14. *Clean coal*

Coal production is increasingly concentrated in countries where exploitation is possible at a low cost: open-cast mines or those of shallow depth, with significant reserves. European production – located in deep mines and therefore costly – is strongly declining.

The use of coal is being gradually reduced to the production of electricity and steel. However, it remains the main source of energy for the production of electricity and its consumption continues to grow in this sector (in recent years, coal consumption significantly benefitted from increased oil prices). Nonetheless, there are large differences between geographical zones. A large volume of coal reserves, prices that are lower and less volatile than those of competing energies and "clean coal" technologies all make coal a valuable source of energy source. However, CO_2 emissions should lead to a strong reduction of coal use.

1.13.1. *Origin of coal*

The formation of coal results from the accumulation of plant debris in sediments and its gradual burying under successive layers of material. This process of overlaying deposits gives birth to solid and combustible substances of high carbon content. Depending on how old the formation is, there may be three major categories of fuel: bituminous, lignite or peat:

– *Bituminous coal* was formed 200–300 million years ago, during the so-called Carboniferous period at the end of the Paleozoic era. At that time, the Earth resembled a vast greenhouse, covered with marshes and luxurious vegetation favored by a warm, humid climate. Bituminous coal is the best solid fuel. Compact and black, it has undergone in-depth transformation and no trace of plant life is visible to the naked eye.

– *Lignite*, also known as brown coal, is of more recent formation (Mesozoic and Tertiary eras). It is a fuel of limited calorific value and more polluting.

– *Peat* is found in recent sedimentary formations, is still forming today in peat bogs and is a very mediocre fuel[2].

1.13.2. *Coal production*

Coal is extracted either in open-cast mines or underground tunnels. Choice of the exploitation method depends on the deposit's geological configuration and its environment. If the overburden which covers the layers of coal is not very thick, the deposit is exploited by open-cast mining. If the coal layer is deep, it is mined by digging a network of underground tunnels. This process is complex and costly and may be spread out over 10 years.

Thanks to increasingly complex modern equipment, open-cast mining may be used for deposits under surface layers as thick as 400 meters (1,300 feet). In this way, yields and results are much better than those obtained using tunnels. First, a large surface area must be cleared; the surface layers (which are also called waste rocks)

---

2 Peat is nevertheless used for electricity generation in the Republic of Ireland, where two peat burning stations were commissioned in 2004/2005.

are removed and the coal is extracted. Waste rocks will be used for backfill during site reclamation. The coal layers gradually appear.

This method has many advantages: working conditions that are less harsh, far greater productivity than that of underground mines, and reduced timeframes for entry into production (2–5 years). Furthermore, since they offer great management flexibility, open-cast mines can adapt better to market demand.

1.13.3. *Coal transport*

Over limited distances, coal is mainly transported by rail and inland waterways. A slurry pipeline may also be used, which is a pipe that carries a suspension of coal in water.

More than 75% of international coal commerce is carried by sea. Most major coal ports have been modernized due to this increasing trade. Coal is carried either by bulk carriers or by mixed cargo vessels that can also transport oil. The larger the capacity of the transporter, the greater the reduction in the cost of sea freight. However, although large cargo loads have increased, there are still small ships for cabotage operations between European countries.

1.13.4. *Coal end-use*

In contrast to oil or gas, coal is a physically stable material and relatively easy to use. However, the extraction and transportation of coal results in significant environmental pollution in the form of fugitive dust (air pollution), soil degradation and groundwater pollution.

The name coal is sometimes reserved for bituminous coal alone. However, there are several qualities of bituminous coal:

– *Anthracite* is highly sought after, but its reserves are limited. It is most widely used for individual home heating.

– *Coking coal* is used for the manufacture of steel. In the blast furnace, iron ore is mixed with coke, which provides the heating and chemical energy needed to transform the ore into molten cast iron, which will then be used to produce steel. The production of a ton of steel requires roughly 600 kg of coke.

– "*Steam*" coal is the main coal used in industrial boilers.

Lignite and peat are used only in electrical power plants and such plants pose serious environmental problems. Like its neighbors, the former Czechoslovakia and

Poland, the former East Germany used enormous quantities of lignite – which has low calorific value but is very rich in sulfur – for the production of electricity. The neighboring forests suffered significant damage because of this. Following German reunification, the use of lignite ceased.

However, the use of coal is strongly defended in the major coal-producing countries (China, India and North America), and its future is linked to the possibility of generating "cleaner" coal, as well as the possibility of CO_2 sequestration.

1.14. Conclusion

Energy demand grows with population growth and rising living standards. There are many sources of energy. Each has its advantages and disadvantages.

Climate change is forcing us to reduce CO_2 emissions, and hence fossil fuel consumption. However, consumption of coal, and above all oil and gas, will remain high for many years to come.

2

The Energy Transition

2.1. Defining the energy transition

The transition of the world's energy systems in the 21st century is driven not only by rising energy demand and the availability of new technologies but also by the threat posed by climate change. Climate change is due to emissions of greenhouse gases (GHGs; the greenhouse effect causing global warming), chief among them CO_2 (followed by methane). The work of the Intergovernmental Panel on Climate Change (IPCC) has shown that it is essential to drastically reduce global CO_2 emissions. Energy accounts for 72% of global GHG emissions. The need for low-carbon energy production and consumption has therefore become a priority in the 21st century. The simultaneous increase in the world's population and average standard of living will lead to a rapid rise in energy demand over the next few years, making the issue of energy transition all the more complex.

To a great extent, growth in carbon emissions is a product of the increase in energy growth. Primary energy consumption increased by 5.8% in 2021, exceeding 2019 levels by 1.3% – the largest increase in history and more than reversing the sharp decline seen in 2020 during the Covid-19 lockdowns. China accounted for a majority of this growth in primary energy consumption. Notably, this growth in primary energy consumption was primarily driven by renewables followed by natural gas and coal. Both the slowdown in energy demand and shift in the energy mix towards natural gas and renewables have led to a decline in growth of carbon emissions. In fact, the growth of renewables exceeded the growth in nuclear energy for the first time in 2019. However, the 0.5% rise in carbon missions, although slower than the 10-year average, only partially offset the significant growth of emissions witnessed in 2018 (2.1%). Countries such as the USA, Russia and India, which had exhibited strong growth in energy demand in 2018, showcased much slower growth in energy markets in 2019. On the contrary, China dominated the expansion in global energy markets, contributing the biggest increases for each source of energy apart from natural gas, second only to the USA by a short margin. In 2021, emissions from energy rebounded strongly back to around 2019 levels. As economic activity recovered from lockdowns and other Covid-19-related measures, energy consumption increased sharply. Carbon intensity, and to lesser extent, energy intensity, were largely unchanged in 2021. Perhaps the most significant change was in the global energy prices, which increased sharply in 2021. The most pronounced increase was in the price of natural gas, quadrupling in Europe, tripling in Asia and doubling in the USA.

To a large extent, the growth in carbon emissions is the product of the increase in primary energy consumption which resumed its rise post-Covid-19 and reached a new record in 2023. China is behind most of this growth in primary energy consumption which was mainly covered by renewable energy, followed by natural gas and coal. The slowdown in energy demand growth over the past two years after the 2021 rebound and the shift in the energy mix towards natural gas and renewables have led to a decline in carbon emissions growth. It is of course renewable energies, particularly solar and wind, which are growing the fastest.

2.2. Why do we need an energy transition?

2.2.1. *Climate change and the greenhouse effect*

Certain gases in the Earth's atmosphere trap the heat produced by some of the thermal radiation reflected back from the Earth, causing temperatures to rise. This is known as the "greenhouse effect". Without the greenhouse effect, the Earth's surface temperature would be around −18°C.

The ability of certain gases to retain heat was demonstrated as early as the mid-19th century by several scientists (Eunice Foote in 1856, John Tyndall in 1859). In 1896, Svante August Arrhenius was the first to assert that the combustion of fossil fuels could lead to global warming. However, this discovery remained in the shadows for many years, as scientists believed that the oceans were capable of absorbing CO_2 production. Furthermore, work carried out in the 1970s showed a downward trend in temperatures between 1940 and 1970, suggesting a new Ice Age! It was not until 1988 that global warming was finally accepted as a reality and the IPCC set up to study climate change.

2.2.2. *Developments in climate negotiations*

It was at the Rio Earth Summit in 1992 that the first global treaty on climate change was signed, namely the United Nations Framework Convention on Climate

Change (UNFCCC), along with the Rio sister conventions (UN Convention on Biological Diversity and UN Convention to Combat Desertification).

The UNFCCC adopted the Kyoto Protocol at the third Conference of the Parties (COP3) in 1997 to stabilize greenhouse gas emissions at an acceptable level. It came into force in 2005, setting legally binding emission reduction targets for 37 industrialized countries for a limited period (2008–2012).

The Kyoto Protocol was conceived as an experimental protocol where flexible mechanisms could be tested, providing a benchmark for the next protocol due to come into force in 2013, which never happened. Notably, eight years were lost between the signing of the Kyoto Protocol and its adoption, both in terms of time and credibility. During this period, industries and markets did nothing to meet decarbonization targets, as they waited for the Protocol to come into force.

Three flexibility mechanisms based on innovation and markets were highlighted in the Kyoto Protocol: carbon markets, the Clean Development Mechanism and the Joint Implementation.

Carbon markets allow operators unable to reduce their CO_2 emissions to the required level to buy emission permits from other players. The Clean Development Mechanism (CDM) enables companies from countries with quantified greenhouse gas emission reduction commitments under the Kyoto Protocol to carry out and/or co-finance emission reduction projects in countries without quantified commitments (developing countries, emerging economies), and to receive carbon credits in return. Joint Implementation (JI) is a Kyoto Protocol program that enables developed countries to reduce their greenhouse gas emissions by financing projects that reduce emissions in other industrialized countries.

After years of negotiations, on December 12, 2015, 195 nations signed the Paris climate agreement at the end of the 21st Conference of the Parties (COP21). For the first time, this historic agreement brought all nations together around a common cause based on their past, present and future responsibilities in the fight against climate change. Actions and investments to move towards a low-carbon, resilient and sustainable future were discussed. The objective of the Paris Agreement is simple: to limit global temperature rise to less than 2°C above pre-industrial levels by the end of the 21st century, and to continue efforts to limit warming to 1.5°C. The aim is to reduce emissions of six greenhouse gases: carbon dioxide (CO_2), methane (CH_4), nitrogen oxides (N_20), hydrofluorocarbons (HFC), perfluorocarbons (PFCs) and sulfur hexafluoride. The two most critical gases are CO_2, which comes largely from the combustion of fossil fuels, and methane (a methane molecule has 20 times the “greenhouse effect” power of CO_2, but a much shorter lifespan).

Unlike the Kyoto Protocol, the Paris Agreement does not impose binding emission reduction targets. Instead, nation-states determine their own emission reduction objectives through so-called Nationally Determined Contributions (NDCs). For some critics, the absence of binding targets means that the agreement is merely a normative climate action plan, rather than a binding treaty. Nevertheless, it represents an important step forward in the fight against climate change.

How can we meet the Paris targets?

2.3. The main ways of combating climate change

2.3.1. *Economic tools: regulations*

Governments have a crucial role to play in implementing regulations to ensure that companies limit GHG emissions and manufacture products with limited GHG emissions. Regulations in the energy sector can take the form of energy efficiency standards in the heating and air-conditioning sectors, vehicle emission standards, etc. For example, the US Corporate Average Fuel Economy (CAFE) regulation imposes a minimum number of miles a vehicle can travel on a gallon of gasoline. In Europe, regulations limiting the number of grams of CO_2 emitted per kilometer by a vehicle are of a similar nature. The aim is to encourage manufacturers of internal combustion engines to improve the performance of their vehicles. Building insulation regulations aim to limit heating and air-conditioning consumption.

2.3.2. *Economic tools: taxes*

An energy tax is a tax on the production, transport or consumption of energy. These taxes can be important sources of revenue for governments. They are also intended to reduce consumption and to favor or discourage certain types of fuel or certain forms of energy use. In oil-producing countries, fuel prices are often very low because they are subsidized, which encourages high fuel consumption.

Conversely, in other countries, energy taxes have been used to limit the use of fossil fuels such as oil, coal and natural gas. Part of the revenue can be used to help finance renewable energies.

2.3.3. *Economic tools: emissions markets*

The very first emissions trading scheme was set up in the United States to reduce SO_2 (sulfur dioxide, the source of highly corrosive acid rain) emissions. The principle is simple: a maximum level of emissions is defined for a zone, and each emitter has an emission quota. If it emits more than this quota, and if the cost of reducing its emissions is very high, it can buy emission rights from other players emitting less or who can reduce their emissions at a low cost. Such a system is known as cap-and-trade.

This system has worked very well for SO_2 in the USA. It has also been implemented in Europe for CO_2 emissions, but initially with more limited success. Everything depends on the quotas allocated to the various players. If these allowances are too high (and governments may be inclined to allocate high allowances so as not to penalize economic players who generate wealth and jobs), the price per ton of CO_2 emitted may be low and provide insufficient incentive to reduce emissions. The number of emissions trading schemes around the world is growing. In addition to the European Union Emission Trading System (EUETS), national or sub-national systems are already in place or under development in Canada, China, Japan, New Zealand, South Korea, Switzerland and the United States.

Recently, from 2021 onwards, the price of carbon emission permits in the European Union Emissions Trading Scheme (ETS) has risen sharply. This is a step towards the price levels deemed necessary to trigger investment in innovative clean technologies. International carbon markets could play a key role in reducing global greenhouse gas emissions.

2.3.4. *Energy savings*

The aim is to reduce energy consumption without limiting the production of goods and services. Energy efficiency is one way of achieving energy savings, for example insulating buildings, reducing heating and cooling needs, installing light-emitting diode bulbs, fluorescent lighting, etc. According to the International Energy Agency (IEA), better building insulation, improved industrial processes and advances in transport could reduce the world's energy needs by a third by 2050 and help reduce global greenhouse gas emissions. The IEA recommends removing subsidies on energy products, which encourage high energy consumption and inefficient energy use in many countries. Reducing energy consumption through greater energy efficiency also has national security benefits, as it reduces fuel imports and/or slows the rate of depletion of domestic energy resources. Energy efficiency, renewable energies and competitive markets are the three essential pillars of a sustainable energy policy.

2.3.5. *Carbon capture, utilization and storage*

Carbon capture, utilization and storage (CCUS), as the name suggests, involves capturing CO_2 and either using it (e.g. reinjecting it into oil fields to increase pressure and thus production) or injecting it into deep geological formations (including depleted oil and gas reservoirs or saline formations). If it is not used on site, the captured CO_2 is compressed and transported by pipeline, ship, train or truck for use or reinjection.

Carbon capture and storage can be effective in capturing carbon emissions from coal combustion, which can then be described as "clean coal". However, these techniques are costly and reduce the efficiency of the power plants concerned.

According to the IEA, CCUS could make a substantial contribution to reducing greenhouse gas emissions by 2050. Without CCUS, the fight against climate change will require very substantial additional investment. However, there are still a limited number of large-scale CCUS installations in the world (around 50 in 2024). Together, these facilities could only capture around 100 million tons of carbon dioxide per year, which is still very low compared to the 38 billion tons emitted each year. In the United States, for example, the Obama administration invested only $84 million in post-combustion CCUS technology at the Petra Nova plant 30 miles southwest of Houston, which could capture 1.6 million tons of carbon dioxide a year. Investment in CCUS remains limited but could develop rapidly.

It should be noted that the use of this technique on a large scale is likely to pose problems of acceptability to local communities, as injection into the subsoil could give rise to concerns.

2.3.6. *Fuel switching (from coal to gas in particular)*

Natural gas can replace more polluting fuels, mainly coal, and limit carbon emissions (furthermore, burning gas emits virtually no polluting products, unlike coal or even oil). According to the IEA, the switch from coal to gas has saved around 500 million tons of CO_2 since 2010 – an effect equivalent to putting 200 million more carbon-free electric vehicles on the road over the same period.

In the United States, the shale oil revolution has considerably increased the supply and lowered the price of natural gas, which has largely replaced coal for power generation. The market share of gas has increased more than that of any other energy source in the United States. Chinese demand for gas has also grown very rapidly in recent years to improve air quality. There is huge potential in the power sector, particularly in the United States and Europe, to reduce carbon emissions by replacing coal with gas.

However, since transporting natural gas by pipeline or in liquefied form (LNG) is expensive, the geographical proximity of gas-rich regions is a determining factor.

Russia's invasion of Ukraine in 2022 and the resulting geopolitical conflict between Russia and Europe have triggered an unprecedented global energy crisis, leading to a sharp rise in the price of household energy consumption. Until 2021, Russia supplied between 30% and 40% of the EU's total gas consumption, with dependence reaching 65% in Germany.

In response to the interruption in Russian gas supplies, the European Union has taken a number of measures that have enabled the situation to return to normal: reducing gas consumption (by more than 10%); increasing gas imports from Norway, Algeria and above all the United States; and improving energy efficiency. The flexibility of the gas market has enabled this rapid, almost unhoped-for return to a normal situation. The EU plans to end Europe's dependence on Russian gas, diversify its gas supplies and reduce its dependence on fossil fuels by increasing the share of renewable energies, in line with the REPowerEU plan.

2.3.7. *Renewable energies*

Renewable energies are developing rapidly because their cost is falling thanks to technical progress. Their main application is the production of electricity, but they are also used as a source of heat and to produce fuels. Worldwide, renewable energies (biomass, hydroelectricity and new renewable energies such as solar, wind, geothermal, etc.) will account for around 13% of the world's primary energy consumption and almost 30% of the world's electricity production by 2022. Biomass consumption is mainly non-commercial (in Africa, wood is used by households who cut wood for cooking close to home without paying for it). This biomass consumption is difficult to assess, but probably represents around 10% (source: IEA) of total energy consumption worldwide.

Hydropower accounts for almost 6% and new renewable energies (wind, solar, geothermal) for almost 8% of global commercial energy consumption. However, the share of these new renewable energies (excluding hydroelectricity and biofuels) in global electricity production is growing fast. They now account for 30–40% of the electricity produced in countries such as Germany, Spain, the UK and Ireland.

In 2023, more than half of the increase in electricity production from renewable energies (wind, solar) came from China. This can be explained by the scale of China's electricity needs and the need to reduce the pollution created by coal-fired power stations, which still cover the majority of these needs. After China, the United States and Japan are the two countries that have increased their production of renewable energy the most. Globally, while coal's share of electricity production has fallen, renewable energies have accounted for the biggest increase in electricity production, with 600 TWh, while other sources of electricity have remained stable.

Although the share of renewable energies in global electricity production in 2023 was almost 30%, it is important to remember that electricity end uses account for only 16% of total final energy consumption. Consequently, recent growth in the share of renewables in final energy consumption has been concentrated in the electricity sector. The growth of renewables in transport and heating, which are the two major sectors of energy consumption, will be slower even if the development of the electric car benefits from progress in non-carbon energies.

Furthermore, only solar and wind energy are likely to be widely developed, provided that they are acceptable to the local population. For some time, the development of other renewable energies, such as marine energy, will remain limited due to technical and economic constraints.

2.3.7.1. *Hydropower*

Water is neither created nor destroyed, but constantly moved. This is the water cycle: run-off, evaporation, precipitation, etc. The flow of water provides energy that can be converted into electricity at high efficiency. Dams (run-of-river dams or reservoir dams where water is stored) are an important source of electricity, often coupled with irrigation. Many dams were built in the 1950s, and it is now estimated that, in areas such as Europe, most of the best sites are already in operation. In other regions (South America, Asia), the potential remains significant. The construction of a dam has major consequences, such as the flooding of large areas and the displacement of populations, and these are becoming increasingly difficult to accept. Some organizations are against the construction of new facilities.

The Three Gorges Dam in China, the largest dam in the world with a capacity of over 20 GW (equivalent to more than 10 EPRs or 20 traditional nuclear power stations built in the 1980s), is 185 meters high and over 2 km long. It required 27 million cubic meters of concrete and is estimated to have cost 23 billion euros. However, it led to the displacement of more than a million people. The Itaïpu dam, between Paraguay and Brazil, is the second largest dam in the world, with a capacity of 14 GW. Built in the 1970s, its figures are equally impressive: 180 m high, 7,900 m long, a reservoir covering 1,350 km^2 and, for the record, the amount of steel used is 380 times the weight of the Eiffel Tower! Another important dam is the Aswan Dam, built in the 1960s as a symbol of cooperation between Nasser's Egypt and the USSR, led at the time by Khrushchev. It was criticized, particularly by Westerners, because it risked retaining the silt that enriched the land irrigated by the Nile downstream of the dam.

The construction of the Grand Renaissance of Ethiopia Dam (GERD) on the Nile, the largest dam in Africa and one of the largest dams in the world, is a source of tension between Ethiopia and Egypt. Its filling (which has already begun) could affect Egypt's water resources. However, this dam is a very important source of electricity in a region that is still largely deprived of it.

South America is the region of the world where hydroelectricity is the most important source of electricity. However, periods of drought in Venezuela, for example, have led to power shortages that have had a profound effect on the country's economy. Similar droughts have affected hydroelectric production in China and Southern Europe. Some countries have therefore developed alternative systems, such as Brazil, which has built gas-fired power stations supplied by Bolivia. However, there are still many dam projects in the region.

In Africa, in addition to the Aswan and GERD dams already mentioned, there is significant potential in Mozambique and Guinea (in the Fouta Djalon massif). However, the main potential lies on the Congo River. The Inga Falls, between Kinshasa and the mouth of the river, have a potential of 40 GW, twice the power of the Three Gorges dam. To date, only two dams, of 350 and 1,420 MW respectively, were built in 1972 and 1982. They were supposed to supply local industries (aluminum, petrochemicals) and the Katanga mines, which produce metals including copper. Both dams operate at low capacity due to poor maintenance. A 4,500 MW, the INGA 3 dam is currently under study. The Grand Inga dam project would have a capacity of 39 GW, but is still some way off.

2.3.7.2. *Traditional biomass*

Biomass comes in a wide variety of forms: wood, charcoal, plant debris, crop residues, animal debris, agricultural and urban waste. Biomass is considered a renewable energy source, since the energy it contains comes from the sun. Unlike other renewable energies, when biomass is used (by combustion), it releases CO_2 into the atmosphere. However, this combustion only releases the CO_2 that the plant has absorbed from the atmosphere through photosynthesis during its growth, whereas the use of fossil fuels involves releasing into the atmosphere carbon dioxide that has been buried in the Earth's crust for millions of years.

A large proportion of the population of sub-Saharan Africa and certain countries in Asia and South America rely solely on wood for cooking and heating. The energy potential of biomass worldwide is estimated at 2.2 Gtoe per year, broken down as follows: 900 Mtep for crops, 850 Mtep for forests and 450 Mtep for organic waste.

However, the efficiency with which traditional biomass is used is generally very low, and its use is a source of numerous problems: time spent by women and children collecting it to the detriment of other activities (training, for example), emissions of toxic products (fine particles) during combustion, which is generally carried out in a perfunctory manner. The toxic products inhaled by women and children in wood-burning homes are a real public health problem: respiratory illnesses kill as many people as malaria in Africa. Numerous variants of improved stoves are available to increase the efficiency of wood use from 10 to 30 or 40%, but their success remains limited.

The main problem remains deforestation.

2.3.7.3. *Biomass in the form of biofuels*

Known as first-generation biofuels or agrofuels, ethanol and biodiesel are two fuels obtained from raw plant matter. Biodiesel results from the processing of vegetable oils (palm, sunflower, rapeseed, soy, coconut, jatropha, etc.), while ethanol is obtained by fermenting sugar extracted from sugar cane (in tropical countries such as Brazil), sugar beet (France) or cereals (USA). Biofuels contain atoms of oxygen that promote combustion and reduce pollutant emissions such as carbon monoxide and unburned hydrocarbons. Furthermore, the plants used to make biofuels absorb CO_2 as they grow. Hydrotreated vegetable oil (HVO) is produced by hydrotreating oils and fats. It can be blended with diesel without mixing limits, and is commonly referred to as "renewable diesel".

Fuel ethanol production was launched in Brazil in the early 1980s, at a time when crude oil prices were very high. However, falling crude oil prices made ethanol two to three times more expensive than petroleum-based fuels in the 1990s. The subsequent rise in crude oil prices made ethanol competitive again. Lower taxes also helped to offset the cost difference between traditional fuels and ethanol when oil prices were low.

As with crude oil, the quality and production cost of biofuels are highly variable, depending on crop yields, harvesting and transport costs. It has recently been estimated that a barrel of Brazilian bioethanol costs 60% of the price of a barrel of oil, a liter of American ethanol costs between \$0.5 and \$1.1, and a liter of biodiesel from the Ivory Coast (produced from palm oil) costs around \$1 (as a matter of comparison, the ex-refinery price of gasoline, excluding taxes and subsidies, is around $0.8 per liter when the price of oil is $80/bbl (price in 2024)). The viability of many biofuels depends on tax subsidies, and therefore on political decisions. The United States and Brazil are the world's leading producers of bio-gasoline and biodiesel. Together, they account for 62% of total global biofuel production, or just over 1.2 million barrels of oil equivalent per day in 2022 (1% of global oil production). Total agrofuels production is around 2 million barrels per day.

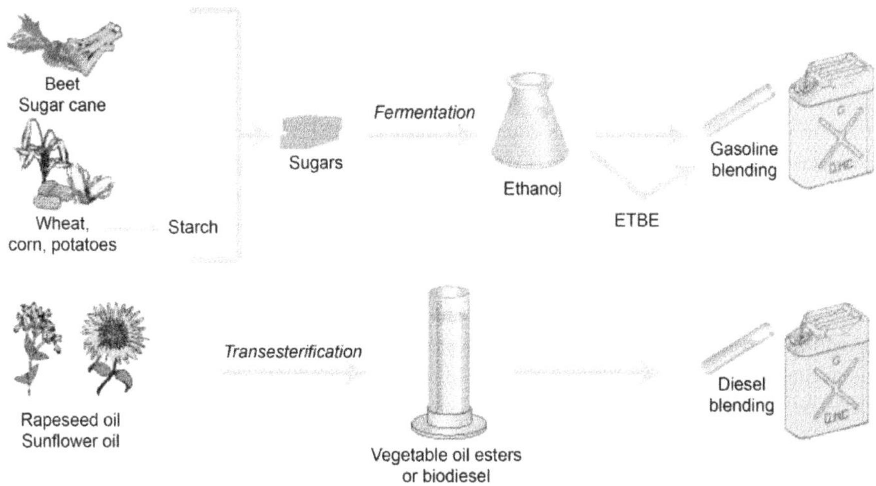

Figure 2.1. *Biomass in the form of biofuels*

While ethanol produced from sugarcane in Brazil probably has a favorable economic (moderate cost) and environmental (reduced CO_2 emissions) balance, ethanol production from corn, or even beet, probably has a more mixed record.

Work is underway on so-called second-generation ethanol, produced from lignocellulosic biomass, i.e. agricultural and forestry residues, and plantations such as coppice. Another method, the production of biofuels by biomass gasification followed by synthesis (BTL), is conceivable but very costly. These techniques are currently being developed. They will be essential if we are to meet our targets for reducing CO_2 emissions, particularly in the air transport sector.

In 2023, biofuel consumption rose by 6%, or 100,000 barrels of oil equivalent per day. Brazil, the United States and Indonesia were the main contributors to this trend.

Described as either an "environmental bulwark for a country's sustainable development" or a "crime against humanity", agrofuels are far from universally accepted. After several years of development, a number of concerns have emerged.

Biofuels have benefited from the growing awareness of global warming. Renewable in origin and usable as an alternative to petroleum products (which are responsible for 60% of CO_2 emissions in areas such as the European Union), biofuels were quickly perceived as a green energy source. However, these optimistic projections are theoretical: Nobel Prize-winning chemist Paul Crutzen estimates that, in some cases, the production of one liter of agrofuel can create twice as many greenhouse gases as "traditional" fuels. In fact, beyond the emissions released during biomass production and processing, everything depends on the land used to produce it. Depending on whether you use fallow land to plant oil palms or clear an equatorial forest, the balance sheet can be very positive or catastrophic. In Southeast Asia, almost 48% of oil palm acreage was taken from virgin or secondary forests, and in Malaysia, almost 87% of deforestation is attributable to oil palm cultivation. In addition to greenhouse gases, biofuel production can cause other environmental damage, such as soil acidification and water shortages.

There is a conflict between biofuel production and the need to feed populations. Available land is becoming increasingly scarce and replacing 10% of gasoline and diesel consumption in Europe and the USA would require around 20% and 25% of arable land in these regions respectively. At a time when IPCC is predicting a worsening of weather phenomena, including droughts and floods, which could lead to water and food shortages and a 50% drop in agricultural production for some countries, it is legitimate to fear that these plans will only provide "full tanks" at the cost of "empty stomachs". The importance of water should also be stressed. While 118 US gallons (450 liters) of water are needed for 1 kg of corn fodder, the United Nations predicts that 2.3 billion people will have no access to water by 2025.

Box 2.1. *Agrofuels: forbidden fruit or means of development?*

2.3.7.4. *Wind power*

Wind power is the third most important source of renewable energy, after biomass and hydropower. The largest wind turbine currently being tested in the Netherlands, built by France (for the blades) and Spain (for the mast), is 260 m high and has a blade span of over 220 m. With a rated output (for wind turbines and solar panels, peak output is the power available under the best conditions) of 12 MW, it could operate, under the best conditions, 4,000–5,000 hours a year (one year counts 8,600 hours). However, it would not always operate at full capacity, and could therefore only produce a few dozen GWh.

For the time being, most of the wind turbines installed are of more modest capacity, just a few MW, although of course this average capacity is tending to increase. Total installed capacity worldwide reached 900 GW in 2022 (for comparison, total electricity generation capacity in France is around 135 GW), compared with 7.5 G in 1997. The global potential for wind power is 12 TW (in 2022 total electricity generation capacity in the world stood at 8.5 TW).

China has the largest wind power production capacity (440 GW by 2022), representing 40% of the world's installed wind power capacity. It is followed by the USA (120 GW), Germany, India, Spain and the UK. Most wind turbines are installed on land, but a growing number of projects are located offshore.

The world's largest wind farm is currently located in China's Gansu province (hence the name Gansu wind farm or Jiuquan wind farm, named after the nearest town, Jianqiu). It will eventually bring together 7,000 wind turbines for a total power output of 20 GW, equivalent to that of the Three Gorges Dam. However, the project is progressing slower than expected, and its current capacity is no more than 10 GW. Furthermore, it is located a long way from consumer centers, and transmission losses are high.

European offshore wind farms are concentrated in the North Sea, particularly in Germany and the UK. The largest is the Dogger Bank wind farm, with a capacity of 3.6 GW, located 130 km off the British coast. Offshore wind power, although more expensive than onshore wind power, could in some countries be a driving force behind the energy transition, given the growing opposition to onshore projects linked to noise, landscape destruction, bird damage, etc. The UK, with its excellent offshore resources, is a perfect example of this potential. Conversely, China, with its many desert areas, could develop onshore wind power.

Offshore wind farms are the fastest-growing source of electricity generation in the 21st century, as they have a higher utilization rate and do not have the disadvantages of onshore wind turbines. However, some experts point to their impact on fisheries and the environment. Finally, investments are very high, the quantities of materials required are considerable, recycling of these materials is problematic, maintenance is difficult and costly, and the lifespan is uncertain.

The difficulty in using wind power is, of course, its intermittency. Wind turbines can usually only operate 20–30% of the time. Generally speaking, the operating rates of offshore wind farms (which can reach 50%) are much higher than those of onshore wind farms. Nevertheless, it is not easy to cope with this intermittency. One solution is a backup from a gas-fired power plant. Another solution is batteries. The cost of some batteries has been reduced by 80% over the last ten years.

Apart from batteries, various storage solutions have been proposed. For example, pumped-storage hydroelectricity (PSH) or pumped hydroelectric energy storage (PHES) systems use the electricity generated during off-peak hours, i.e. cheap electricity, to bring water up to a dam or reservoir at altitude. The water is released through turbines to produce electricity during peak hours when the price of electricity is high. The advantage is therefore economic, provided a suitable site is available. Other solutions, such as compressed air, have also been devised.

Figure 2.2. *Wind turbines*

2.3.7.5. *Solar energy*

The Earth's surface receives a quantity of solar energy equivalent to 10,000 times the world's energy demand. This equates to a very theoretical potential of 1–4 MWh/m^2/year.

The sun's energy can be used in many different ways. For example, "passive solar" means designing buildings that use direct sunlight for heating. These buildings need to be extremely well insulated, which underlines the importance of technical innovations in thermal insulation, materials, glazing, etc.

Solar energy can mean either:

– the use of thermal solar panels to capture heat and transfer it to a heat transfer fluid;

– the use of parabolic mirrors to concentrate the calorific power of solar radiation on a container of water (or molten salts). This technique is known as concentrated solar power (CSP). The steam from the boiling liquid drives a turbine. These installations operate mainly during the day, and their use is subject to weather variations. They do, however, have one advantage over photovoltaic systems (which we will describe shortly): while voltaic panel production ceases at sunset, CSP electricity production can continue beyond nightfall, thanks to the heat stored by the heat transfer fluids. This means that electricity needs can be met during the evening, a period of high demand;

– the use of photovoltaic solar systems/panels, which convert solar radiation directly into electricity using silicon cells or any other material capable of converting light into electricity (Figure 2.3). Research into improving efficiency and reducing costs is considerable; prices are falling all the time, and the yields of commercially available systems have risen from 5% to over 20% in the last 20 years. By 2020, installed solar power capacity was in excess of 700 GW, with China, the USA and India together accounting for over 75% of the global solar photovoltaic market (40% for China alone). In Africa, numerous power plants of just a few dozen MW have recently been built. Sunshine in Sahelian countries is obviously a decisive factor. As elsewhere, there is the problem of storage.

The largest plant is currently located in India: the Bhadla Solar Park, in the Thar Desert, covers 57 km^2 and has a capacity of 2.7 GW, with a target of 3.5 GW. Other very powerful plants also exist in India (Pavagada 2 GW, Kurnool Ultra Mega Solar Park, 1 GW).

However, China is the world's leading producer of solar energy. The second most powerful solar power plant is located near the Longyangxia Dam, at an altitude of 3,000 m, to compensate for intermittent sunlight. China also boasts some of the most powerful power plants in the world: Huanghe Hydropower Hainan Solar Park with 2.2 GW, Yanchi Ningxia Solar Park with 1 GW, Datang with 1 GW, expected to reach 3 GW, and Tengger with 1.5 GW.

Figure 2.3. *Photovoltaic solar panels*

The United Arab Emirates have taken advantage of their sunny climate to build several large-scale solar power plants. The Mohammed bin Rashid Al Maktoum solar park south of Dubai has a capacity of 1.3 GW, but is expected to reach 5 GW by 2030. It comprises 11 million solar panels and covers an area of 77 km^2.

2.3.7.6. *Geothermal energy*

The Earth is composed of a crust covering a mantle of molten rock. The amount of heat contained beneath the Earth's surface to a depth of 10,000 meters (33,000 feet) represents 50,000 times more energy than the world's total hydrocarbon reserves. Hot springs and geysers are manifestations of this intense underground activity. In Iceland and the Philippines, this energy, which is easy to harness, is widely used. Worldwide production of electricity from geothermal sources will soon reach 100 TWh (0.5% of total world production). The major advantages of this form of energy are its high availability – 70% on average – and its environmental benefits (CO_2 emissions are 10% of those of a gas-fired power plant).

However, drilling depths vary considerably from one location to another, and there is a risk of not finding a geothermal source. It is therefore important to establish the precise characteristics of the area to be drilled before launching this type of operation. Around 20 countries worldwide, mainly in Africa (Kenya, Rift Valley), Asia and North America, produce geothermal electricity. It is estimated that the number of countries using geothermal energy could more than double over the next years. It generally takes seven to eight years to develop a geothermal project. Its subsequent lifespan depends largely on the acidity of the water and the extent of the resulting pipe corrosion.

In addition to traditional geothermal energy, experimental hot dry rock (HDR) projects have been carried out. These involve injecting heat transfer fluids at great depth, often into former oil reservoirs (which allows detailed knowledge of the reservoir at low cost), and recovering them at the surface after heating them underground. The future of this technology is highly uncertain.

2.3.7.7. *Marine energies*

Marine renewable energies, sometimes called "blue energies", are classified into several categories according to the characteristics of the ocean they use, whether movement, heat or salinity. If we exclude offshore wind power, we can distinguish the following:

– Tidal power: several centuries ago, there were "tidal mills" operating on the following principle: a basin fills up when the tide rises, and when the difference in level between the water in the basin and the water in the ocean is sufficient at ebb tide, the water in the basin is released through a turbine to generate electricity. Like conventional hydroelectric dams, recent tidal power plants built on river estuaries are capable of holding back huge quantities of water twice a day. Once released, they generate electricity. In practice, however, few power plants exist. The oldest is undoubtedly the 240 MW Rance plant in France, inaugurated in 1965. Other smaller plants have been built. A slightly larger unit was built in South Korea in 2011 (254 MW). There are also plans for very large-scale projects. The Incheon power plant, also in South Korea, would have had a capacity of around 1,320 MW. However, this project, like others in Canada and Russia, was abandoned. The cost of the electricity produced is very high, several times higher than that of wind or solar power. The number of sites that can be equipped is also limited, as the necessary amplitude of the tides is considerable and can only be found in a few places.

– Ocean wave energy is a combination of wind and water power. Wind applies a force that concentrates on the ocean's surface, and this energy can be harnessed by floats fitted with pumps. Initially located on the coast, larger and larger experimental facilities are now moving out to sea. The experimental phase of these offshore wave power plants is nearing completion in Japan, India, Portugal, the UK and Norway. Plants are already operating in the Azores, Scotland (with a capacity of 0.5 MW per unit), and recently in Aguçadoura, northern Portugal (target installed capacity of 21 MW at an electricity cost lower than solar power). Massive development is by no means certain (visual problems, limited efficiency, etc.).

– The energy of ocean currents is comparable to the energy of wind above the surface of the water. To harness it, one can use tidal turbines, which are large propellers anchored to the seabed.

– Thermal energy from the seas: the sea has enormous heat reserves. The difference in temperature between surface and deep waters can be used to generate steam, which can then be used to generate electricity.

– Osmotic energy: this technique exploits the movement of water across a membrane between saltwater and freshwater reserves to generate electricity.

Although marine energies offer a number of advantages, their development has so far been limited. Corrosion due to sea salinity is a major drawback for this energy source.

2.4. The challenges facing renewable energies

The development of renewable energies faces a number of challenges.

2.4.1. *The availability of critical metals and the problem of scrap*

Technologies such as solar power, wind energy, fuel cells, batteries, electrolysis, hydrogen storage, electric cars and energy-efficient lighting all require metals: copper, nickel, aluminum, lithium, cobalt and rare earths, 17 chemical elements including scandium, yttrium and 15 lanthanides (including tellurium, indium, dysprosium, neodymium, ruthenium, etc.). The development of wind turbines, solar panels and electric cars will increase demand for these metals – often called critical metals since they are quite necessary for the energy transition – and for these rare earths, which are not so rare but very difficult to exploit or recycle.

There is a concern about the limited availability of these critical metals and rare earths. Their use also poses a problem in terms of waste management.

2.4.2. *The social impacts of mining*

Like most mining industries, the extraction of the metals and rare earths needed to manufacture wind turbines, photovoltaic panels, batteries etc. has significant impacts on the environment and on the workers in this sector. For example, more than half the world's total supply of cobalt (a key component of rechargeable lithium-ion batteries) comes from the Democratic Republic of Congo (DRC). However, the mining industry in the DRC is marked by human rights violations, such as the non-respect of labor rights and the proliferation of child labor. Fighting between DRC and neighboring countries for control over the production of cobalt and coltan (another strategic metal used for smart phones) has led to the death of thousands of victims.

2.4.3. *Intermittency and cost*

Wind and solar power are intermittent. Batteries can be a solution. However there is a cost. Some experts even believe that storing solar energy requires more batteries than the world will ever be able to produce, and even if that were the case, the costs would be unacceptably high.

2.4.4. *Space requirements for solar and wind farms*

Solar energy requires an average of 4 hectares per megawatt of electricity-generating capacity. To supply the entire planet (which is obviously an absurd hypothesis, but one that shows the limits of this solution), an area of 50,000–100,000 km^2 would be required. In the case of France alone, an estimated

5,000 km^2 would have to be developed, equivalent to around 1% of the country's total surface area. These figures should of course be considered as orders of magnitude.

Large-scale wind farms use between 10 and 60 hectares per megawatt of generating capacity, according to the National Renewable Energy Laboratory. This is largely due to the spacing required between turbines, typically 5 to 10 rotor lengths in diameter.

2.5. The hydrogen solution

Hydrogen has often been presented as a miracle solution to the world's energy needs. In recent years, substantial funds have been devoted to hydrogen energy.

Until recently, hydrogen was not considered an energy source, but rather an energy carrier. Recent research has shown that it exists naturally in quite a few places, but it is a kind of continuous production, by chemical reaction, of small, dilute quantities of hydrogen. Exploitation would therefore be complex. A case in point is the Bourakébougou deposit in Mali. Discovered by chance, the production of 98% pure hydrogen is used to power a microelectric power station. This hydrogen is known as "white" hydrogen.

Hydrogen requirements are currently limited to less than 100 million tons per year. Most is consumed in oil refineries to remove sulfur from petroleum products (hydrogen combines with sulfur to produce H_2S, which is then destroyed). Hydrogen can also be used as a fuel in motor vehicles, thanks to fuel cells. In these cells, hydrogen combines with oxygen to produce electricity and water, enabling totally clean mobility if the hydrogen is produced under clean conditions. Hydrogen-powered cars are already on the road. Hydrogen-powered trucks, buses and trains are currently being tested. Airbus has set itself the target of operating hydrogen-powered aircraft in the 2030s.

Today, hydrogen can be produced either from petroleum products (mainly natural gas) or by electrolysis of water. A distinction is made between:

– gray hydrogen, produced from hydrocarbons. A total of 95% of hydrogen is currently produced in oil refineries by "reforming" natural gas or petroleum products. But this reaction releases carbon in the form of CO_2, contributing to the greenhouse effect. However, if the CO_2 is reinjected into the ground using CCS or CCUS techniques, it becomes blue hydrogen;

– other production methods, which involve electrolyzing water and breaking it down into hydrogen and oxygen, by passing an electric current through an aqueous solution. There are different colors depending on the origin of the electricity:

- green hydrogen is produced using electricity from renewable sources such as wind and sun. In this way, we can take advantage of the availability of these energies (due to their intermittent nature) to use surplus electricity for hydrogen production,

- pink hydrogen: the electricity comes from a nuclear power plant, so there are no greenhouse gas emissions, but like all energy sources, nuclear power has the disadvantages already mentioned (accidents, emissions).

Hydrogen is not easy to use. It is even more difficult to liquefy than natural gas (hydrogen is liquid at −253°C), and its energy density per unit volume is very low: the calorific value of hydrogen is just 3 kWh/m^3, compared with 16 kWh/m^3 for methanol and 40 kWh/m^3 for natural gas. As seen, its production is complex, and the cost of producing 1 kg of hydrogen is three to five times that of gasoline. It is also difficult to transport. Current hydrogen pipeline projects mix around 15–20% hydrogen with natural gas. Finally, the small size of the molecule makes storage difficult, even in the most hermetically sealed tanks. Hydrogen has a tendency to leak, raising concerns about the high risk of accidents. The overall efficiency of the hydrogen chain is low, and massive storage is problematic.

However, new technologies and investments could make hydrogen acceptable in the future, and countries such as Germany, Japan, the USA and France are increasingly investing in this solution. Hydrogen can help to decarbonize sectors such as long-distance transport, the chemicals industry and the steel industry, where reducing emissions is particularly difficult. It can also be used to store energy from renewable energies and electricity in general.

2.6. Is the energy transition possible?

Growing environmental concerns and security of supply issues (see Chapter 4) have led to considerable interest in renewable energies. In particular, wind power and photovoltaic technology are inspiring great hopes. Their contribution to the global energy balance remains limited, but there is a strong political will in some countries, notably in Europe, China and India, to develop them. In October 2023, the European Union raised its renewable energy target to 42.5% of total energy production by 2030 (45% if possible). Clearly, hydropower will continue to play a major role in the energy transition to cleaner fuels, but wind and solar power are also set to develop rapidly, as evidenced by their very rapid expansion over the past decade.

In May 2021, the IEA released its ambitious Net Zero by 2050 Scenario, which has since set the tone for a new norm, stimulating higher ambition among governments and corporations. In the lead up to the 26th Conference of Parties of the UNFCCC (COP26), held in Glasgow in November 2021, 17 countries pledged to achieve net-zero emissions by 2050 or a later date, with some countries targeting 2025, and 151 countries submitted new or updated Nationally Determined Contributions (NDCs) towards reducing their greenhouse gas emissions under the Paris Agreement. In 2022 the European Union Commission raised its 2030 target for renewables due to the soaring gas prices in the aftermath of the Russian invasion in Ukraine. With increased attention on targeting net-zero emissions, by the end of 2021, nearly 85% of the world's population and 90% of its GDP were covered by some form of "net-zero target". However, these targets vary widely in their application (target date, status, greenhouse gas and scope) and in governance indicators used for tracking progress.

The COP 28 meeting in Dubai agreed on an "energy transition away from fossil fuels", which should accelerate the transition to net-zero carbon.

In principle, renewable energies have a lower environmental impact than fossil fuels. However, problems such as the need for critical metals (copper, nickel, aluminum, lithium, cobalt, etc.) and rare earths and the recycling and dismantling of wind turbines, solar panels and electric vehicles are difficult to resolve. Nevertheless, renewable energies have a decisive advantage, at least in terms of their use: they do not emit greenhouse gases, a major concern at the moment.

Renewable energies can be used to meet a wide range of needs for heat, electricity and, to some extent, fuels. The technologies are available, even if considerable progress still needs to be made to improve yields, reduce manufacturing costs and make energy permanently available. Resistance to their development is both economic (often low profitability) and political (opposition from part of the population to the noise and visual pollution induced by such equipment). It is the manifestation of the NIMBY syndrome – *Not In My BackYard*: people do not disagree in principle, but they do not want a project to alter their living environment. The installation of offshore wind turbines can also have an impact on the seabed and marine biodiversity.

However, renewable energies are also a means of providing energy to remote regions not connected to traditional energy distribution networks. In many parts of Africa, solar or wind power can provide electricity to populations, particularly rural ones, who are currently deprived of it.

By 2021, $1,900 billion had been invested in energy projects. Of this amount, over $700 billion was devoted to renewable energies. The largest investments were in wind and solar power. In China, 35% of energy investments have gone to renewables in recent years (32% in the USA and the European Union). More generally, the APAC (Asia–Pacific) region is investing massively in this sector.

2.6.1. *Carbon neutrality*

Carbon neutrality (source: European Parliament) implies a balance between carbon (or CO_2) emissions and the absorption of emitted carbon by carbon sinks, CCUS or carbon projects abroad. To achieve zero net emissions, all greenhouse gas emissions worldwide must be offset by carbon sequestration.

A carbon sink is a system that absorbs more carbon than it emits. The main natural carbon sinks are soil, forests and oceans. According to estimates, natural sinks eliminate between 9.5 and 11 gigatons of CO_2 per year. Annual global CO_2 emissions are about 38 Gt per year.

To date, no artificial carbon sink can remove carbon from the atmosphere on a scale sufficient to combat global warming.

Carbon stored in natural sinks, such as forests, is released into the atmosphere through forest fires, changes in land use or logging. It is therefore essential to reduce fires and deforestation.

It will be more difficult (and probably impossible) for a given country to achieve 100% renewable energies than to achieve carbon neutrality (via carbon sinks, CCUS or carbon projects abroad). The use of renewable energies for power generation is accelerating, but urgent action is needed in other sectors such as space heating/cooling, industry and transport. In at least 30 countries, renewable energies already account for over 20% of energy production. According to some experts, the main obstacle to the widespread implementation of large-scale renewable energies to limit CO_2 emissions is political, not technological. All the same, the main obstacles to achieving the Paris Agreement targets are probably climate change denial, the fossil fuel lobby, political inaction, unsustainable energy consumption, obsolete energy infrastructure and financial constraints. This is a source of debate.

2.6.2. *Can we achieve carbon neutrality by 2050?*

To limit global warming to below 2°C, or even 1.5°C, compared with pre-industrial levels (the target set by COP21 in Paris in 2015), profound changes are needed in most sectors of production, consumption and individual behavior. Although significant progress has been made in developing renewable energies worldwide, the current rate of increase in carbon emissions far exceeds the targets set.

In some countries, it is difficult to finance the transition to renewable energies. According to the IEA, limiting global warming to 1.5°C would require increasing the share of renewable energies in electricity generation to 70–85% by 2050, and an annual investment in the energy system of around US$ 2,400 billion (2010 value) between 2016 and 2035, representing around 2.5% of global GDP. A business-as-usual scenario would result in an average temperature rise of close to 3°C, or even higher.

In addition, deforestation for agricultural purposes has increased emissions by removing important natural carbon sinks. For example, the Amazon rainforest in South America now emits more carbon than it absorbs due to massive deforestation.

Some countries may be able to achieve carbon neutrality by 2050. It is unlikely that this objective will be achieved at global level by that date.

2.6.3. *Issues of international justice and equity*

Climate change is a global problem in which the responsibilities of individual countries are difficult to determine. Emissions depend on their level of development and consumption habits. If emissions in the United States, for example, are much higher than in Europe (on average), this is due in particular to the abundance of fossil fuel resources in America, whereas Europe has virtually none. While the United States, China and India are the three main CO_2 emitters, responsibilities differ depending on whether current emissions alone are taken into account or whether emissions from the past are included.

In addition, emerging countries, often located in Africa, are likely to suffer far greater economic and social impacts from global warming than advanced economies. Implementing low-carbon policies requires global cooperation and institutional capacity-building, which are weaker in developing countries. This calls for financial, technological and other support from the world's advanced economies. Social and environmental concerns must guide global cooperation to achieve an equitable energy transition. With energy demand set to rise over the next 25 years, and in the absence of far-reaching changes, emissions could increase by as much as two-thirds. Therefore, a successful energy transition scenario implies a 30–50% reduction in fossil fuel use by 2040.

Renewable energies are accessible to virtually every country in the world, provided the financing exists. However, there are differences in each nation's ability to improve its renewable energy infrastructure, due to varying degrees of availability of scarce minerals, technological capabilities, institutional capacities and a favorable political framework.

2.6.4. *The geopolitical race to renewable energies*

The transition from fossil fuels to renewable energies is affecting the global economy by altering trade and power relations. The energy transition represents an enormous challenge for hydrocarbon-producing countries. The Arab countries of the Gulf, which have long depended on the sale of oil for their domestic revenue, are attempting to modify their economic strategies by developing renewable energies (solar in particular). Given that many oil-rich nations are also rich in renewable energy sources, they have the potential to become new energy leaders, provided there is sufficient political will. The IEA forecasts a 50% increase in global electricity generation capacity from renewable sources between 2019 and 2024.

In its outlook, the IEA has so far explored several scenarios. Let us take two of them: the Stated Policies scenario – which relies on measures already in place and initiatives under development – and the so-called Sustainable Development scenario. In the Stated Policies scenario, the share of modern renewable energies reaches 15% of total final energy consumption in 2030. In the sustainable development scenario, the share of modern renewable energies in total final energy consumption increases at more than twice the rate observed since 2000, reaching 23% in 2030.

Innovation and technology will be decisive in improving energy efficiency, enabling the development of renewables and electricity transmission infrastructures, as well as energy storage. Some countries, such as China, the United States and the European states, have made renewables a priority. Other developing countries are still heavily dependent on fossil fuels.

Oil has been a major source of conflict over the last 160 years. We can dream that a global energy transition could lead to peaceful relations based on technical cooperation and mutual benefits. Renewable energies can contribute to economic development and alleviate some of the most crucial socio-economic problems afflicting the world today. Investing in renewable energies creates jobs, reduces some forms of pollution, improves access to energy and reduces competition for scarce national resources, generating a positive knock-on effect on the overall sustainable development of nation-states.

However, energy transitions are also accompanied by an increase in the mining of essential metals and minerals, leading to high levels of pollution and social problems. As reserves of critical minerals such as cobalt and lithium are concentrated in a few countries (China, DRC, Latin America), control of these minerals and supply chains could create conflicts, while exacerbating geopolitical rivalries. For example, the Democratic Republic of Congo (Congo Kinshasa) accounts for 70% of cobalt production, while South Africa is the world's largest producer of platinum (80%), chromium, manganese and vanadium. It is the second-largest producer of palladium and zirconium. A large proportion of lithium reserves are located in Latin America (Chile–Argentina–Bolivia triangle) and Australia. China controls 70% of rare earth production.

However, according to the IEA, mining assets are exposed to increasing climatic risks. Copper and lithium are particularly vulnerable to water stress, given the high water requirements for their extraction. Over 50% of current lithium and copper production is concentrated in regions with high levels of water stress. Several major producing regions, such as South America and China, are also prone to extreme heat or flooding, threatening reliable and sustainable supplies.

The continued decline in the cost of renewable energies will transform global energy markets, with a shift in dependence on hydrocarbon producers and an overall reduction in price vulnerability. This is best illustrated by the growing investment in renewable energy projects around the world by some of the world's largest oil companies, such as BP, Shell and Total.

The example of Germany shows that the energy transition is complex. In place for almost 10 years, the *Energiewende* (German for "energy transition") aims in principle to transform the German energy system into a more efficient one powered largely by renewable energy sources and without nuclear power generation (the last reactors were closed in 2023). Germany has made great strides in the decarbonization of its electricity sector by development of wind and solar power. This has led to difficulties for the national grid, which regularly faces critical situations when production falls short of consumption. Wind turbines are located in the north of the country and solar panels in the south, while significant consumption is located in central Germany. The direct financial cost of Germany's energy transition is already close to 500 billion euros. German households and businesses pay much more for electricity than in most other OECD countries. The phasing out of nuclear power and coal is likely to increase the country's dependence on natural gas, but Russian supplies have been stopped. It is therefore increasingly important to pursue efforts to diversify gas supply options, notably by importing liquefied natural gas.

With reference to renewable energies, countries can be classified as follows:

– countries with high technical potential for renewable energy production as potential energy exporters, such as Australia, Chile and Brazil;

– mineral-rich countries as potential suppliers of the raw materials needed for renewable technologies;

– countries with a high capacity for technological innovation in renewable energy markets, such as China.

Therefore, the energy transition will give rise to new energy geographies based on comparative advantages in terms of technology, solar and wind energy resources, relative prices and transport costs. This phenomenon could also lead to a new geopolitical map, with areas that were once considered strategic for oil trade, such as the Straits of Hormuz and Malacca, losing their importance in the 21st century. However, the emergence of new trade routes could lead to new types of conflict between nation-states. Power cuts could be used as a geopolitical weapon by countries that dominate energy networks.

2.7. Energy and sociology

Asia–Pacific and Europe have set high targets for renewable energies, both in the short and long terms.

However, in the absence of very strong and unlikely constraints, the transport sector will continue to use large quantities of petroleum products for many years to come. The industrial sector also requires large quantities of energy, for which fossil fuels are currently best suited. In the residential and commercial sector, on the contrary, energy supply and efficiency could evolve rapidly over the next few years.

Significant savings can be achieved through better building design and insulation. Solar or even wind-powered equipment could make these buildings self-sufficient in terms of heating, electricity and air conditioning. It is even possible for the electricity produced to exceed a building's needs and be sold to local producers via a grid connection, as demonstrated by the growing use of solar photovoltaic arrays in residential areas.

The sociological aspect of this point is important. A centralized electricity production system, in which each citizen is a passive consumer, can be replaced by a system in which citizens have become autonomous producers. This autonomy can be extended to transport, with individuals producing electricity to recharge their cars.

A utopia? Absolutely. However, climate change could make this utopia necessary.

2.8. International oil companies: "Beyond Petroleum"

Despite their need for medium-term profitability and their relations with oil-producing countries, international oil companies (IOCs) are nevertheless stepping up their investments in renewable energies. Their focus is often on sectors in which they are already present, if only symbolically.

With its highly publicized rebranding as *Beyond Petroleum* in 2000, BP was the first to cross the symbolic threshold of beyond petroleum. Already benefiting from the 30 years' experience of its BP Solar subsidiary (target sales of $1 billion in 2008) in the field of solar energy, BP announced in 2005 the creation of *BP Alternative Energy* to manage an $8 billion investment program over 10 years. Since 2005, $2.9 billion has been invested in wind, solar, carbon capture and storage and biofuels, including a $1 billion commitment to Brazilian ethanol in summer 2008.

One of the world's largest non-governmental corporations, ExxonMobil, a strong advocate of profitability and financial pragmatism, has been a latecomer to alternative energies. It has shown only minor interest, preferring to focus on energy savings and pollution risks, as well as on providing grants to research organizations such as Stanford's *Global Climate and Energy Project*, worth $100 million over 10 years.

In 2016, the CEOs of the 10 largest oil companies launched a joint initiative, the *Oil and Gas Climate Initiate*, aimed at reducing greenhouse gas emissions with a billion-dollar fund to be invested over a decade.

In 2020, several major companies committed to achieving carbon neutrality by 2050.

2.9. Conclusion

An energy transition can only be a win-win situation if policy-makers make a concerted effort to analyze the opportunities it offers and mitigate some of the risks involved. The biggest obstacle is posed by industrial sectors, which are traditionally dependent on fossil fuels. Social provisions must therefore be made for the millions of people employed by this sector in order to integrate them into the new energy system. Industrial policy and social policy can no longer be separated into two opposing domains, and must be synthesized to enable a large-scale energy transition. Resources must be invested in retraining the workforce and creating a new workforce with the know-how required for a new energy system.

There is no doubt about the need to reduce CO_2 emissions. However, is the "net-zero emissions" target by 2050 that many countries – at least the most developed – have set themselves easy to achieve? Probably not. Fossil fuels still account for over 80% of total energy consumption. Replacing these fossil fuels with renewable energies, particularly wind and solar, will be a complex task. Wind turbines and solar panels take up a lot of space. They require large quantities of metals and rare earths, the ultimate resources for low-carbon technologies. These are poorly understood, and their extraction currently poses formidable environmental and social problems.

The stakes are high. The solutions are complex. Scientific research and the desire for energy sobriety may perhaps enable us to meet the challenges of the future.

3

Energy Markets and Prices: Situation and Outlook

3.1. Introduction: markets and prices

Energy markets are among the world's most important commodity markets. The volumes traded are considerable. For the main products (oil, gas, electricity, etc.), there are both physical markets and futures markets. Physical markets are as old as the commodities concerned, and futures markets appeared around 1980, at a time when prices, hitherto often fixed over long periods of time, were becoming volatile. In particular, futures markets enable operators to protect themselves against price variations.

Energy encompasses oil, natural gas, coal, nuclear, hydroelectricity, solar, wind, wood and more. Therefore, is there a price for energy when its forms are so diverse? The answer is partly yes, because all types of energy are needed to meet global demand, and one form can often be substituted for another: to produce electricity, we can use coal, oil, gas or, of course, nuclear, hydro or wind power. Also, when there is competition between energies, their prices are linked. However, substitutions can be limited, leading to sharp price divergences. In September 2022, the price of oil approached \$100 per barrel (\$/bbl), while the price of gas in Europe reached over \$60/MBtu, equivalent, on a calorific basis, to almost \$400/bbl of oil! Note that the price at the same time in the southern United States, where the main production is located, was only approximately \$8/MBtu, equivalent to \$50/bbl of oil (prices in other areas of the United States – the northeast, for example, where demand is very high – can be much higher). By 2024, gas prices in Europe, as we will see, returned to a level close to previous values (approximately \$10/MBtu).

The energy sector is capital-intensive. Massive investments are required for production: billions of dollars are spent to bring an oil or natural gas field on stream, to operate a coal mine or to build a nuclear power plant or a dam, and hundreds of millions for a wind farm or solar power plant. Once the investment has been made, the capital invested must be recovered. The units must therefore, if possible, operate at full capacity. Of course, the problem is more complex for energies such as wind and solar power, which are by definition intermittent. Sometimes, in a situation of strong competition, with excess capacity and marginal production costs, the price can be low, as operators will tend to reduce sales prices to cover marginal costs alone.

It is interesting to note that the Covid-19 crisis temporarily led to very low oil, gas and coal prices, but this did not stop the development of renewable energies, thanks in particular to guaranteed price systems.

The oil industry has particular characteristics. The size and location of the deposits in the Middle East are such that production costs are only a few dollars per barrel. In addition, oil being liquid, it can be transported inexpensively, even over long distances. Consequently, Middle Eastern oil is arguably the cheapest energy source in the world, even though, paradoxically, it is not currently the most used, mainly for geopolitical reasons. At the time of the oil crises of 1973 and 1979, oil supplies from the Middle East appeared less secure and consumers relied more on oil from the North Sea, Alaska or Africa.

Global energy supply therefore comprises three distinct components:

– the supply of oil from OPEC countries, particularly in the Middle East, which is characterized by low overall costs. The adjustment of supply to demand is therefore ensured by the OPEC countries, which means that it is they who can set the price of oil and indirectly that of other fossil fuels[1] (Figure 3.1);

– non-OPEC oil, as well as gas, coal, nuclear and hydroelectric power, all of which have higher production costs;

– renewable energies, whose development is becoming independent of fossil fuel prices, thanks to feed-in tariffs in many countries.

1 It is said that OPEC countries play the role of "swing producers". This role is due to economic – but also geopolitical – reasons. Following the 1973 embargo by Arab oil-producing countries against certain consuming countries, the major oil-consuming countries sought to diversify their supplies and obtain oil from non-OPEC countries.

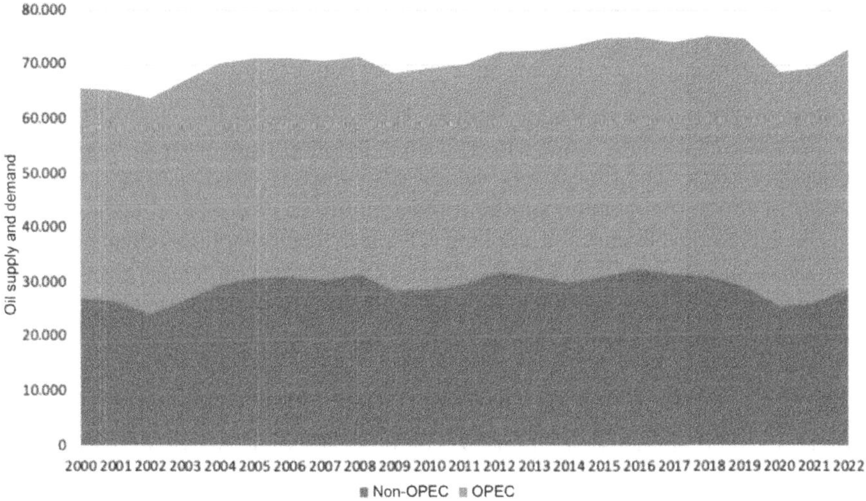

Figure 3.1. *OPEC's share of total oil production (source: OPEC Annual Statistical Bulletin 2023). For a color version of this figure, see www.iste.co.uk/favennec/geopolitics1.zip*

3.2. An introduction to the electricity market

The history of the electric power industry began at the end of the 19th century. In 1869, a Belgian engineer, Zénobe Gramme, developed the first industrial dynamo (a generator using electromagnets), just one year after Werner von Siemens had produced an experimental dynamo. In 1877, it was Gramme again who succeeded in industrially manufacturing alternators. In 1879, direct current was available from a power station for distribution in London. In 1882, Thomas Edison built a power station in New York with a distribution network serving 59 customers equipped with light bulbs. By the end of the decade, the use of electric motors extended demand to a full 24-hour day. Many American cities had electricity generation and distribution systems, but the use of direct current strictly limits the area that can be served, due to the considerable losses incurred during transmission. Alternating current, which reduces losses, was developed by George Westinghouse, in particular at the Niagara Dam. Alternating current became the industrial standard.

3.3. An introduction to the gas market

The calorific and lighting power of natural gas has been known to the Chinese for thousands of years. However, in Europe, the first gas to be used was town gas, a synthetic gas produced by the closed distillation of coal. This gas appeared at the end of the 18th century and was used for lighting.

In 1821, in Fredonia (USA), William Hart, considered the "father of natural gas", dug the first North American well after observing gas bubbles rising to the surface in a creek. The first known natural gas company, Fredonia Gas Light, was founded in 1858. The invention of the Bunsen burner in 1885 opened up new outlets for gas, including heating and cooking. However, consumption remained highly localized, as it was impossible to transport large quantities of natural gas over long distances. In 1890, a major change came with the invention of watertight joints, enabling the construction of a gas pipeline linking Chicago to a reservoir in Indiana.

However, it was not until after World War II that natural gas consumption expanded, thanks to the development of pipeline networks and storage systems. It then definitively replaced town gas. In Europe, deposits were discovered in the Po plains in Italy, Lacq in France and Groningen in the Netherlands in the 1950s, then in the North Sea in the 1960s.

3.4. The first gas and electricity companies

In the gas and electricity sectors, in the 19th and early 20th centuries, local and private companies set up production units and local distribution networks in major cities, often with the help of foreign capital. In France, on the eve of World War II, private companies were responsible for gas and electricity production and distribution in areas covering one or more towns. They were inspired by the rail transport model, with several companies sharing the French network. The national territory was cut into slices of a "cake", with Paris at its center. One of these companies is the famous PLM (Paris, Lyon, Marseille).

In the United States, private companies called IOUs[2] supplied 90% of electricity production in 1900. Competition between them for downtown consumer markets was fierce. Nevertheless, the increasing cost, size and efficiency of power plants made consolidation inevitable. Electricity distribution networks expanded beyond city and soon state boundaries. Federal rules were put in place to regulate the rates and accounts of municipal generation and distribution companies. As electricity distribution was recognized as a natural monopoly, standards of control were established. The federal government intervened to promote rural electrification, which was less profitable. This intervention accelerated during the Great Depression, because the IOUs were abusing their dominant market positions. At the end of 1941, the Tennessee Valley Authority's major hydroelectric programs gave

2 Investor-owned utilities.

the states and the federal government control over a significant share of electricity production.

3.5. The rise of interventionism after World War II

In the United States, since 1938, private gas producers have been selling to a single buyer, with a monopoly on transport and distribution in identified geographical areas.

The end of World War II marked a turning point in industrial organization, particularly in Europe. In some countries, such as France and the Netherlands, the government opted for public enterprise status for this monopoly. In the United States, on the contrary, the government preferred to entrust the monopoly to private companies. In all cases, the monopoly company, as the sole buyer, controls the balance between supply and demand. This has led to real success stories, such as Gaz de France (GDF) or Gasunie in the Netherlands. Vertical integration, which ensures a centralized view of production capacity, and thus optimizes investment between base and peak, has been adopted by the majority in Europe, but not in the United States.

After the war, a number of European countries nationalized their rail, gas, electricity and later telecommunications sectors for economic, political and social reasons:

– *Economic*: national companies had a monopoly, which enabled them to reduce costs;

– *Political*: resistance movements against Nazism, in which Communists played an important role, were generally hostile to the economic liberalism of the interwar period, which was said to have favored the rise of Nazism; they also sometimes punished private owners accused of collaborating with the German occupation authorities;

– *Social*: national companies seemed best placed to meet public service obligations, supplying all consumers, whatever the cost and under comparable price conditions. Keynesian ideas were dominant at the time, and state intervention in the economy seemed natural.

The structure of the gas industry changed in Europe after World War II. In France, the nationalization law of April 6, 1946 created Gaz de France, which grouped together 615 gas operations representing 550 coal-fired gas plants (94% of French gas assets).

As in the case of natural gas, the development of electricity generation and distribution was initially driven by private companies operating locally. In France, in 1946, there were 86 thermal power plants and 300 hydroelectric power plants divided between 154 companies. Over 1,200 companies were involved in transmission and distribution. The nationalization law of April 8, 1946 transferred the assets of electricity generation, transmission and distribution companies to Électricité de France (EDF).

This business model was working well. The major national gas and electricity companies were able to deploy the resources required to develop production capacity and transmission and distribution networks at a satisfactory pace. After all, the population's fast-growing needs have to be met.

The 1960s seemed to mark the beginning of a new "golden age" for humankind, based on strong, uninterrupted economic growth. GNP was rising by 5–6% a year, and the application of Keynesian theories meant that the days of recessions were finally over. Growing demand, particularly for energy, was generating sustained economic activity.

The United States, on the contrary, had chosen to leave electricity and gas to the private sector. Private companies did, however, operate under the supervision of a regulator, managed differently in each state. The regulator allowed producers to set prices that cover costs plus a profit (a "fair" rate of return).

In Europe, public utilities charged a price set by the government. The fundamental difference between Europe and the United States was not necessarily the way in which the price was calculated, but rather the fact that in Europe, the price was governed by the state, whereas in the United States, electricity markets were fully privatized.

3.6. The 1970s: the resource issue and the economic crisis

The radiant landscape of endless growth (and, importantly, near-full employment in industrialized countries) began to darken in the late 1960s. The exponential increase in consumption gave cause for concern. Experts from the Club of Rome published "The Limits to Growth" (Meadows report), in which they warned of the imminent exhaustion of raw materials. At the same time, a new generation was emerging that did not recognize itself in the consumer society and was looking for a new model of society. Organizational structures were also changing.

In the early 1970s, economic growth in Europe began to slow, with rising unemployment following the first oil shock (1973). Despite all the measures taken by governments in North America, Europe and Japan to stimulate their economies, a new phenomenon appeared: stagflation (the term is a contraction of stagnation and inflation). Since the war, it seemed possible for governments to manage the economy to avoid unemployment and high inflation, but this policy was no longer working. Inflation has exceeded 10% in many countries. Unemployment also reached close to 10% in several countries in the early 1980s.

The liberal economic theories, ignored during the period when Keynesian-inspired economic policies seemed to be succeeding, have come back into fashion. According to these theories, Western economies suffer from excessive state intervention. Deregulation and privatization are necessary.

The aim of deregulation is to eliminate barriers to competition. Price controls are to be abolished, monopolies are to be replaced by companies operating competitively, and customs barriers are to be lifted. Deregulation is often based on the theory that, as a result of technical progress, leaner, more flexible production facilities can compete with natural monopolies and perform better. Greater competition between economic players is supposed to foster progress and benefit consumers in the form of lower prices. Consumers can then consume more and invest more: in both cases, economic activity is increased. It is a virtuous circle whose positive effects should benefit us all.

Privatization is firstly a means of achieving greater efficiency. Private companies under the control of their shareholders are supposed to be more efficient than state monopolies because the state is not best placed to manage production operations. There is another objective: to generate revenue for the state.

Another area where state control was very strong until the 1980s was the refining and marketing of fuels. With the exception of the United States and a few European countries, the state regulated activities and prices in most countries. Deregulation was introduced in the 1980s, first in Europe, then in Japan. In France, the last controls on fuel prices were abolished in 1986, and a law enacted in 1992 considerably reduced government control over the oil industry.

3.7. The example of the UK energy sector

In the early 1970s, Chile, which had passed from the socialist regime of Salvador Allende to the dictatorial military regime of Augusto Pinochet, was the country where Milton Friedman's "Chicago Boys" put their highly liberal economic theories into practice. However, it was the arrival in power of Conservative Party leader Margaret Thatcher in the UK in 1979 that marked the beginning of liberalization in Western economies. The British Prime Minister's fight against regulation culminated in the coal miners' strike in 1984. Despite the miners' impressive mobilization, the strike was a failure. The unions were weakened and had to give way to privatization.

In the oil sector, the privatization of the British National Oil Corporation (BNOC) was the first step. The BNOC was later taken over by BP. Deregulation of the gas industry began in 1982 and, with the Gas Act of 1986, competitors of British Gas, which until then had been a monopoly, were allowed to use its network to supply consumers using a minimum quantity of gas. Subsequently, British Gas had to split its gas transport and trading operations into two independent companies: Transco and British Gas International. This separation of activities was known as unbundling. An independent regulatory body, the Office of Gas Supply (Ofgas), was created to promote competition, and the gas industry came under the authority of the Office of Fair Trading, responsible for ensuring compliance with competition legislation. Today, Centrica is the leading supplier of natural gas in the UK, under the British Gas brand. Centrica is also a major gas producer, producing 29% of the UK's gas requirements. Centrica is one of the UK's electricity suppliers, with seven power stations totaling 3,420 MW. It has diversified its power generation activities and invested in renewable energies.

Deregulation of the electricity sector began in 1990. A pool of producers created a system of daily auctions for wholesale supplies. However, the rise in prices observed in the first few years, which was the opposite of what was intended, demonstrated the need to maintain a degree of regulation, at least for the transitional phase.

3.8. The example of the US energy sector

In the United States, the regulation of oil, gas and electricity distribution is overseen by an independent government agency, officially linked to the Department of Energy: the Federal Energy Regulatory Commission (FERC). It was created following the 1977 reorganization of the Federal Power Commission (FPC), itself established in 1920. It also oversees wholesale sales of electricity and oil, licenses hydroelectric projects and approves the construction of interstate pipelines, storage facilities and liquefied natural gas terminals. It guarantees non-discriminatory access to the network for third parties, and can force a company deemed to be excessively dominant to split up into independent companies.

When Ronald Reagan became President of the United States in 1981, he modeled his economic policy on that of Margaret Thatcher. At the time, the structure of the natural gas industry in the United States was simple: gas producers sold their product to distribution companies, which were licensed by the federal government to build interstate networks. Since 1956, the federal government has regulated the price of gas at the wellhead, and the selling price to local distribution companies (LDCs). The states set the end-user price.

From 1985, users were able to buy gas directly from producers, independently of any transmission contract. Then, in 1992, the separation of transport and sales activities was decreed by law. These sectors were opened up to competition, and users were free to choose their service providers. At the same time, a spot gas market began to develop in 1982, and wellhead prices were fully deregulated in 1989.

The FERC also restructured the electricity market. In 1992, the Energy Policy Act opened up electricity generation to competition, allowing independent power producers to sell energy outside their home state. As a result, the United States moved from a system of territorial licenses to a free market in which customers were no longer dependent on a single supplier.

In 2005, the Energy Policy Act was passed by Congress and signed into law by George W. Bush. It notably exempted natural gas production from the constraints imposed by the Clean Air Act, the Safe Drinking Water Act, the Clean Water Act and CERCLA, a law enabling federal authorities to identify the parties responsible for contaminating a site and compel them to clean it up.

At present, the situation in the United States is that of a market with very different structures from one state to another, but which coexist. Some states have deregulated the electricity sector, others have not, and the variety of strategies remains very great.

On the whole, the electricity sector remains legally regulated to avoid monopoly situations: to this end, each state has a public utilities commission which must ensure that competition is respected.

3.9. Towards a single electricity market in the European Union

In Europe, the drive towards deregulation and privatization is in line with the vision set out by the founding fathers of the European Union (EU), who wanted to create a single market open to competition (Common Market). In the energy sector, the first step was to abolish all price controls on petroleum products. Nevertheless, the European Commission maintained the notion of public service for electricity, qualifying it as a "service of general interest". Until the 1990s, national governments retained control over the organization of the electricity sector. Although there were differences, in most countries electricity was in the hands of a vertically integrated company.

As criticism of this model grew throughout the 1970s and 1980s, governments gradually introduced competition, under the impetus of the European Commission. The Commission's aim was to establish a common market for electricity (and gas), as for other goods and services. The aim was to lower consumer prices through competition. From the EU's point of view, market deregulation and the integration of member states into a single market would also enhance the security of supply. This would mean more players in the market, and companies across the EU would be able to sell the electricity they produce in other EU countries thanks to cross-border interconnections.

Following the British example, the gas and electricity markets were progressively liberalized. However, it was difficult to obtain the agreement of the majority of member states to liberalize their electricity markets. The European Commission therefore chose to use the competition and free movement articles of the European Economic Community (EEC) Treaty to push member states to abandon vertically integrated state monopolies in the electricity sector, as there were no specific energy policy provisions at the time. To achieve its objective, the Commission focused on Article 90 of the EEC Treaty, which states that monopolies hinder the free movement of goods and services and cannot be justified in terms of public service obligations.

In 1996, the first directive on energy markets was adopted. It provided a set of common rules for the internal electricity market. It had three main objectives:

– the creation of a competitive internal electricity market, aimed at improving energy efficiency and lowering consumer prices;

– security of supply;

– improving environmental protection through better coordination of environmental policies between member states.

In 2003, faced with the fact that implementation of the First Energy Directive varied widely from one country to another, the European Parliament and the Council proposed a second directive. It repealed the previous directive and laid down common rules for the internal electricity market. This directive places particular emphasis on the role of domestic consumers, which had not been addressed in the first energy directive. It gives end-users the possibility of changing supplier easily, while remaining protected from any threat of potential disconnection from the grid.

The Third Energy Directive, adopted in 2009, aims to remedy the shortcomings of the previous directive, and sets a final deadline of March 2011 for Member States to implement the Commission's plan. It also introduces incentives to develop renewable energies.

To date, the Commission's deregulation efforts have yielded significant results, as the EU now has a functioning common electricity market. Consumers can buy electricity directly or indirectly from any producer, and producers can sell electricity directly or indirectly to millions of consumers throughout the market.

The benefits of this competitive market have yet to be demonstrated. Electricity prices have tended to rise since the implementation of the directives. The meteoric rise in electricity prices on the wholesale market in the summer of 2021, and again in the early months of Russia's invasion of Ukraine, can make us regret the days when public authorities managed natural "monopolies". Prices returned to more reasonable levels in 2023, but a reform of the electricity market was implemented at the end of 2023 to prevent consumers from being confronted with excessive prices.

3.10. Characteristics of electricity markets

For some, like crude oil and natural gas, electricity is a commodity that can be bought, sold and traded. Nevertheless, due to the physical characteristics of electricity, electricity markets differ from other commodity markets for three main reasons:

– Firstly, it is always difficult to store large volumes of electricity in an economically viable way, so the value of electricity varies considerably according to time and situation. This explains, in part, the differences in electricity prices observed at different moments.

– Secondly, since electricity flows are difficult to control, there is a high risk of cascading failures and blackouts.

– Thirdly, for the electricity market to function properly, generating plants must constantly adapt to variable demand. If this is not the case, blackouts can occur.

This requires flexibility. Balancing supply and demand is a complex issue, made all the more difficult by the increasing penetration of renewable energies in the power grid. A company's flexibility, in other words its ability to modify its production or consumption very quickly, is therefore of considerable value.

Ensuring a balanced and stable market is a real challenge for operators. That is why several players are responsible for managing the power grid. The most important roles in the market are those of the transmission system operator (TSO) and the distribution system operator (DSO). While TSOs are responsible for transporting electricity at the national level, DSOs are responsible for distribution to the end-consumer, implementing the necessary investments. Operators also ensure that electricity can be supplied to consumers throughout the year, by reinforcing and maintaining the network. In principle, each country has a single TSO. However, there are exceptions, such as Germany, which has four. As far as DSOs are concerned, the situation can vary considerably, since Germany has over 800, while the UK has only 5. TSOs and DSOs are private or sometimes public entities (in Europe), but are nevertheless controlled by a national regulator who ensures that they comply with market regulations.

To ensure that electricity supply meets demand, the TSO coordinates the operation of generating units. In the event of a discrepancy, the TSO asks producers to increase or reduce electricity production, thereby modifying the system frequency. If the frequency does not correspond to a predetermined range, the TSO is obliged to adapt the system load by adding or removing generation or load (demand).

Market players are required to inform the grid operator of their forecasts for electricity production and consumption, as well as their transmission requirements. In practice, authorized bodies provide the grid operator with daily information on their planned transactions for the following day, as well as on the networks they will be using to transmit electricity. It is then up to the DSO to adjust the amount of electricity each actor will consume and produce. As seen, when the network is faced with too much demand and too little supply (or vice versa), the system frequency will be either too high or too low, which can lead to brown outs (partial or temporary reduction in system voltage or capacity) or black outs (in effect: system collapse and production shutdown).

3.11. Wholesale and retail electricity market

As with other energy sources, there are two types of electricity market: wholesale and retail. Wholesale electricity markets enable exchanges between producers, retailers and other financial intermediaries, for both short-term and future electricity deliveries. Retail electricity markets organize the sale of electricity to end-users.

The wholesale electricity market is central to the operation of any national electricity system, as it balances supply and demand. The wholesale market is made up of the following players: generators, suppliers, traders and demand-side management operators. Generators trade and sell the electricity produced by their power plants. Suppliers source and market electricity, reselling it to end-consumers. Traders buy electricity for the sole purpose of reselling it, thus ensuring market liquidity. Demand-side management operators are responsible for ensuring that the market operates smoothly.

The retail market plays an essential role as the last link in the electricity supply chain. It enables electricity retailers to supply energy to residential and commercial customers. The retail market has three key elements structuring the smooth operation of the market: a specific framework, a guarantee of competition, and balancing and reconciliation services (imbalance management), enabling the settlement of electricity supply contracts. Retail markets in which consumers can choose their supplier are a fairly recent phenomenon, resulting from the liberalization of electricity markets in certain regions of the world.

3.12. The electricity business

In practical terms, the electricity market operates like an auction, allowing electricity production to be determined on a day-to-day basis. Suppliers offer the electricity produced by their power plants at a certain price. Wholesalers submit bids to meet their end customers' demand for energy. Demand is met by taking the lowest-priced bids first, of course, and then selecting bids in ascending order of price. Market negotiations end when the quantity of electricity offered and the quantity demanded match. There are two electricity markets: the Day-Ahead market and the Intraday market. The Day-Ahead market exchanges electricity for delivery the following day. It enables the TSO to ensure that the network will be balanced, and to modify demand in terms of availability and flexibility of supply and demand.

Spot prices (electricity prices for almost immediate delivery) are the most commonly used prices for trading on electricity markets. There are spot prices for the Day-Ahead market and spot prices for the Intraday market. Futures contracts, on the contrary, are traded for delivery in the future.

3.13. The price of electricity

The price set by an operator generally differs depending on whether it concerns industrial, commercial or residential consumers. The average price per kWh for residential end-users is significantly higher than for commercial and industrial consumers, because the costs associated with serving large commercial and industrial customers using big quantities of energy are lower (economies of scale).

The cost of electricity depends on many factors based on the type of client: production route, the size of the plant and whether the production is at base or peak levels. Base-load production (the production provided most of the time) is provided by the cheapest power plants (nuclear or coal-fired), as well as by wind, solar and hydro power.

Production required for shorter periods (semi-base-load and peak) is provided by gas-fired power plants, or even those using fuel oil. Generation costs at plants burning gas or fuel oil and operating only some tens of hours per year are significantly higher than those at nuclear or coal base-load plants.

The price of electricity varies according to the type of consumer, the level of competition in the market and, above all, the time it is supplied. The cost volatility of prices is staggering: during some fortunately rare times of the year, the price of electricity may be several dozen times that of a period of low demand. This is because electricity cannot be stored, and very costly generation plants must be brought on line for short periods to meet peak demand.

Order-of-magnitude electricity generation costs in new plants from 2021 are given in Table 3.1 (in Euros per MWh).

Energy sources	Cost (USD/MWh)
Nuclear	141–221
Gas	115–221
Coal	68–166
Wind	68–166
Geothermal	83–96
Hydraulic	22–46
Residential solar PV	117–282
Service solar PV	24–96
Solar CSP	42–94

Table 3.1. *Electricity production costs for new power plants (source: Lazard & US National Renewable Energy Laboratory, 2023)*

Generation costs in gas and coal-fired plants mainly depend on the price of the fuel. The low price of gas at the start of the 2000s explains the trend for gas-fired combined cycle power plants.

On the European market, the rules set by Brussels have led to prices in excess of 1,000 Euros per MWh in 2022. This is because the price was set at the level of the production cost of the most expensive power plant, i.e. a natural gas-fired plant. The price of gas had reached record highs following the halt in Russian gas deliveries to

Europe after the invasion of Ukraine. Electricity prices in Europe returned to a "reasonable" level in 2023. However, to prevent consumers from having to cope with excessive prices, at the end of 2023 a market reform introduced long-term agreements between electricity producers and consumers. Differences between the price agreed by the two partners and the market price are regulated by the state, which pays or receives these differences.

These costs do not take into account the pollution caused by the use of the various energy sources. The European Union Emissions Trading Scheme (EU ETS), which has also been introduced in other regions, obliges economic players with high CO_2 emissions to buy "emission credits" on a market. The price of these emission credits (expressed, for example, in euros per ton of CO_2), which has been fairly low for many years, is now rising sharply, driving up the cost of producing electricity from coal, for example.

3.14. The role of renewable energies in electricity markets

In the context of the EU's policy to reduce greenhouse gas emissions by 55% by 2030 (compared to 1990 – decision of July 2021), the EU is seeing a sharp increase in the penetration of renewable energy sources, such as wind and solar power, into the electricity grid. Since wind and solar power are intermittent by nature, replacement sources are needed when the sun disappears and there is no wind.

In Germany, where wind power (in the North Sea) and solar power (in the south) can cover most needs at certain times (when there's sun and wind), on windless nights electricity has to be generated by coal- or gas-fired power plants. Coal-fired (and often lignite-fired) power plants are polluting. Gas-fired plants depend on the availability of gas. Electricity markets therefore need policies adapted to the intermittency of renewable energies.

3.15. Historical trends in oil prices – price control by the majors and OPEC

Until 1950, the oil industry was in the hands of large integrated international companies (producing, transporting, refining oil and distributing products). The majors, also known as the "Seven Sisters", controlled most of the business and set the so-called posted prices.

After 1950, the nature and scale of the oil industry changed, following the major discoveries made in the Middle East between 1930 and 1950. These deposits were controlled by the majors, who took advantage of this abundant, inexpensive resource to consolidate their dominant position in the major markets of America, Europe and Asia. The massive growth in oil consumption between 1945 and 1960/1970 was encouraged by the drop in the price of oil from around 3 to 2 dollars (per barrel).

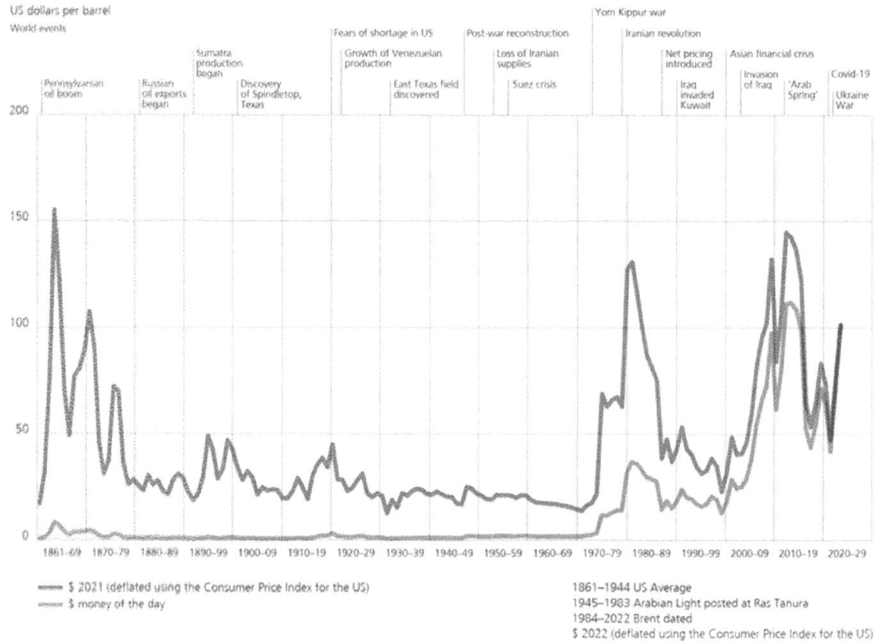

Figure 3.2. *Oil prices from 1861 to 2022 (source: EI Statistical Review of World Energy 2023). For a color version of this figure, see www.iste.co.uk/favennec/geopolitics1.zip*

Until 1960, the majors had complete control over the industry, but the situation was about to change. After World War II, countries that had previously been colonized demanded their independence or autonomy. This rise in power is illustrated by the Bandoeng Conference (1966) in Indonesia, where developing countries asserted their power under the influence of leaders such as Gamal Abdel Nasser (Egypt), Jawaharlal Nehru (India), Sukarno (Indonesia) and Zhou Enlai (China).

At the same time, oil-exporting developing countries gradually began to play a more important role. On September 14, 1960 in Baghdad, five oil-producing countries – Venezuela, Saudi Arabia, Iran, Iraq and Kuwait – created the

Organization of the Petroleum Exporting Countries (OPEC[3]) to combat falling prices and declining revenues per barrel. OPEC's aim was to stabilize the price of crude oil; this objective was achieved, and the price remained stable from 1960 to 1970 (the price of Arabian light crude, which was used as the reference price within OPEC, was $1.80/bbl, equivalent to $20 in 2024 prices (Figures 3.2 and 3.3)).

Fears of a crude oil shortage emerged in the late 1960s. Annual consumption had more than doubled between 1960 and 1970, and proven reserves were now equivalent to only around 30 years' consumption. Also around 1970, experts feared that the strong growth of the post-war boom years would lead to the depletion of raw materials. The Club of Rome report on "The Limits to Growth", published in 1972, recommended an economic slowdown to preserve natural resources. This was the beginning of the environmental protection and "sustainable development" movements. From 1970 to 1973, oil prices were negotiated for the first time between oil-producing countries and oil companies. Various agreements (Tripoli, Teheran, Geneva) raised the price to $3/bbl.

Figure 3.3. *WTI crude oil price in dollars between 1970 and 2018 (source: IMF)*

Then, two political crises resulted in substantial increases in the oil price. In 1973, during the Yom Kippur war between Israel and the Arab nations, the posted price rose from $3 to $5 in October (this was the first time that the producing states

3 OPEC currently comprises the following countries: Algeria, Saudi Arabia, Congo-Brazzaville, United Arab Emirates, Gabon, Equatorial Guinea, Iran, Iraq, Kuwait, Libya, Nigeria and Venezuela.

had unilaterally changed the posted price), then to $11.65/bbl on January 1, 1974, although the actual selling price was then $7 or $8. A few years later, in 1979–1981, the Iranian crisis, with the departure of the Shah of Iran and the arrival of Ayatollah Khomeini in power, led to an even higher increase in the oil price, which reached $35/bbl. The other fundamental event of the 1970s was that most major producing countries (particularly the Arabian Gulf countries) nationalized their oil fields.

However, the tenfold increase in the price of oil resulted in a fall in consumption of nearly 15% between the end of the 1970s and the mid-1980s. At the same time, new production encouraged by the increase in prices was being developed in the North Sea and Alaska. Lower prices quickly became inevitable.

OPEC initially reacted to the lower prices by instituting production quotas. Each country was allocated a production ceiling, which was gradually reduced to prevent the market collapsing. In 1985, the official price remained at $25/bbl. However, this level was only maintained thanks to a decrease in OPEC production of nearly 50% between 1979 (30 million barrels per day (Mb/d)) and 1985 (15 Mb/d). The situation was particularly serious for Saudi Arabia, which acted as the swing producer and whose production decreased by nearly 70%.

To regain market share, Saudi Arabia effectively started a price war by introducing netback contracts[4]. Their sales started to climb, but the price of oil collapsed from $25/bbl in January 1986 to less than $10 six months later.

3.16. Historical trends in oil prices: end of the 20th century

From 1986 onwards, new players (new producing countries, independent companies, traders and financial institutions) took control of the oil market, to the detriment of the majors and OPEC. The resulting oil price was relatively low (between $10 and $20/bbl, depending on circumstances), but increasingly volatile.

In 1998, the price of oil fell once more to $10/bbl. There were several reasons for that. OPEC had substantially increased its production quotas at the end of 1997. At the same time, the Asian economic crisis hit Thailand and South Korea, both major oil consumers. There was considerable conflict between OPEC member countries; Middle East countries criticized Venezuela for its policy of increasing production at

4 In netback contracts, the crude oil producer's selling price was calculated to equate to the value of products obtained by the refiner when they sell the gasoline, diesel fuel, fuel oil, etc. produced on the markets, less the transport and refining costs incurred. Refiners, who had been making substantial losses at the start of the 1980s, could at last balance their books. Therefore, they started to process more crude oil, and flooded the product markets, making the prices of products and the prices of crude oil tumble.

any cost, regardless of their quota. Rivalry between Iran and Saudi Arabia also weakened the organization. OPEC's lack of unity meant that the decision they took in 1998 to reduce production lacked credibility.

3.17. Historical trends in oil prices: 2000–2014

A price of $10/bbl was a catastrophe for the oil-producing countries, more than 90% of which depend on this product. OPEC countries' debt increased. The OPEC countries need to return to discipline in order to raise prices. How could this be achieved?

The election of Hugo Chavez as President of Venezuela at the end of 1998 was the first sign of change. While the previous government had favored maximizing production, the new President favored a policy of solidarity with third-world countries in general and with other oil-producing countries in particular. Aware of the importance of increasing oil prices, he argued for an agreement between Venezuela, Saudi Arabia and Mexico (a non-OPEC country) to limit production. This agreement would be strengthened by a strong improvement in relations between Saudi Arabia and Iran, the main Arabian Gulf -producing countries.

The commitments to reduce OPEC production, supported by clear signs of solidarity from the main non-OPEC producers, finally appeared credible to operators. In March 1999, the price of oil started an upward trend that would lead it to a peak level in 2000.

The terrorist attacks of September 11, 2001 – destruction of the two World Trade Towers in New York by planes hijacked by terrorists linked to Al Qaida – caused a collapse in prices, with Americans greatly reducing their personal travel. However, prices gradually recovered. Until 2003, $25/bbl was generally agreed to be the "normal" price of crude oil, and this was OPEC's objective. However, the threat of American intervention in Iraq caused uncertainty in the market and the addition of a "risk premium", which different experts estimated at $5, $10 or $15/bbl.

This theory was confirmed by the fall in the price of oil on March 20, 2003, the day on which President George W. Bush announced that the United States rejected Saddam Hussein's response to the US ultimatum, and that the US-led coalition would attack Iraq. In London, the price of Brent crude fell from $35 to $25. Operators were not worried about the immediate consequences of the US action. Surplus capacity from countries neighboring Iraq (Saudi Arabia, UAE, etc.) meant that lost Iraqi production could be made up and it was considered that, with surplus production capacity at 5–10% of total capacity, there would be a return to "normal" market supply within a few months. It was also expected that investment in Iraq would once again become possible (plans were made to raise production capacity from 3 to 6 Mb/d), so a return to "normal" oil prices therefore seemed probable.

The role of OPEC

Although supply and demand has had a basic role in the oil price-setting mechanism since 1986, at least until 2003 it was OPEC's position that was decisive. Without OPEC, oil prices would have been – during certain periods – much lower.

However, in periods of significant potential oversupply, OPEC does not always wish to assume the sole responsibility for supporting prices. Therefore, in 2001, OPEC reduced its production by 5 Mb/d, i.e. by nearly 20%, to prevent a sudden price fall. However, at the end of 2001, the organization was faced with a dilemma: it could reduce its production further and see its market share decline dramatically and non-OPEC producers profit from higher prices without participating in the loss of production, or maintain its export volume and inevitably experience a fall in the crude oil price. In fact, at the start of 2002, the major non-OPEC producers (Mexico, Norway, and most importantly Russia) joined OPEC in their efforts to maintain prices.

At the end of 2008, the worldwide recession and a further collapse in oil prices once again made the cartel's pricing policy a central issue. OPEC decided to reduce its quotas by 4 Mb/d over several stages, starting in September. It also tried to persuade other producing countries (Russia, Mexico, Norway, etc.) to join in.

The collapse of prices in 2014 is clearly linked to a modification of the position of OPEC. To face the large excess of oil in the market, a consequence of the rapid development of the LTO (shale oil) production in the United States as well as of the increasing production of countries such as Iraq and Iran after 2015, OPEC could have, as usual, decided to reduce its production. However, the organization refused to do so and at the OPEC meeting of November 27, 2015 Saudi Arabia, by far the leading country, decided to keep its production at the current level and announced it would defend its market share. Through its sovereign wealth funds, Saudi Arabia has substantial reserves which, in principle, should enable it to finance its budget deficit.

The price of oil then fell to very low levels, approximately $30/bbl in early 2016. Most exporting countries were experiencing growing financial difficulties. As a consequence, at the end of 2016, OPEC decided to cut production. The agreement between OPEC countries was followed by a similar agreement between 10 non-OPEC countries (Azerbaijan, Bahrain, Brunei, Kazakhstan, Malaysia, Mexico, Oman, Russia, Sudan and South Sudan), which, led by Russia, decided to contribute to limiting oil production. Henceforth, the price is regulated by OPEC+, which brings together OPEC (a structured organization) and the 10 countries mentioned above.

Box 3.1. *OPEC's role*

After the drop on March 20, 2003, the price of oil began to rise again, reaching \$147/bbl (Brent crude) on July 11, 2008. This is the highest price seen to date. There are many reasons for this. The situation in Iraq and the Middle East was not what had been expected. Iraqi production remained well below that of the Saddam Hussein era. Attacks in Saudi Arabia have threatened oil installations. Oil consumption rose rapidly, while surplus production capacity disappeared. There has been no shortage of oil on the markets, but the balance between supply and demand is precarious. Costs, especially investment costs, have been rising sharply.

Forecasts of peak oil production in the range of 95–100 Mb/d have raised serious concerns, as the needs of China and other emerging countries appear to be unlimited. The market has been trying desperately to balance future supply and demand.

Why do not price increases slow the rise in demand? The explanation is simple. The income effect (when incomes double, gasoline consumption rises by 70%) is greater than the price effect (when prices rise by 100%, gasoline consumption falls by only 7%). Economic growth has been extremely strong (4% per year from 2003 to 2007), while the fuel price rises seen by consumers have been mitigated by tax adjustments in consumer countries and price controls in emerging countries.

Speculation will play an important role. As economic growth looks set to continue, and the needs of emerging countries increase rapidly, a rise in oil prices seems inevitable. Commercial funds will therefore invest in oil and other commodities on the assumption that prices will continue to rise. This de facto accentuates the upward trend in prices. When OPEC, on the one hand, and a major bank specializing in commodities trading, on the other hand, indicated in the spring of 2008 that "they would not be surprised if the price of oil reached \$200 by the end of the year", they were encouraging speculation.

However, a speculative bubble was created that was soon to burst. The price of Brent crude oil, which had reached \$147/bbl on July 11, 2008 on the back of speculation, plummeted to \$40 by the end of 2008. The markets are finally waking up to the subprime crisis, which is leading to a sharp drop in demand, while oil production remains strong.

OPEC reduced its production quotas and stabilized prices in a range between \$40 and \$50. Investment funds withdrew heavily from the oil markets (and those of other commodities). This reinforced the downward trend in prices.

The fall in prices from \$147 to less than \$40 between July and December 2008 was in every respect similar to what occurred in 1986 at the time of the oil counter shock, when Saudi Arabia launched a price war to recover market share and prices fell from \$28 to \$8 between January and July. The reasons in both cases were the same: an oversupply of crude oil. The market forgets long-term considerations (anticipation of increasing and strong demand confronting limited future production) and focuses on short-term fundamentals.

In mid-2009, prices rose to \$70/bbl, close to the \$75/bbl considered to be the "right price" by the King of Saudi Arabia and that needed to ensure the production of marginal supplies, i.e. for instance, synthetic oil from Canadian oil sands. The price of oil continued to increase up to \$120/bbl at the beginning of 2011. Then, the price remained between \$100 and \$120/bbl up to 2014, as a supposed consequence of the "Arab Spring". The largest producing countries in the Gulf were not affected by the Arab Spring but a kind of "geopolitical risk" threatened these countries.

3.18. Historical trends in oil prices since 2014

In mid-June 2014, the Islamic State (Daesh) attacked Iraq and came within 40 km of Baghdad, threatening to take control of several Iraqi fields. The price of a barrel of oil soared. However, Daesh retreated and the threat disappeared. The market then realized that there was a potential oversupply of oil in the world, particularly in the United States: production of shale oil (now called light tight oil (LTO)) had risen from a few hundred barrels per day in 2010 to over 4 Mb/d in 2014, while production in other countries remained stable. The price of oil then fell rapidly.

Figure 3.4. *Brent crude oil price in USD per barrel from 2014 (source: Trading Economics 2023)*

Operators expected OPEC to cut production. However, at the cartel's traditional autumn meeting on November 27, 2014 in Vienna, Saudi Arabia declared that it wished to retain its market share and would not reduce its low-cost production so as not to encourage the development of high-cost production (the much more expensive shale oil production in the United States).

Following Saudi Arabia's decision to keep production high, oil prices continued to fall, dropping to very low levels – approximately $30/bbl in early 2016. An OPEC meeting in Doha in April 2016 seemed set to result in an agreement to cut production, but talks broke down at the last minute due to tensions between Saudi Arabia and Iran.

The decisive meeting took place on November 30, 2016 in Vienna, where the 13 (at the time) OPEC members agreed to cut their production by 1.2 Mb/d and decided on a joint production cap of 32.5 Mb/d. A few days later, following further discussions with the largest non-OPEC oil-producing countries, 10 countries (Azerbaijan, Bahrain, Brunei, Kazakhstan, Malaysia, Mexico, Oman, Russia, Sudan and South Sudan) in turn agreed to cut their production by 0.6 Mb/d. The traditional OPEC group and the 10 countries mentioned above are known as OPEC+.

The market reacted and the price rose above $50/bbl.

Prices were then affected by Donald Trump's decision to exit the nuclear agreement between Iran and the 5+1 group (United States, United Kingdom, China, Russia, France and Germany) on May 8, 2018. This agreement stipulated that, in exchange for the lifting of sanctions, Iran would halt uranium enrichment activities for the manufacture of nuclear weapons. Exiting the agreement means that sanctions against Iran will be progressively reintroduced, with the most severe coming into force six months later, on November 5th.

The mid-term elections in the United States (the famous mid-term elections in which the House of Representatives and a third of the Senate are completely renewed, in addition to state and local elections) were scheduled for November 6th: sanctions would have increased the price of oil and gasoline, a very bad signal for American voters. Donald Trump decided to grant exemptions to eight countries (China, Japan, South Korea, India, Taiwan, Turkey, Greece and Italy, the biggest importers of Iranian crude), which were still allowed to buy Iranian crude without incurring US sanctions. The market remained well supplied for a few months, but this exemption regime was abolished in 2019, with Iran exporting only limited quantities of oil and gas to neighboring countries and China

Oil prices have also been deeply affected by the Covid-19 pandemic. In May 2020, the price of oil was negative (–35 dollars per barrel) on the futures market. The reason for this is simple: speculators bought crude oil contracts a few months earlier, and needed to put this oil on the market a few months later. However, in May, nobody wanted to buy crude oil, and storage facilities were saturated. Therefore, operators with storage capacities available had to be paid to take oil. The situation was temporary, of course, and the price of oil subsequently returned to positive territory, albeit at a low level.

The economic recovery of 2021 boosted crude oil prices. This rise has been accentuated by Russia's invasion of Ukraine. The price of crude reached just over $100.

The objective of Saudi Arabia and Russia, the main oil producers outside the United States, is a price of approximately $80/bbl, enabling Saudi Arabia to finance its budget and ambitious "Vision 2030" development program, and Russia to finance the war in Ukraine.

In the years to come, high demand combined with limited production – as operators are reluctant to invest if the future of fossil fuels is compromised in the fight against global warming – could lead to oil price spikes.

In short, the price of oil is determined above all by the supply/demand balance. Speculative movements merely support the underlying trends. Other factors (crude oil and product inventory levels, as well as geopolitical events) can play a decisive role.

3.19. The impact of oil prices on demand

Oil prices naturally play an important role in economic activity. When the price of oil is $100/bbl, oil trade represents $10 billion per day.

Although the two oil shocks of 1973 and 1979 resulted in demand falling by 15%, the increase in the price of a barrel from $10 to more than $100 between 1999 and 2008 had effects on demand that were slower and more limited. Several explanations for this have been advanced:

– The weight of oil in the economy is less than it was 50 years ago and so the importance of the energy bill is also less. France spent nearly 6% of its GDP on its oil at the beginning of the 1980s, but spends between 1 and 2% today. More efficient use of oil and an increase in the service sector's share in the economy (services consume little energy) explain this. However, although oil has less weight in developed economies, it remains very significant for the poorest developing countries: it can exceed 10% of GDP for non-producing African countries.

– The proportion of taxes in the price of gasoline and diesel fuel lessens the impact of crude oil price variations. Generally, in France (as in many European countries), if the price of crude oil quadruples from $25 to $100/bbl, the price of fuel at a service station only increases by €0.50 per liter, which is 30% of the consumer price.

– The price of a liter of gasoline represented half an hour's earnings at the French minimum wage in 1981, but less than 10 minutes today.

For oil-producing countries, the price of oil is very important, as most of them rely heavily on oil and gas revenues to balance their budgets, and the minimum oil price required to do so varies considerably from country to country. It is relatively low for the Gulf countries (except Iran), whose populations are limited. These countries have accumulated substantial financial reserves, with hundreds of billions of dollars in sovereign funds. A price of $50 or $60 is sufficient for the United Arab Emirates, Kuwait or Qatar (excluding Qatar's gas exports). It is much higher for countries with larger populations, such as Nigeria.

The worst situation is probably that of Venezuela. Russia is also heavily dependent on its oil and gas exports. The fall of the Soviet Union is sometimes attributed to the drop in oil prices in 1986, which deprived the Union of its main resource.

3.20. High oil prices: how do they affect supply?

Non-OPEC production seems to be reaching its ceiling in many countries. Only OPEC countries – and in particular the countries of the Middle East – seem to increase their production significantly. Saudi Arabia is the only country with a fair excess capacity (approximately 2 Mb/d), and has an actual production capacity of more than 12 Mb/d. This excess capacity is a political decision of the Saudi government which wants Saudi Arabia to replace the exports of the second largest exporting country in case an event prevents this second country from exporting.

What is the right price for oil? A few points of reference:

– Production costs (excluding costs of capital) are several dollars per barrel in the Middle East, higher but "low" in other producing countries. However, they are in the range of $50/bbl in difficult zones of the North Sea, for synthetic oil obtained from the very heavy crude oil of Orinoco or from oil sands (also called tar sands or crude bitumen) from Athabasca. Production costs of LTO depend heavily on the production area (Eagle Ford, Permian, North Dakota) and are also quite variable within the same production area. They are also several tens of dollars per barrel.

– Most oil-producing countries that are members of OPEC depend on oil for 80–90% of their national revenue. Until roughly 2005, they prepared their budgets assuming an oil price of $20–$25/bbl. For example, Algeria used $19/bbl for many years. Any revenue from higher prices was then used for exceptional expenditure (debt repayment, new equipment projects, etc.). This situation has changed and many producing countries now "need" a much higher price to balance their budgets. The price "needed" varies considerably from one producing country to another, but is often at very high levels.

It should be noted that, if oil price increased up to $147/bbl in 2008, this was also a consequence of the huge increase in production costs which had increased by a factor of 2 or 3. De facto, between 2003 and 2008, all costs increased everywhere (cement, steel, manpower) including the oil industry. The collapse of oil prices from 2014 has obliged both the oil companies and the service companies to drastically reduce their costs, and many international oil companies have posted objectives to be profitable with a $60/bbl price of oil or less.

3.21. Who will make the necessary investments in exploration and production?

3.21.1. *International oil companies*

The five largest international oil companies (Exxon Mobil, Shell, BP, Chevron and Total Energies) have jointly earned more than $110 billion in profits every year from 2005 until 2013 except in 2009. Over the entire period, part of these profits was used to reduce debt, which had become very low, and to remunerate shareholders. In 2022, thanks to soaring prices following the invasion of Ukraine, these profits exceeded $150 billion.

These figures are of course causing a stir, and the taxation of "super profits" was on the agenda for 2023, with few concrete results. To defend themselves, international oil companies point out that they must distribute substantial dividends to keep their shareholders and, of course, invest in new production projects to compensate for the depletion of their fields. However, the most promising basins are often inaccessible to the major international companies. OPEC member countries control 75% of reserves, and these are the least expensive to exploit. Since the nationalizations of the 1970s, and notwithstanding the few exceptions discussed below, most OPEC countries have no intention of reopening their oil and gas industries to the big international companies. Saudi Arabia and Kuwait are completely closed. Outside the Middle East, Venezuela has only opened marginal fields and extra-heavy crude oil reserves to foreign companies. Outside OPEC, Russia has shown that it wishes to retain tight control over its reserves.

Another important factor is the strategy to be adopted by international oil companies. They want to appear as "green" companies, and are announcing major investments in renewable energies.

Overall, investment in the oil and gas sector has fallen sharply since 2014. The energy transition should eventually lead to a shift away from fossil fuels, but oil consumption will continue to grow for several years. Insufficient investment could put pressure on prices.

3.21.2. *National companies*

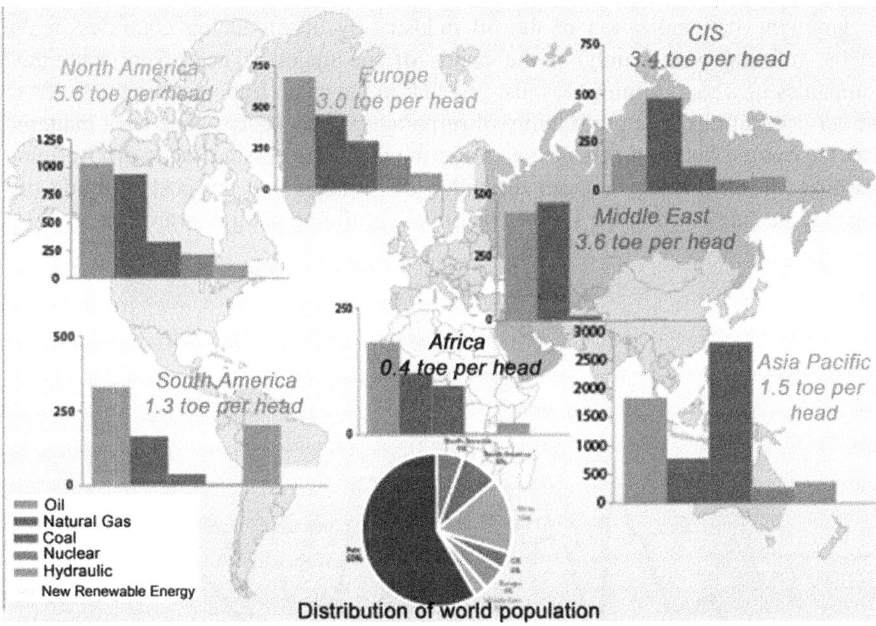

Figure 3.5. *World primary energy consumption in 2022 (source: EI Statistical Review of World Energy 2023). For a color version of this figure, see www.iste.co.uk/favennec/geopolitics1.zip*

State-owned companies (Saudi Aramco in Saudi Arabia, NIOC in Iran, PDVS in Venezuela, Pemex in Mexico, Sonatrach in Algeria, NNPC in Nigeria, etc.) receive only a portion of the revenues from the sale of crude oil. Their governments take a very large share of the revenues to finance the state budget. In many cases, the revenues left to national oil companies are insufficient to enable them to maintain and develop their oil production capacities. This is particularly the case in Venezuela, as well as in Mexico, Nigeria and Algeria.

The situation is slowly changing in Mexico, where the energy sector, totally closed to foreign companies after nationalization in 1938, has been reopened after lengthy internal discussions. At the end of 2013, President Enrique Pena Neto obtained a parliamentary majority to authorize the operation of the oil sector by private companies. This opening-up was, however, subject to political uncertainties. This was illustrated by the strategy of President Andres Manuel Lopez Obrador, elected in 2018 from the Mexican left and reluctant to open up the sector.

3.22. Prices of petroleum products

Until the nationalization of the oil industry by oil-producing countries in the 1970s, refining was mainly in the hands of the majors. These were integrated companies in which refining was just one link in the chain leading from the fields to the service stations. The profitability of refining was secondary, since what mattered was the margin between product sales and the cost of accessing crude oil. Refining margins (the difference between the value of products and the cost of crude oil) began to be calculated in the 1970s. Historically, refining margins were low.

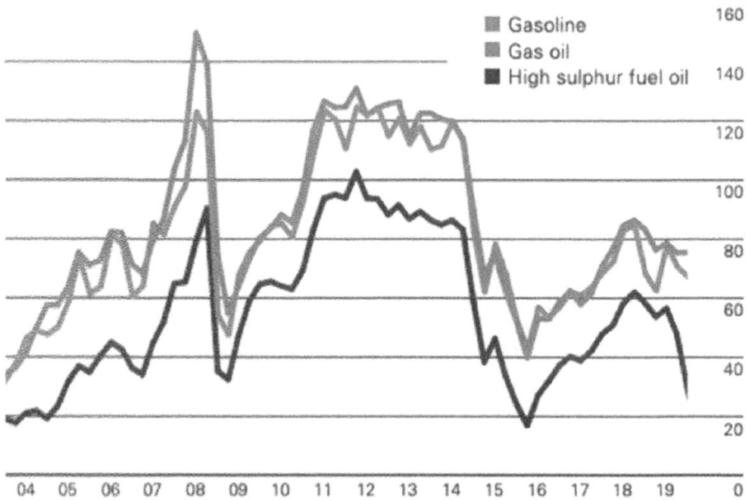

Figure 3.6. *Petroleum product prices (Rotterdam) (source: S&P Global Platts 2020). For a color version of this figure, see www.iste.co.uk/favennec/geopolitics1.zip*

Despite an improvement, margins were for a long time insufficient to cover all refining costs, due to excess capacity and fierce competition between refining companies.

In the United States and Europe, many refineries were closed. In France, there were 23 refineries in operation in 1973. Only seven are still in operation. Conversely, numerous refineries have been built in Asia. In the Middle East, Saudi Arabia built several refineries to export petroleum products in the 1980s. As of 2015, it has again built two large refineries, of 400,000 b/d each, in association with Total and Sinopec respectively. Large capacities have also been built in Asia to meet the growing demand. The world's largest refinery is located in India. This 1.2 Mb/d refinery (almost the total refining capacity of a European country) can export large volumes to Africa, where many refineries have recently closed.

The prices of petroleum fuels used for heating (liquefied petroleum gas, heating oil and heavy fuel oil) are linked to those of competing energies. The price of heavy fuel oil depends in part on the price of coal or gas, and the price of domestic fuel oil is also linked to that of gas. Motor fuel prices, on the contrary, are higher because – at least until recently – they are not in competition with other products.

The price of crude oil accounts for most of the price of products leaving refineries, as transport and refining costs are generally relatively low.

3.23. Pump price: taxes on petroleum products

Globalization of petroleum product markets has meant that, in much of the world, ex-refinery prices for gasoline or diesel fuel vary only by the transport differential. Even when transport costs are included, the difference is only a limited percentage.

The position of end-consumer prices (i.e. pump prices in the case of motor fuels) is very different. They are based on these ex-refinery prices plus distribution costs and taxes.

Taxes on petroleum products vary considerably. They are generally low on heavy fuel oils whose prices are an important component of industrial manufacturing costs. Taxing heavy fuel oils would be tantamount to reducing industrial competitiveness. They are also low on home heating oil, an important item in a household's cost of living. On motor fuels, they vary significantly. The practices used are as follows:

– Countries with high levels of imports tax both gasoline and diesel fuel heavily, even though they may discount part of the taxes for taxi drivers and road transporters, again to maintain competitiveness. For other customers, in some countries, taxes can be up to 70% of the pump price.

– Countries such as the United States apply lower taxes than Europe or Japan, but they still are significant.

– Oil-exporting countries have abundant resources of fuel and up to recently sold it at a very low price, often lower than cost. They considered that oil belonged to the people and, as a resource provided to them by God or a supreme being, it should not be expensive. In Venezuela and some Gulf countries, fuel was sold for a derisory sum. The Iranian Oil Minister once jokingly remarked that it would be preferable to give gasoline to automobile drivers for free, provided that they came to pick it up in the refineries, thereby at least saving the distribution costs.

The very low prices practiced in major exporting countries encouraged excessive consumption, resulted in increased pollution and impoverished the countries as they reduced the resources available for export. However, even moderate increases in these prices sometimes led to protest movements or even riots with tragic consequences (in Venezuela in the 1990s, several hundred people died in riots following a decision to increase gasoline prices).

In contrast, the very high taxes on motor fuels in consuming countries are a major source of government revenue. In France, these taxes represent roughly 10% of the nation's budget. This form of taxation is relatively painless, and service stations are good tax collection agents. In addition, these taxes are supposed to take into account the outside effects (pollution) arising from the use of petroleum products.

3.24. Oil and taxation

The large taxes collected on oil products by some large consuming countries are a recurring subject of contention for producing countries, who criticize consuming countries for motor fuel taxes that they deem excessive, since they slow the consumption of a product that is vital for producing countries. To which the consuming countries reply that the distribution of tax levies between VAT, corporate taxes, income taxes and taxes on petroleum products is an internal matter for them and they have the right to decide that as they wish. As part of the energy transition, lower product prices are out of the question.

On the contrary, the oil revenues of oil-producing countries represent hundreds of billions of dollars a year. The use of these revenues varies depending on the country. Prior strong economic development and an established democratic tradition favor a "good" use of oil revenue. The classic example of that is Norway, which has created a fund for future generations and was wise enough to avoid the problems of "Dutch disease".

What is Dutch disease? When the natural gas deposit of Groningen in Holland was put into production at the start of the 1960s, revenues from gas exports led to inflation (additional financial resources without simultaneous growth in production), increased wages and production costs, worsened the competitiveness of Dutch products and therefore destroyed some local businesses.

Similar phenomena have been observed throughout history. The conquest of Latin America by the Spanish filled their pockets with the continent's gold and silver. However, the galleons filled with gold that brought wealth to privileged Spanish families did not bring economic development to the Spanish nation. On the contrary, it was the large Italian cities (Genoa and Venice), followed by the major ports of Northern Europe (Holland, Belgium, etc.), that became the drivers of the European renaissance.

Many oil-rich countries have problems in converting their subterranean wealth into a real development tool. Venezuela remains highly dependent on oil, despite having been a producer for a hundred years. With the fall in price, the situation of Venezuela is extremely difficult. The situation is similar in African countries. In Nigeria, oil revenues have destroyed part of the country's economic activity. For example, crop cultivation has been discouraged because oil wealth can easily be used to import food that could be produced locally. An extreme situation is that of Nigerian refineries, which are perfectly capable of producing at full capacity but in fact operate at very low levels since importing refined products provides the much sought-after currency commissions. In other countries which have experienced brutal wars, oil money has made the situation worse because it has facilitated arms purchases.

In the Arabian Peninsula, oil money has completely transformed Saudi Arabia and its neighbors. It has paid for the development of major infrastructure (roads, water and electricity distribution networks, etc.) and the creation of health services, education, etc. The various countries of the Gulf Cooperation Council are attempting to develop other activities to diversify their economies: these include developments in the gas sector such as LNG, or GTL in Qatar, and development of the petrochemicals industry in Saudi Arabia. However, diversification away from hydrocarbons remains difficult even though in small countries (Dubai) services and commerce have become important.

In the case of the poorest countries, where government structures are the weakest, oil resources represent a very significant increase in wealth. Firm political will is needed in order to make the best use of these resources. In this regard, good examples include the Extractive Industries Transparency Initiative (EITI) and Publish What You Pay initiatives, strongly promoted by NGOs with an important presence in West Africa.

3.25. Price of natural gas

Since gas and oil are closely related and are substitutable products in the residential and industrial sectors, the price of gas is – or was for a long time – linked to that of crude oil or petroleum products.

The reason is simple: when huge reserves of gas were discovered in the 1950s in North Africa for instance, and when Algeria wanted to produce and sell the gas, European consumers through companies like Ruhrgas, Gaz de France or SNAM were very prepared to buy the gas. However, the costs of production, transportation (from the center of Sahara to the coast of Algeria), liquefaction, transportation by ship (from the coast of Algeria to European ports) and regasification of the gas were simply huge and the investments could not be repaid quickly. Therefore, long-term contracts had to be agreed upon between sellers and buyers. Sellers would commit to sell determined quantities of gas over 25 years or more and of course buyers would commit to take the gas. In order to make the price of gas competitive, it had to be linked to the price of energies in competition, heating oil and fuel oil.

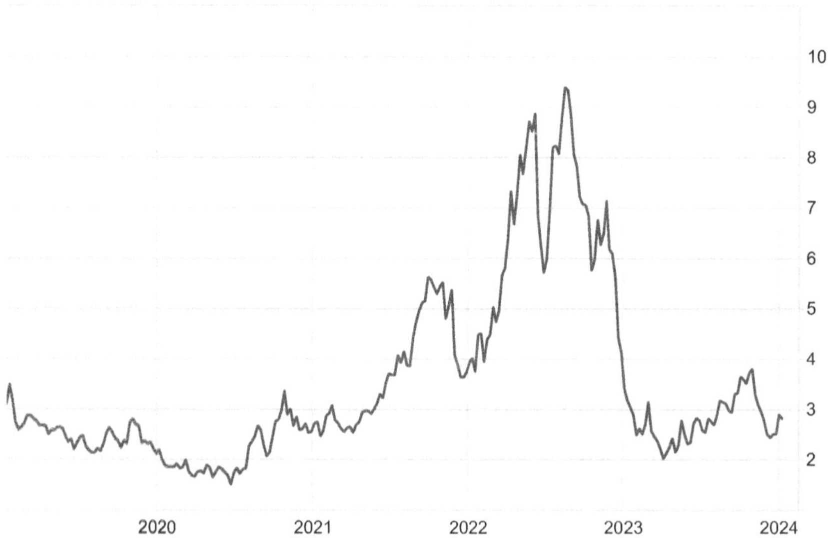

Figure 3.7. *Natural gas price in USD per MBtu (Henry Hub, USA) (source: Trading Economics 2023)*

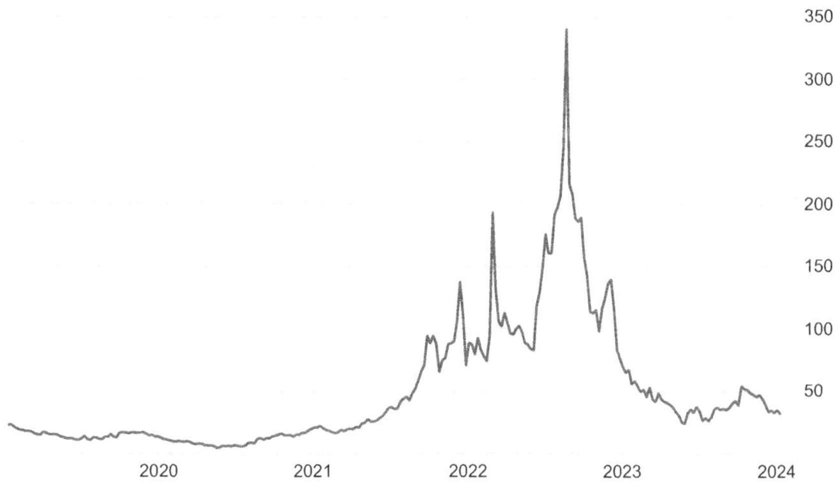

Figure 3.8. *Natural gas price in Euro per MWh (TTF, Europe) (source: Trading Economics 2023)*

The gas consumption developed very differently in the main markets. In the United States, and in North America, there was always large production of gas and gas was produced by a large number of – small or big – companies. Therefore, the price emerged from a gas-to-gas competition. In Europe, the market for natural gas developed in the 1950s after the discoveries in Italy (Po Valley), France (Lacq) and the Netherlands (Groningen), but imports from north Algeria (later Russia and Norway) were quickly necessary. In Asia, the gas market developed first in Japan, then in South Korea and Taiwan. In both cases (Europe and Asia), imports were necessary and long-term contracts were the solution to make these exports economical.

While the transport cost of crude oil is a low proportion of its price, this does not hold true for gas. Therefore, for the present, there is no world market for gas, but rather three regional markets: one for North America, one for Europe and one for northeast Asia. However, it is possible to re-route LNG tankers destined for Asia to Europe, which tends to globalize the market.

There are three references for gas prices:

– the Henry Hub in the United States. Located in Louisiana, it is a hub where numerous gas pipelines converge, enabling major exchanges;

– the TTF in the Netherlands, a futures market that serves as a benchmark for Europe;

– the Japan Korea Market (JKM), the benchmark for Asia.

During the 1980s and 1990s, the price remained relatively stable from $1 to $3/MBtu[5] in the United States, $2 to $4/Mbtu in Europe and $3 to $5/Mbtu in Japan. From 2000 to 2008, prices doubled, or even tripled, in these markets. Prices also tended to converge and become more volatile, because of the trend for liberalization in gas markets. The increase in the price of gas was especially strong in the United States because the growing demand could not be met by the local production. Imports from Canada were limited because Canada wanted to keep a good fraction of its production for the production of oil sands. Therefore, the United States anticipated growing imports and started to build a number of LNG re-gasification terminals (see also Volume 2, Chapter 1, on North America).

These terminals were only used at a very limited scale because of the sudden development of the production of tight gas and shale gas which represent more than 50% of the US production. Today, the United States is exporting gas and the first gas exports came in 2016. Some of the LNG re-gasification terminals were transformed into LNG export terminals (at the cost of building liquefaction capacities). Now, the United States is one of the world's leading LNG exporters, along with Qatar and Australia, and could become number one.

The financial crisis (subprimes) in 2008 triggered a collapse in prices. From 2009 onwards, however, prices remained low in the United States due to the abundance of shale gas, whereas they rose sharply in Europe and Asia due to higher oil prices. Gas prices were particularly high in Asia, and especially in Japan, where the Fukushima accident necessitated the use of additional quantities of gas to compensate for the loss of nuclear power generation.

From 2014, gas prices began to fall in Europe and Asia, following the fall in oil prices. After very low prices in 2020 (Covid-19), prices rose sharply in 2021 (economic recovery) and again in 2022 following the invasion of Ukraine and the halt in Russian exports to Europe. Gas prices have reached unprecedented levels (over $60/MBtu equivalent to $400/bbl on a heat content basis!) in Europe and Asia. However, Europe overcame the halt in Russian supplies more easily than expected (reduced consumption, increased imports, particularly from the United States), and by 2023 prices had returned to pre-crisis levels.

5 Millions of BTUs – British Thermal Units. This is the traditional unit used for natural gas pricing. There are roughly 40 million BTUs in 1 ton of oil equivalent.

The Gas Exporting Countries Forum (GECF), sometimes referred to as "OPEC Gas", plays a much more limited role than its oil cousin. The specific characteristics of gas, and the close links between producers and consumers, prevent the forum from influencing prices, so that it is content to act as a cooperation body.

3.26. Price of coal

Almost 80% of coal consumption is concentrated in three countries: China, by far the biggest consumer (over 50% of global consumption); India, where consumption is rising rapidly to produce electricity; and the United States, where consumption has been halved in 10 years due to the replacement of coal by gas for electricity generation.

Coal prices are following the same trend as oil prices. In November 2021, they reached very high levels, in line with the trend in oil and gas prices.

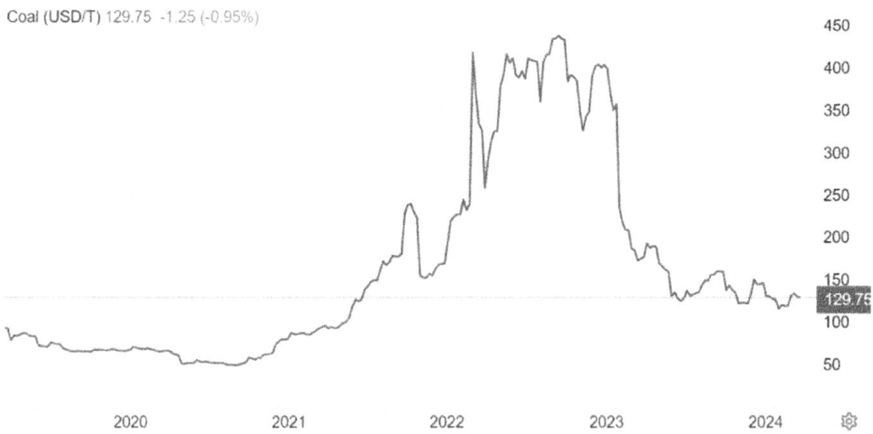

Figure 3.9. *Coal price in the USA (source: Trading Economics)*

3.27. The uranium market

Following the launch of nuclear programs in Europe and Japan, the price of uranium rose from $6 to $43/lb over the 1970s. However, overproduction in the 1980s caused prices to tumble so much that, by 1994, they had fallen back to their 1970 level.

Prices reached record levels in 2007 and again in 2010. The Fukushima disaster led to a steady decline in prices. However, prices have since started to rise again.

Uranium prices are not set by free markets; they are negotiated under contracts between the buyer and seller that generally last for three to five years. There is a spot market.

Production is roughly 60,000 tons of uranium (or 130 million pounds). The main uranium-producing countries are Kazakhstan (40% of world production), Australia, Namibia and Canada. Between them, they share nearly 80% of the world market.

No new mines have been opened in the past 20 years, and demand over the next few years is expected to grow by 1–2% per year because of the large number of nuclear power plants under construction.

However, there is an important difference between nuclear electricity generation and the use of coal, oil or gas, which is that the cost of the electricity is not dependent on the price of the fuel, which accounts for only 5% of the production cost.

3.28. Oil reserves

A distinction is made between resources (oil in place) and oil that can be extracted (recoverable reserves or simply reserves). On average, just over a third (35%) of oil in place is recoverable. Recovery rates vary from over 60% (porous reservoir, light oil) to less than 10%. The recovery rate depends, of course, on economic conditions.

Proven or proved reserves are quantities of oil contained in known reservoirs that are recoverable under current technical and economic conditions. Reserves are also said to be proved if the probability of extracting them is greater than 90%. Probable reserves are those where the probability of production falls to 50%, and possible reserves are those where the probability is only 10%.

The distinction between proved, probable and possible reserves is only really of use to oil companies. At a worldwide level, it is more helpful to refer to the idea of ultimate recoverable reserves, which is the sum of:

- reserves already used, i.e. the consumption of oil since 1859;
- proved reserves;
- reserves to be discovered.

The world's proven reserves of conventional crude oil are in the region of 245 billion toe, or 1,760 billion barrels[6], equivalent to 50 years' production at the current rate. Geologists believe that significant quantities of oil could yet be discovered, thus increasing these figures.

Technological advances could also increase recovery rates. Today's average recovery rates are roughly 30–35% (which means that 65–70% of oil is left in the ground – the recovery rate can be as high as 60% or more in favorable fields in the North Sea and as low as less than 10% in extra heavy oil fields in Venezuela). However, recently discovered deposits are smaller and more difficult to exploit, so maintaining a 35% recovery rate may already be a good performance.

In summary, estimates of ultimate recoverable reserves range from 2,000 billion barrels according to the Association for the Study of Peak Oil (ASPO), to nearly 6,000 billion barrels according to the International Energy Agency (IEA). A good illustration is shown in Figure 3.11.

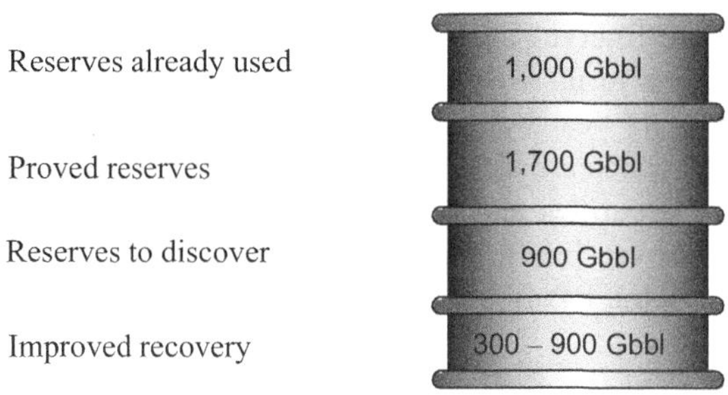

Figure 3.10. *Oil resources*

In total, remaining oil reserves (i.e. proven, undiscovered and enhanced recovery reserves) could represent almost 100 years of current production. Estimates of undiscovered reserves are based on geologists' studies of sedimentary basins.

6 Reserve figures must be treated with caution. Measuring reserves is a tricky business, since it involves estimating the quantities of oil located at great depths on the basis of measurements made by a few wells. Moreover, the sources of the figures are often opaque. In the OPEC countries, which control over 70% of reserves, the figures are provided by governments and therefore have a strong political aspect. The author considers that world oil reserves are reasonably estimated at between 1,200 and 1,800 billion barrels, and that in any case these reserves are more than sufficient to meet our current and future needs.

The question of fossil fuel reserves, particularly oil, has long been crucial. Climate change and the need to reduce greenhouse gas emissions have led some specialists to recommend leaving some reserves in the ground. However, it is useful to know the state of these reserves.

Since the start of the 20th century, there had been many alarmist predictions that reserves would soon be exhausted. The large discoveries in Texas at the beginning of the 1930s, then in the Middle East around 1940, made these fears temporarily disappear. However, they re-emerged in the 1960s. In 1970, the ratio of proved reserves to annual production was only 30, which suggested that reserves would be exhausted by the beginning of the 21st century. This was one of the reasons for the oil shocks, when the price of oil increased by a factor of 10. The fall in the consumption and substantial level of exploration that followed meant that the forthcoming end of oil could be forgotten, until in the years 2000–2010, debates regarding oil reserves returned to the news.

The level of oil reserves has been the subject of controversy for many years. Firstly, 75% of these reserves are located in OPEC countries or other producing countries where access to information is difficult. In many countries, reserves are simply announced every year by the government. Private oil companies which are non-state owned and which are listed on the New York Stock Exchange must submit their figures to the Securities and Exchange Commission (SEC), which carefully evaluates these reserves: but the reserves of the five largest international oil companies (Exxon Mobil, BP, Shell, Total and Chevron) correspond to less than 5% of the worldwide total.

While the level of reserves is now of limited interest, as it is likely that some of the oil will never be exploited to avoid too violent a climate change, the debate on their estimation is worth recalling.

Overall figures for reserves were thus doubted by pessimists, often members of the Association for the Study of Peak Oil (ASPO), who contested the reserve levels published by many countries. They recalled that, between 1986 and 1989, most Middle East OPEC countries multiplied their actual reserves by a factor of two or three to obtain higher production quotas, since these quotas were linked to reserves. There was intense controversy, fueled by well-known banker, the late Matt Simmons, regarding Saudi Arabia's reserves: according to him, these reserves were grossly overestimated, a fact denied by Aramco, which often stated its willingness to produce 12 or even 15 Mb/d to meet market needs.

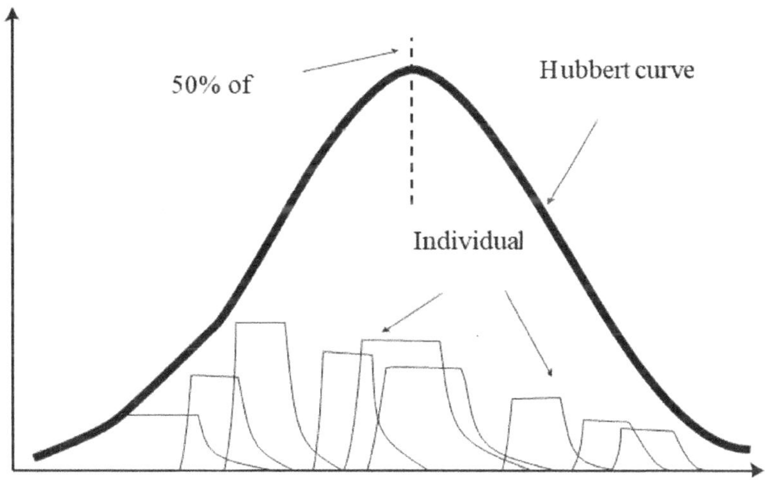

Figure 3.11. *Peak oil according to King Hubbert*

Basing its opinion on an evaluation of typical published reserves figures, ASPO announced that oil production would peak soon (2010, 2015) after which it would inevitably decline. This concept of peak production was based on the work of King Hubbert, a petroleum geologist who worked for Shell in the USA in the 1960s. Based on the fact that discoveries in America reached a maximum in the 1930s, he announced that American production would reach a maximum in 1969, which did actually occur. ASPO members have extrapolated this result to a worldwide scale and, since oil discoveries reached a peak in the 1960s, argued that production will peak in the 2000s.

The picture has been largely changed by the uprise of shale oil production (LTO) in the United States from 2010.

As a conclusion, it is clear that hydrocarbon reserves are finite and therefore exhaustible. However, ultimate reserves depend on economic and political factors and are difficult to assess.

3.29. Unconventional oil reserves

Unconventional oil means oil that cannot be produced using "conventional" methods. This notion covers in particular Venezuela's Orinoco extra-heavy oil, Canada's oil sands and US LTO (or shale oil). Venezuela's Orinoco extra-heavy oil reserves and Canada's oil sands (also known as asphalt sands) are parts of proven reserves[7].

Extra-heavy oil is found mainly in Venezuela in the Orinoco oil basin, which contains resources of approximately 1,400 billion barrels of extra-heavy crude oil. This is in situ oil, present in the subsoil, and only a part of it can be produced. With current technology, the recoverable reserves in this basin would be approximately 220 billion barrels. However, these extra-heavy crudes need to be pre-treated and transformed into light oil, using cracking processes, so that they can be more easily transported and processed in a conventional refinery. All in all, Venezuela has announced oil reserves in excess of 300 billion barrels, making it the world's largest oil reserve holder ahead of Saudi Arabia. It should be remembered, however, that Venezuela's disastrous political and economic situation has resulted in the production of less than 1 Mb/d (compared with 10 Mb/d for Saudi Arabia or Russia).

In Canada, asphalt or bituminous sands, formerly known as tar sands and now called oil sands, are a mixture of sand and asphalt or bitumen. The oil, formed deep in the Canadian soil, rose to the surface in the absence of cap rock. At the surface, the light fractions evaporated and were destroyed by bacteria, while the heavy fractions mixed with the sand. There are two main techniques for its exploitation:

– If the asphaltic sands are at a shallow depth, traditional mining techniques are used: the sand mixed with asphalt is extracted by hydraulic shovels, mixed and heated with water, and the oil separated by decantation.

– If the oil sands are too deep for traditional mining, steam injection is used to liquefy the bitumen and recover it at the surface (steam-assisted gravity drainage (SAGD)). The bitumen must then be processed to produce a synthetic crude oil. These oil sands are mainly concentrated in Canada (in Athabasca and on Melville Island). Resources are currently estimated at some 300 Gt, of which 34 Gt are thought to be recoverable. Oil sands fields' development is costly, and some projects can only be profitable if the oil price is \$60 to \$80.

Oil shale (not to be confused with shale oil, now known as LTO to avoid confusion) is organic matter in rocks, matter whose transformation into hydrocarbons is not complete and that can, at very high temperatures, yield oil comparable to certain crude oils. Oil shale represent a significant resource, but the production costs are very high and current exploitation techniques are very harmful to the environment. Historically, the oil shale industry pre-dated the conventional oil

7 Much of Canada's oil sands and Venezuela's extra-heavy oil are now included in conventional oil reserves by the *BP/EI Statistical Review* and the *Oil and Gas Journal*.

industry, but it became uneconomic after the discovery of crude oil in Pennsylvania in 1859 and practically no oil is currently produced from shale.

Production of oil will therefore continue for several more decades. As Sheikh Yamani [8] once said, "The Stone Age came to an end not for a lack of stones and the oil age will end, but not for a lack of oil". Some oil (like coal and gas) will probably remain buried in the ground forever.

3.30. Concentration of hydrocarbon reserves

The geographical distribution of oil reserves (Figure 3.12) is very uneven. Nearly 75% of these reserves are located in OPEC countries, which therefore have a proved reserve to production (R/P) ratio of roughly 75, while for non-OPEC producers, this ratio is only 17.

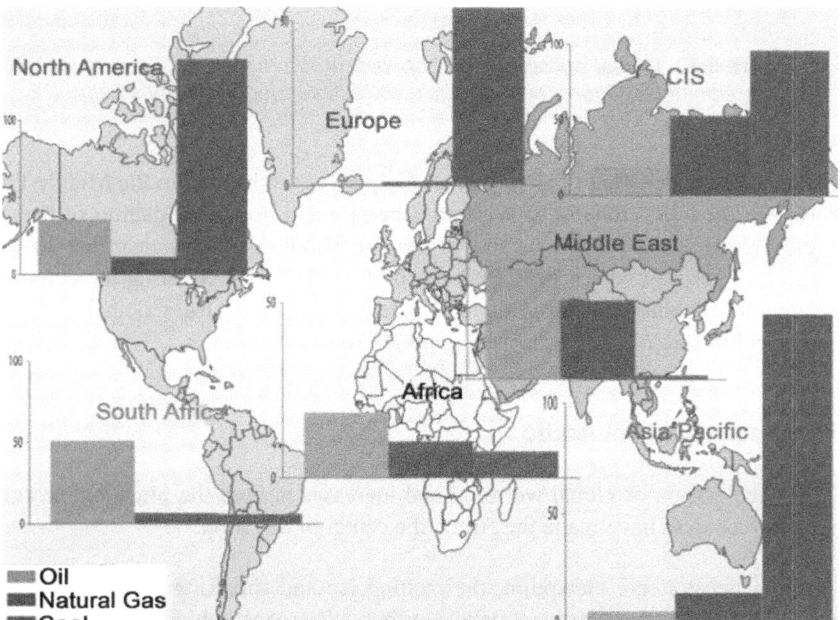

Figure 3.12. *Geographical distribution of hydrocarbon resources (source: BP Statistical Review 2020). For a color version of this figure, see www.iste.co.uk/favennec/geopolitics1.zip*

8 Saudi Arabia's Oil Minister until 1986.

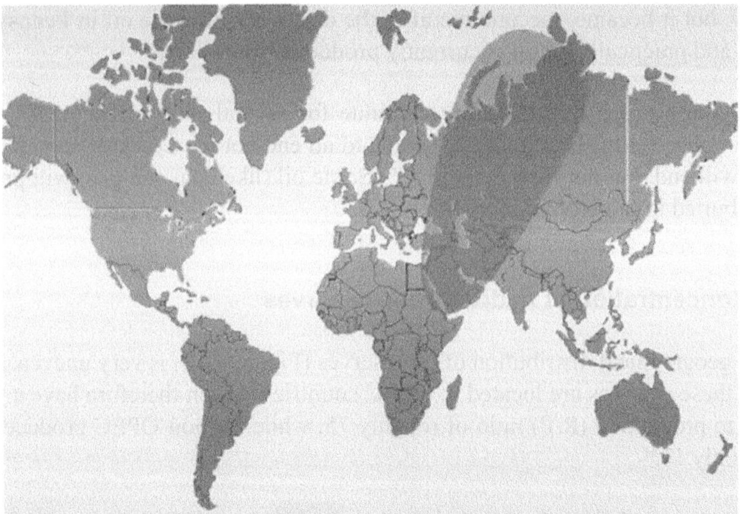

Figure 3.13. *Global concentration of hydrocarbon resources. For a color version of this figure, see www.iste.co.uk/favennec/geopolitics1.zip*

Since more than 60% of conventional oil reserves are located in the Middle East and 10% in the CIS – mainly in Western Siberia – and because a quarter of natural gas reserves are located in Russia and 40% in the Middle East, it is clear that 70% of the world's hydrocarbon reserves are located in a small zone covering the countries bordering the Arabian/Persian Gulf and extending towards Russia, including the Caspian region and Western Siberia (Figure 3.13).

3.31. Conquest of the Arctic

The acceleration of global warming and increases in both the price and scarcity of natural resources have made the Arctic the center of attention.

From a geostrategic viewpoint, the melting ice and shrinking icecap open new transport routes via the Northwest and Northeast Passages, which both opened for the first time in 2008. These new connections between the Pacific and the Atlantic could revolutionize marine shipping, putting Tokyo 14,000 km (8,700 miles) from London versus 21,000 km (13,000 miles) currently. By claiming sovereignty respectively over the Northwest and Northeast Passages, Canada and Russia are attempting to control marine traffic in them.

The Arctic Circle is also strategically important in relation to hydrocarbons. According to a report by the *US Geological Survey* published in 2007, the Polar

Circle could contain one-fifth of the planet's undiscovered recoverable hydrocarbon reserves amounting to 90 billion barrels of oil and 47 trillion cubic meters of gas, i.e. in total 60 billion toe or some 13% of today's proved reserves. Although the majority of identified reserves are located near coasts, so in the territorial waters of the countries involved (the American state of Alaska, Canadian Beaufort Sea, Norwegian Barents Sea, Danish Greenland and Russia's Siberian offshore), there is a significant possibility of Arctic reserves being in international waters or areas subject to disputed territorial claims (e.g. Western Greenland between Denmark and Canada, the Barents Sea between Norway and Russia, etc.).

Current competition for the Polar regions has included submissions filed with the UN and an increasing number of symbolic missions since 2007: Russia planting a flag 4,200 m (14,000 ft) below the North Pole, cementing its hold over Franz Joseph Land, undertaking scientific studies on Wrangel Island, etc. In addition, the United States and Canada are investing heavily in icebreaker fleets and keenly negotiating commercial agreements with countries of the zone.

3.32. Exploitation of the seabed's soil and subsoil resources

According to the 1982 United Nations Convention on the Law of the Sea, coastal nations have sovereign rights over resources from the soil and subsoil of their seabed, notably with regard to hydrocarbon resources. The continental shelf of a coastal nation comprises the sea-bed and subsoil thereof, up to the outer edge of the continental slope or up to 200 nautical miles from the coasts. Its boundary coincides with that of the maximum extension of the exclusive economic zone, the zone in which the coastal nation has the right to exploit all economic resources in the water, on the seabed and in the subsoil.

Where two nations have coastlines that are adjacent or facing each other, a maritime delimitation agreement is necessary. When the continental margin extends beyond 200 nautical miles, nations are entitled to exercise their jurisdiction either up to 350 nautical miles from the coasts, or up to 100 nautical miles from the 2,500 m isobaths, depending on certain geological criteria. In return, the coastal nation must contribute to a system for sharing revenue generated by the exploitation of mineral resources beyond the limit of 200 nautical miles, managed by the International Seabed Authority.

3.33. Natural gas reserves

Proved reserves of natural gas amount to roughly 170 billion toe, or a reserves to production (R/P) ratio of 50 years. This is sufficient for a substantial increase in natural gas's share of world energy supply. Additional reserves of roughly 100 billion toe can be expected from new discoveries. However, in contrast to oil, no increase in reserves will come from improved recovery rates as the recovery rates for gas already average 80%.

The very significant developments of unconventional gas raise important questions about reserves of tight gas, coal bed methane and, in particular, shale gas. These resources are probably very large but the potential for transforming them into recoverable reserves is still poorly understood.

Proved world reserves of natural gas are concentrated in two main areas: the CIS (29%) and the Middle East (38%). Three countries – Russia, Iran and Qatar – hold more than 50% of world natural gas reserves.

3.34. Coal reserves

Coal reserves are very large and well distributed throughout the world. Proved reserves (roughly 891 billion tons) amount to about 130 years current consumption, and probable reserves amount to 600 years.

3.35. Uranium reserves

Uranium reserves (assuming a relatively reasonable extraction cost of $130/kg) are sufficient to enable existing or projected generation plants to operate for nearly 100 years.

In 2021, reasonably assured uranium resources (in thousands of tons) were as shown in Table 3.2.

	Uranium reserves (thousands of tons)
Australia	1,684
Kazakhstan	815
Canada	589
Russia	481
Namibia	470
South Africa	321
World total	6,078

Table 3.2. *2021 uranium reserves (source: World Nuclear Association)*

3.36. Future energy needs

As Pierre Dac[9] wrote, "The art of forecasting is difficult, especially when it involves the future". However, we need forecasts for the critical period required for the construction of new facilities (oil, gas and coal production, nuclear power plants, and development of new renewable energies) which can exceed 10 years.

Outlook 2035

In 2035, fossil fuels will probably remain the dominant energy sources. The IEA forecasts that they should still meet between 60% and 80% of commercial energy needs (80% to day). Oil consumption will continue to grow over the next few years since transport needs are increasing, Oil growth will be at a slower rate due to the development of electric vehicles. The increase in the use of automobiles in North America and Europe will not be maintained but road transport sector consumption will be significant in China and India.

Oil will still be used as a fuel and as a raw material for the petrochemicals industry.

Gas will remain widely used, since it is the cleanest of the fossil fuels.

Coal should continue to be used, especially because of the consumption of electricity in China and India, which is based on coal, but the global consumption of the solid fuel will strongly decrease elsewhere.

Because of the Chernobyl and Fukushima accidents and the problem of disposing of nuclear waste, public opinion in many countries will maintain its reluctance towards the use of nuclear power. The best prospects for the development of nuclear energy over the next few years are in Asia, where fossil fuel reserves and existing generating capacity are low and the demand for energy is exploding. Many industrialized countries (USA, Great Britain, France, etc.), could also increase the use of nuclear energy, but perhaps at a limited scale. However, the massive development of nuclear energy expected (currently there are 440 nuclear power plants throughout the world and some experts forecast more than 2,000) will require the use of new, economical, generation IV fast-neutron reactors, since uranium reserves are only sufficient to fuel existing plants for some 100 years.

Renewable energies involve very different issues. The development of hydraulic energy is undoubtedly close to its limit; major dams (Three Gorges in China, Itaipu in Brazil and Ataturk in Turkey) require the flooding of enormous areas and consequent population displacement that is increasingly unacceptable. The Inga site,

9 Niels Bohr and an ancient Chinese proverb said the same thing.

near the mouth of the Congo River, has significant potential (of the order of 40 GW). Two dams have already been built. The construction of additional dams at this site remains possible, but electricity demand in the region remains very low.

The use of biomass – i.e. wood – is very controversial in many regions of the world, particularly sub-Saharan Africa, because of the deforestation and desertification of the regions and the very serious health problems for the inhabitants who inhale the smoke released during wood combustion (it is estimated that several million Africans die each year of respiratory illnesses). Finally, wood combustion is very inefficient: less than 10% of the wood's energy is recovered, although the quantities of wood used could be reduced significantly with improved stoves which are simple to manufacture and use.

Finally, there are new renewable energies (NREs), the most promising of which are wind and photovoltaic energy.

Two scenarios prepared by IEA some years ago are shown below; the Current Policies Scenario, which extrapolates today's policies, which are not sustainable, and the 450 Scenario, which forecasts stabilization of the atmospheric CO_2 concentration at 450 ppm, to limit the global temperature increase to 2°C by 2100.

Gtoe	**1980**	**2022**	**2035** Current Policies Scenario	**2035** "450" Scenario
Oil	3.1	4.5	5.0	3.8
Natural gas	1.2	3.4	4.0	3.0
Coal	1.8	3.8	5.3	2.5
Nuclear	0.2	0.6	1.1	1.7
Renewables:				
Hydro	1.2	1.0	0.4	0.5
Biomass and waste	0.8	1.2	1.7	2.3
Other renewables	–	1.1	0.5	1.1
Total	**7.3**	**15.6**	**18.0**	**14.9**

Table 3.3. *Forecast energy consumption by energy (source: IEA and the author)*

Outlook 2050

The forecast for 2050 is different. By then, hydrocarbon production will probably have started to decline and meet less than 50% of demand. Other energy sources will have to take a much larger global market share, perhaps nuclear energy, if generation IV plants become available, since nuclear power does not contribute to the greenhouse effect. Renewable energies will undoubtedly play a far larger role as well. The use of hydrogen remains uncertain. The issues of hydrogen production and use have been discussed in Chapter 2 of this volume. While its sole combustion product is very pure water, it is merely an energy vector and must be produced either using electricity, preferably from renewables, or nuclear energy, to avoid greenhouse gas emissions.

The 20th century was unique in being a period of cheap energy. It is probable that, in the medium term, the price of energy will reflect its scarcity. How will this transition take place: with or without a major economic and environmental crisis?

3.37. Pollution issues

Environmental issues are of growing concern to the public opinion, and to the political authorities as well. It is the duty of the latter to meet what appears to be the challenge of the 21st century: producing and consuming more energy while respecting the environment.

Local pollution

This is pollution emitted in a limited area, for example in a town. In the 19th century, this pollution resulted from the development of industrial activities. In the 20th century, smog appeared (a contraction of the words smoke and fog). Smog is a particularly thick and toxic fog resulting from the condensation of water vapor into tiny droplets that form on the surface of microscopic particles making up smoke. When coal was the main urban heating source in London, smog was common; in 1952, more than 4,000 people died from respiratory problems caused by smog. Smog is also common in cities where automobile traffic cause especially heavy emissions (see below).

Today, local pollution is mainly caused by transport and the exhaust gases of vehicles. The principal pollutants are carbon monoxide, unburned hydrocarbons and nitrogen oxides. Unburned hydrocarbons and nitrogen oxides can react in the presence of sunlight to produce ozone. Ozone is an oxidizing agent that attacks vegetation and irritates the respiratory system. Automobiles are now equipped with catalytic converters: devices installed on exhaust pipes that significantly reduce pollutant emissions. It is estimated that a vehicle manufactured now only emits a small percentage of the pollutants from a vehicle manufactured in 1970.

With the Auto Oil plan, launched at the start of the 1990s, the European Union set precise objectives for the reduction of polluting gas emissions. Better operation of catalytic converters requires a significant reduction in the sulfur content of engine fuels. Other measures have been initiated, for example the installation of particle filters on diesel engine exhausts and service station nozzles that recover gasoline vapors or simply setting standards for maximum CO_2

Further improvements in air quality could be achieved by faster renewal of the automobile fleet and more inspections of engine operations. But of course, the development of electric vehicles limits this pollution (obviously the global effect on environment will depend on the source of electricity: if the source is coal, pollution will only be displaced).

The sale of thermal cars (using gasoline or diesel) will be banned after 2035 in Europe.

Biofuels: these fuels are made from agricultural products and can be substituted for other higher-polluting fuels. Biofuels incorporate oxygen molecules that promote combustion and decrease emissions of pollutants such as carbon monoxide and unburned hydrocarbons. CO_2 is also absorbed by the plants used for the manufacture of biofuels during their growth. However, present biofuels only supply, and will only be able to supply, a low proportion of total consumption.

As high-voltage power lines generate magnetic fields, it is sometimes claimed that they have harmful effects on the human body. An example is that, in June 2005, the *British Medical Journal* published a study demonstrating a relatively limited but real risk of childhood leukemia for children living less than 600 m (2,000 ft) from a high-voltage power line. No rational explanation has been found for this increased risk. In France, the International Agency for Research on Cancer (IARC), based in Lyon, classifies very-low-frequency magnetic fields produced by high-voltage power lines into Group 2B of potentially carcinogenic agents.

Box 3.2. *High-voltage power lines*

Regional pollution

This is pollution that is geographically far more widespread than urban pollution. It is caused by polluting gases emitted in one area being moved by the wind to other areas that may be several hundred or even thousands of miles away. Acid rain is a typical example of regional pollution: sulfur dioxide and nitrogen oxide emissions resulting from the combustion of heavy fuel oil or coal – both rich in sulfur – can affect areas over considerable distances. As an example, such emissions in Great Britain caused acid rain in Scandinavia. This acid rain is harmful to forests (destruction of vegetation) and lakes (destruction of fauna and flora). Emissions from Chinese power plants also cause acid rain over Japan.

The extent of this regional pollution and its consequences depend largely on weather conditions (particularly wind speed and direction). It only involves gases with a lifespan sufficiently long for them to be carried over long distances: sulfur dioxide (SO_2), nitrogen oxides (NO_x) or ammonia (NH_3).

Therefore, regional pollution means that neighboring states must negotiate to find concrete, effective solutions to avoid ecological disasters or even the loss of human life. In 1999, the United Nations therefore agreed on the Gothenburg Protocol, with its objective of a 75% reduction in SO_2 emissions and a 49% reduction for NO_x compared with 1990 levels.

In 2024, the effect of acid rains has largely been reduced by the implementation of environmental policies which strongly reduce the emissions of the gases which produce the rain.

Refineries are the leading targets for projects aimed at reducing acid gas emissions. In fact, the combustion of heavy fuel oil is one of the leading sources of SO_2. Since 1980, lower sulfur content fuels have been used and that has reduced emissions by 35% over the past 20 years. Today, refining plants are subject to very strict quota restrictions (the quantity of SO_2 per month was a maximum of 1,700 mg/Nm^3[10] or less but that was lowered to 1,000 mg/Nm^3 in 2008).

The continuous progress made in improving the quality of petroleum products could give the impression that the problems of local and regional pollution are being dealt with in a better way. However, a new issue is of increasing concern to the scientific community and civil society: climate change.

Global pollution

Global pollution is pollution whose effects are worldwide. The appearance of "ozone holes" over the South Polar Region, due to the destruction of the tropospheric ozone layer by so-called CFC gases, was the first example. The elimination of CFCs, particularly in refrigerators, has stopped the growth of these holes.

Global warming is of course to day the major concern. We have dealt with this problem in the previous chapter.

---

10 Nm^3 is a cubic meter measured under standard (normal) conditions of temperature and pressure.

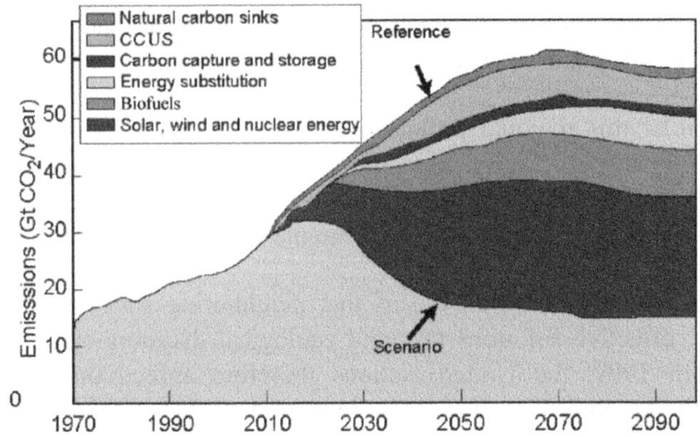

Figure 3.14. *CO_2 emissions. For a color version of this figure, see www.iste.co.uk/favennec/geopolitics1.zip*

3.38. Accidents

The energy chain is by its very nature hazardous, and the possibilities for accidents are numerous. Producing oil or gas involves extracting matter that is often burning hot, corrosive and highly pressurized in an environment that can be extreme: North Sea waves of more than 15 m (50 ft), pressure of approximately 98 bars (100 kg/cm^2) at a depth of 1,000 m (3,300 ft) off the shore of Africa, winds of nearly 300 km/hr (185 mph) in the Gulf of Mexico, etc. The distribution of gas or electricity requires very special care, since it involves substantial risks. Also, coal mining is hazardous, as shown by the many mining accidents in China and elsewhere.

Gas explosions also claim many victims:

– In Siberia, the movement of a train caused the explosion of gas that had leaked from a pipe and accumulated in a depression (Oufa – 1989). Several hundred people were killed.

– In a Pemex LPG storage terminal (Ixhuatepec – 1984), an explosion killed 500 people.

– In France, there was a gas leak at the Feyzin refinery caused by incorrect manipulation of a valve and the gas exploded when a car passed by the side of the refinery.

However, without doubt, the accidents having the greatest effect on the public are crude oil spills and the risk of nuclear accidents. Crude oil spills can have several causes: loss of well control (blowout), unauthorized ballast discharges and oil spills caused by a shipwreck.

There has been significant pollution from well blowouts since the beginning of the petroleum industry: the Spindletop well drilled in 1900 was out of control for several weeks. More recently, in 1979, a blowout at the IXTOC-1 well off the shore of Mexico lasted nine months. However, the most spectacular accident was probably Macondo.

The Macondo disaster

On April 20, 2010, there was a leak of hydrocarbons from a deep water well (the Macondo well) being drilled by Transocean's Deepwater Horizon rig for BP on the latter's Mississippi Canyon Block 252 in the Gulf of Mexico. The well was in 5,000 ft (1,700 m) of water, 48 miles from the nearest shoreline, with a total depth of 18,360 ft (6,250 m). The hydrocarbons ignited causing an explosion and fire on the rig, which burned for 36 hours until the rig sank; 11 out of the 126-member crew on the rig were killed and 17 others injured. Despite a series of different attempts to stem it, oil and gas continued to flow from the well for 87 days. This spill was the worst oil spill in the oil industry's history. The total amount leaked has been estimated at between 4.1 and 4.9 million bbl; for comparison, the spill from the Exxon Valdez was estimated at 260,000–750,000 barrels. The well was finally capped by drilling two relief wells, to intercept and then plug the original well.

The three companies principally involved were BP, the lease operator; Transocean, the owner of the rig; and Halliburton, responsible for cementing the wellbore annulus to prevent hydrocarbons entering the wellbore. BP's internal investigation into this accident concluded that the disaster was the result of "a complex and interlinked series of mechanical failures, human judgments, operational implementation and team interfaces" coming "together to allow the initiation and escalation of the accident".

The US Government's National Commission on the BP Deepwater Horizon Oil Spill and Offshore Drilling reported on the disaster and the future of offshore drilling to the President in January 2011.

The report was highly critical of BP's safety culture. It said BP has caused a number of disastrous or potentially disastrous workplace incidents that suggest its approach to managing safety has focused on individual worker occupational safety but not on process safety. These incidents and subsequent analyses indicate that the company does not have consistent and reliable risk management processes and thus has been unable to meet its professed commitment to safety. BP's safety lapses have been chronic.

There is a striking discrepancy between fatalities in the United States and in the European offshore oil and gas industry, with the former four times the latter per person-hour worked. This indicates that the problem is not an inherent trait of the business itself but results from the differing cultures and regulatory systems under which the industry operates. The US federal authorities lacked regulations covering some of the most critical decisions made on the Deepwater Horizon that affected the safety of the Macondo well. For instance, there are no meaningful regulations governing the requirements for cementing a well and testing the cement used, nor for negative-pressure testing of the well's integrity – a fundamental check against dangerous hydrocarbon incursions into an underbalanced well.

In addition, the government and industry were both woefully unprepared to contain or respond to a deepwater well blowout like that at Macondo. They lacked adequate contingency planning, and neither government nor industry had invested sufficiently in research, development and demonstration to improve containment or response technology.

The impact on the coastal zones of the Gulf of Mexico has been catastrophic. Tourism and fishing have been devastated. BP has pledged $20 billion to the Trust established to pay legitimate claims. The clean-up response involved approximately 43,100 personnel, more than 6,470 vessels and dozens of aircraft.

The disaster has transformed BP. To cover clean-up costs and compensation, they took a pre-tax charge of $32.2 billion and planned to sell up to $30 billion of assets. Bowing to political pressure in America, they suspended dividend payments to shareholders. The Chief Executive and the Head of Exploration and Production at the time of the disaster have left the company. The financial impact on the company was such that its market capitalization[11] fell by over $97 billion, i.e. more than halved, between the spill on April 20th and the low point for the share price on June 29th. Even after the partial recovery up to the end of 2010, the company's value was still some $50 billion lower. The new Chief Executive was an American, the first time that a non-British national has held such a position in BP.

The oil spill affected BP worldwide but the environmental concern raised by the oil spill has had percussions beyond BP. The American Government imposed a six-month moratorium on deep water (> 500 ft) drilling which meant that drilling at 33 off-shore wells was suspended. The oil industry accepted that its ability to respond to such leaks is inadequate and, in July 2010, Chevron, ConocoPhillips, ExxonMobil and Shell announced that they had committed $1 billion to build and deploy a rapid response system to capture and contain oil in the event of a potential

11 Market capitalization is the value of the company as seen by the investment market; it is the multiple of the company's share price and the number of shares issued.

future underwater well blowout in the deepwater Gulf of Mexico. BP subsequently joined the scheme.

In government, the director of the Minerals Management Service resigned. There was considerable impact on US politics; the spill was even described as "Obama's Katrina". As BP's failure to contain it quickly continued, an opinion poll found that 53% of adults thought that President Obama was doing a "poor" or "very poor" job handling the spill. The President was criticized, on the one hand, for "a daily stream of negative publicity for the Gulf of Mexico" when less than 10% of the coast line saw any oil at all. On the other hand, in late August, the *New York Times* castigated the government for allowing too much uncertainty about lingering damage from the disaster.

Other spills

Considering the number of oil tankers in use and the quantities of oil and petroleum products shipped, shipwrecks are relatively rare. But they are still too frequent.

The cost of transporting oil is low compared with its selling price. Even for very long distances (e.g. from the Persian Gulf to the USA or Europe), it is not more than a few dollars per barrel. However, an operator's main concern is not whether they pay $10, $100 or $1,000; it is to not pay $101 if a competitor only pays $100, which is why they seek the lowest cost transport possible. Therefore, very strict international regulation is vital to prevent the use of ships that are too old or in poor condition, and thus reduce the risk of accidents. Following the Exxon Valdez shipwreck, nearly 40,000 tons of crude oil spread over the coasts of Alaska. The United States then instigated a very strict inspection regime for ships entering their ports.

Following the Erika shipwreck off the coast of France (December 1999) and that of the Prestige (November 2002) off the coast of Spain, Europe enacted stricter standards albeit after long negotiations.

However, the problem has not been solved. In August 2006, the products tanker, ProboKoal, which had been carrying motor gasoline from Lithuania to Nigeria, discharged toxic refinery residues, which should have been treated in a specialized plant, at Abidjan. As there were no such specialized facilities in Abidjan, these residues were mixed into the town's normal waste system and caused serious health problems for the local population. Therefore, there is still a flagrant lack of regulatory control.

Box 3.3. *Why oil spills?*

Unauthorized ballast discharges result from ship's tanks being cleaned with seawater and the cleaning water then being released into the open sea; ballast discharges represent one-third of marine pollution by hydrocarbons, or two to three times more than tanker accidents (Figure 15).

Determining the chain of responsibilities for oil spills is complex, as it is difficult to establish ownership of the ship and the cargo. Accusations are made against oil companies, accused of being careless, and against ship owners and flags of "convenience", charged with being lax. In response to the recent Erika (1999) and Prestige (2002) shipwrecks, the European Union has strengthened its legislation by requiring that all ships passing through its waters be equipped with double hulls. In doing so, it has made common cause with American legislation, implemented following the Exxon Valdez shipwreck in 1989 off Alaska.

Although oil spills are infrequent, their consequences are such that they have a strong and lasting psychological impact on the local inhabitants.

Once the slicks have reached the shore, there are few cleanup techniques available other than mechanical ones. The repercussions are ecological (oil contamination of local fauna and flora), economic (tourism, aquaculture, etc.), political and psychological.

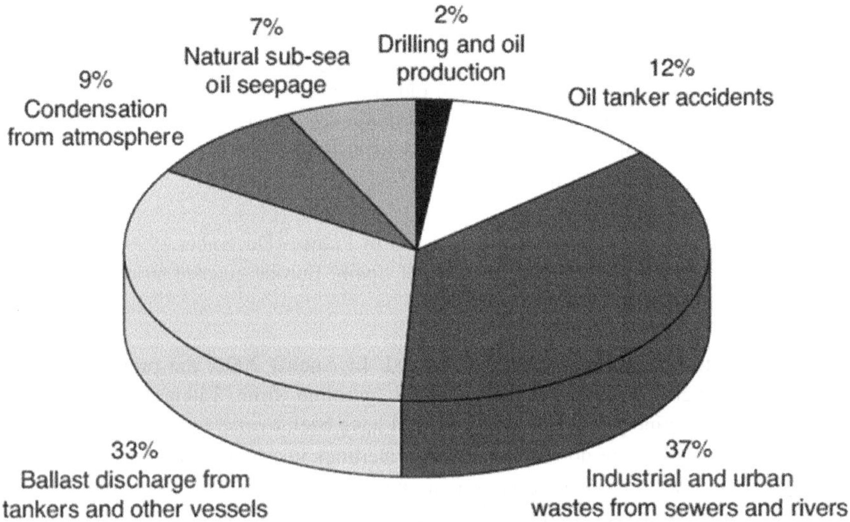

Figure 3.15. *Sources of marine pollution*

Date	Ship	Ship-owner country	Location	Discharge
1967	Torrey Canyon	Liberia	Great Britain	119,000 t
1970	Othello	?	Sweden	60,000–100,000 t
1972	Sea Star	South Korea	Gulf of Oman	115,000 t
1976	Urquiola	Spain	Spain	100,000 t
1977	Hawaiian Patriot	Liberia	Pacific Ocean	99,000 t
1978	Amoco Cadiz	Liberia	France	223,000 t
1979	IXTOC-1 platform	–	Gulf of Mexico	500,000–1,500,000 t
1979	Atlantic Express Aegean Captain	?	Trinidad and Tobago	280,000 t
1980	Irenes Serenade	Greece	Greece	102,000 t
1983	Castillo de Bellver	Spain	South Africa	250,000 t
1989	Exxon Valdez	United States	Alaska	40,000 t
1991	Mina al Ahmadi oil terminal	–	Kuwait	700,000–900,000 t
1991	ABT SUMMER	Liberia	Off Angola	260,000 t
1991	Haven	Cyprus	Italy	144,000 t
1999	Erika	Malta	France	20,000 t
2001	Oil platform	Brazil	Brazil	350,000 t
2002	Prestige	Spain	Spain/France	77,000 t
2003	Tasman Spirit	Greece	Pakistan	12,000 t
2006	Lebanese oil reserves	–	Lebanon	15,000 t
2007	Hebei Spirit	China	China	10,000 t
2010	Deepwater Horizon drilling rig	USA	Gulf of Mexico	600,000–700,000 t

Table 3.4. *Principal oil spills (source: Wikipedia and http://www.itopf.com/.)*

Nuclear accidents

The probability of accidents in nuclear power plants is very low, but the scope of potential damage is such that the perception of the risk is increased and mistrust of this type of energy is heightened. The first major nuclear accident was that at Three Mile Island (depicted in a movie called *The China Syndrome* that invoked the theory that meltdown of the nuclear core would have released such enormous quantities of heat that the core would melt all the way through the Earth's core and emerge from the other side in China). This accident – which fortunately had no grave consequences – was undoubtedly caused by the reactor design. The Chernobyl accident was far more serious.

When the coolant system in a nuclear reactor fails to reduce the heat produced by the nuclear reaction sufficiently, the core of the reactor starts to melt causing a massive release of radioactivity. The USSR design of the so called RMBK reactors, or graphite moderated reactors, had a number of deficiencies, one of which was the absence of an efficient system of containment. The Chernobyl accident occurred when the gas emissions caused by the melting reactor blew off the concrete slab covering it, which had not been designed to resist such pressures. The gases then condensed in the atmosphere, forming a radioactive cloud that the wind blew west and southwesterly for several thousand miles over the next few days. Much of Europe was affected by the radioactive cloud. As for most catastrophes, the causes were an unfortunate combination of human error and technical problems.

In the months following the accident, the number of cases of cancer and abnormal births increased in the Chernobyl region. Many agricultural products became unfit for consumption. Despite this having been denied by the Soviet authorities, according to some sources, the explosion directly caused the death of some 12,500 people over a 10-year period, while roughly 4 million people – both civilian and military – suffered consequences of varying seriousness from the catastrophe. More than 70,000 of them became disabled. Over 11,000 people, 1,800 in Chernobyl and elsewhere as far as eastern France, were treated for thyroid cancer. Globally, this accident cost the international community more than $1 billion.

As a temporary solution, the residual radioactivity was confined by pouring concrete around the ruined reactor. This was mainly financed by the European Union, with contributions from the United States, in exchange for which the operation of the nuclear reactor was abandoned. A new enclosure is currently under construction, funded by the European Bank for Reconstruction and Development.

Box 3.4. *The Chernobyl catastrophe: Ukraine 1986*

At last, there was the Fukushima accident.

On March 11, 2011, a magnitude 9 earthquake shook Japan, triggering a 15 m high tsunami on the east coast and flooding vast areas. Some 20,000 people lost their lives in these natural disasters. At the Fukushima–Daiichi nuclear power plant, the tsunami destroyed essential safety components in units 1–4. This triggered a core meltdown and explosions. Radioactive substances were released into the environment. Following the chain reaction of earthquake, tsunami and reactor accident, some 165,000 people were evacuated or voluntarily left their homes in

Fukushima prefecture. The evacuated areas are gradually being re-authorized, so that a few years later, the number of people still evacuated stood at 45,000.

3.39. Conclusion: an uncertain outlook; future energy needs

Since 1979, the evolution of energy markets has been marked by two key words: privatization (of companies in the sector) and deregulation, aimed in principle at reducing costs and prices and favoring consumers.

Deregulation of the oil and petroleum product market, which had long been underway in the United States and was gradually extended to most industrialized countries in the second half of the 20th century, seemed the natural thing to do. Price controls on petroleum products persist in many emerging countries.

Deregulation of the gas and electricity markets was much more complex and took much longer. This is only to be expected in "natural monopoly" industries, where the existence of a single company in a given area seems quite "natural". The excellent performance of EDF under Marcel Boiteux, who devised a generally satisfactory pricing system, is proof of this.

However, the determination of British, American and, ultimately, European Union leaders to dismantle monopolies and introduce competition at all costs prevailed. The results of this deregulation remain to be seen. As American experts have pointed out, it only works if deregulation is perfectly regulated.

Time will tell whether all the decisions taken were the right ones. These are eminently political measures, and the changes in power in the various countries will have obvious consequences in this area. The violent increases in gas and electricity prices following Russia's invasion of Ukraine should prompt the European Union to review the way these markets operate.

The development of renewable energies and the need to reduce our consumption of fossil fuels are putting the problem of reserves on the back burner. We have enough coal, oil and gas. Our concern must be to reduce consumption and optimize use.

4

Structure of the Energy Industries – Security of Supply

4.1. Introduction

The creation and development of production capacity and transport and distribution networks in industries in the energy sector have often been undertaken by private enterprise. Coal production in much of Europe, for example, was long controlled by well-known individual families such as Krupp in Germany. In the oil sector, the names of the founders of major companies are still well-known: John Rockefeller (Standard Oil), Henri Deterding (Royal Dutch, then Royal Dutch Shell), Marcus Samuel (Shell), etc.

Nonetheless, governments quickly became aware of the strategic importance of energy industries and decided to play a prominent role in their development.

4.2. Natural monopolies and effects of size

There have been many examples of industrial development that have benefitted from the obvious advantages of a natural monopoly and economies of scale. Why build two parallel railway lines, two parallel gas pipe lines or two parallel power lines to service the same customer? What could be more natural than making a single company responsible for gas and electricity distribution over a given territory? Although in many countries prior to World War II, several companies were involved in gas or electricity distribution, only one company operated in a given zone: each company had its territory. This idea of a natural monopoly extends to rail transport and also to telecommunications, water distribution and in general all "network" activities.

The history of the leading oil company Standard Oil illustrates the benefits of size. Over a 10 year period (1870–1880), John Rockefeller created a company that held a near-monopoly on the refining and distribution of petroleum products in the United States. The company's size allowed it to negotiate the lowest price for the crude oil that it purchased from many small producers, who had little bargaining strength in the negotiation. Similarly, he obtained highly advantageous transport costs from the independent companies, far lower than the prices given to his competitors. Initially, Rockefeller did not get involved in crude oil production, preferring to benefit from competition between the very numerous producers operating in what was still a limited market. At the end of the century, because of the substantial growth in demand for petroleum products, Standard Oil found that it needed at least some control over its crude oil supply to give the supply security necessary for product manufacture. Rockefeller therefore added crude oil production to Standard Oil's activities.

However, Standard Oil's size and strength were the subject of increasingly severe criticism from the media from the beginning of the 20th century. In 1911, the company was broken up into 34 companies under the 1890 Sherman Act (antitrust law). Among these new companies were:

– Standard Oil of New Jersey (which became Esso, then Exxon, now ExxonMobil);

– Standard Oil of New York (which became Mobil after merging with Vacuum, then merging with Exxon in 1999);

– Standard Oil of California (Socal which became Chevron after buying Gulf in 1984 and before merging with Texaco at the beginning of the 2000s).

The end of the 20th and beginning of the 21st centuries were marked by a new wave of inter-company consolidation: BP-Amoco-Arco, Exxon-Mobil, Total-Fina-Elf, Chevron-Texaco, Conoco-Philipps, etc. This wave of mergers and acquisitions continued with Statoil-Hydro, Chevron-Unocal, Conoco-Burlington and Rosneft-Yukos.

4.3. The petroleum industry: international oil companies and national oil companies

As soon as the break-up of the Rockefeller Empire was complete, the new companies found themselves competing with other major companies that had been formed in the early stages of the oil industry. These included Gulf and Texaco which developed the oil fields in Texas around 1900, Royal Dutch in Indonesia, Shell (which would merge with Royal Dutch in 1907) and Anglo-Persian (today's BP) in Persia (Iran). The seven largest companies – the "Seven Sisters"[1] according to the expression coined by Enrico Mattei, head of Agip and then of ENI (the Italian petroleum company) – came to exercise control of the oil industry throughout the entire world. To avoid "excessive" competition, they met in 1928 at Achnaccary Castle in northern Scotland. Under the agreement reached ("As Is" agreement), they divided existing markets between themselves and limited competition to new markets only.

Although the American companies mentioned above were established through private enterprise, the development of other international companies owed much to decisions taken by the governments concerned. In 1914, the British Government, who had concluded a long-term contract with Anglo-Persian for the Royal Navy's fuel oil supplies, became the majority shareholder[2] of the company. In 1924, the French State created Compagnie Française du Pétrole (CFP). This company took over Deutsch Bank's shares in the Turkish Petroleum Company as part of German reparations for war damage. This company, active in Mesopotamia, had been set up before World War I by German and Turkish interests to explore for oil along the Istanbul–Baghdad railroad. The company became the Iraq Petroleum Corporation (IPC) after the war, when German and Turkish interests were essentially replaced by Anglo-Saxon companies.

After World War II, the French state created Elf-Aquitaine (Bret-Rouzaut and Favennec, 2011) to merge the equity stakes it held in several different companies. Therefore, the French Government was responsible for the creation and development of two major companies: CFP which became Total and Elf which merged with Total at the end of the 20th century. The same government also established the Institut Français du Pétrole[3] (French Petroleum Institute), a research and training organization known throughout the world and intended to ensure that France was not dependent on American oil industry technology. These actions also resulted in the creation of a powerful para-petroleum industry based on the development of companies with robust technical competence in the upstream sector, i.e. seismic, drilling, engineering, etc. (CGG, Technip – which merged with Coflexip, Axens, etc.).

1 Esso, Mobil, Socal, Gulf, Texaco, Royal Dutch Shell and BP.

2 Under this agreement, the government undertook not to intervene in commercial policy but was given the right to appoint two non-executive directors to the Board, a right it retained until the sale of the government's holding under Margaret Thatcher.

3 Now, IFP Energies nouvelles.

Petroleum companies concentrate on different strategic objectives depending on their country of origin and their relationship with its government. Broadly speaking, North American companies' main objectives are financial profitability, while European state-owned or formerly state-owned companies – Total, ENI, Repsol, etc. – were created to ensure their countries' security of supply. Their privatization has nonetheless led them to adopt the same management objectives as their competitors who have always operated under a free market system.

4.4. The oil industry: post-war years and the creation of OPEC

Unhappy with the oil price cuts imposed by the Seven Sisters in the late 1950s, five of the world's biggest oil-producing countries – Saudi Arabia, Iraq, Iran, Kuwait and Venezuela – met in Baghdad in 1960 and created the Organization of the Petroleum Exporting Countries (OPEC)[4] on September 14, with the initial aim of ensuring price stability.

This objective was achieved, and the price of oil remained stable for 10 years. Moderate increases were agreed between OPEC and the oil companies during the period 1969–1972. OPEC then unilaterally increased prices threefold between October 1973 and January 1974 (the first oil shock caused by the Yom Kippur War), and again threefold between 1979 and 1981 (the second oil shock caused by the Islamic Revolution in Iran). From 1974 until 1980, OPEC controlled markets and prices. From 1980 to 1985, this control weakened until free markets were established. Prices varied from day to day, a situation unheard of until then (see Chapter 3).

4.5. Nationalization in oil-producing countries

The model of a state monopoly discussed above was also widely adopted in the 1950s, 1960s and 1970s by third-world countries. In these developing countries, the most commonly held theories favored the creation of large state-owned companies, as this was the sole means of obtaining the resources needed for the significant investments required[5].

---

4 At the start of 2024, OPEC includes 12 countries: Saudi Arabia, Iran, Iraq, Kuwait, the United Arab Emirates, Algeria, Libya, Nigeria, Gabon, Equitorial Guinea, Republic of Congo and Venezuela. Angola has just left.

5 Remember that the post-war era was also marked by the advent of the USSR as the second dominant power in the world after the United States. The Soviet economic model – often described as the Socialist model – was used as a reference by countries that had just won their independence after conflicts, many of them violent, with the former colonial powers, which

In the 1970s, the petroleum industry assets, i.e. the oil fields and the facilities, were nationalized: by 1971 in Algeria, 1972 in Iraq and 1973 in Libya, 1976 in Kuwait and Venezuela and, starting in 1976, in Saudi Arabia (nationalization was progressive, given the scale of Saudi Arabia's reserves, making it easier to transfer control of production from American companies to the new Saudi Aramco).

Governments of oil-producing countries established state-owned companies to manage their interests in the exploitation of the country's resources. These companies were required to transfer the majority of their revenues back to the state, but they retained a portion to invest or at least renew their equipment.

The International Energy Agency (IEA) was created in 1974 by most member countries of the OECD, with the notable exception of France, which only joined in 1992. This was in reaction to the events of 1973, in particular the embargo ordered by the oil-producing Arab countries against several other countries, including the United States and the Netherlands, accused of supporting Israel in the Yom Kippur War. The main first objective of the IEA is to implement a system of reallocation of oil in case of reduction of oil supplies. This includes setting up strategic stocks and publishing regular and reliable statistics and studies on energy markets.

Today, however, the IEA's responsibility has expanded to include energy policymaking in terms of economic development and environmental protection, as well as energy security. Its work covers diversification of energy sources, renewable energy, climate change policies, market reform, energy efficiency, development and deployment of clean energy technologies and energy technology collaboration with major consumers and producers of energy such as China, India, Russia and the OPEC countries. The IEA undertakes a broad program of energy research, data compilation, publications and public dissemination of the latest energy policy analysis and recommendations on good practices.

Box 4.1. *The International Energy Agency (IEA)*

4.6. The years 1980–1990: OPEC's loss of power – members' interests diverge

At the beginning of the 1980s, the increase in the price of oil had resulted in a fall in demand and the development of significant non-OPEC production. In the

were seen as in the camp of imperialist and capitalist countries. The Soviet model, founded on collective ownership of the means of production, is based on state-owned companies managing all sectors of the economy. This model was widely admired in the third world, so much so that Nikita Khrushchev, General Secretary of the Communist Party, could declare at the end of the 1950s that "the USSR's wealth will surpass that of the United States by 1980" and this statement did not seem incongruous.

1980s the cartel lost control of the market and its market share fell by the mid-1980s to less than 30% from more than 50% of world production in the 1970s (today, it is around 40%), despite the fact that its member countries held around 75% of the world's reserves and benefited from low production costs.

The fall in prices had been inevitable because of the significant capacity surpluses that resulted from the drop in demand. From 1982, OPEC accepted the role of swing producer: the other countries produced at maximum capacity and OPEC adjusted its production to demand. The current situation remains similar due to large potential production surpluses.

Producer and consumer countries are highly dependent on each other:

– The major exporting countries remain highly dependent on their oil revenues, which provide most of their budgetary income. Any interruption in exports would quickly have fair consequences for the exporters themselves.

– The exporting countries import massive quantities of finished goods and agricultural products. The European Union is the main trading partner of the producing countries of the Gulf.

– The exporting countries have numerous financial assets ("petrodollars" or "petroeuros") in Western economies. The yield on these assets depends on the economic growth of the countries in which they are invested, i.e. the energy-consuming countries. But historically, this growth is in inverse proportion to the growth in crude oil prices.

Box 4.2. *Mutual dependency*

4.7. Back to liberalism

In the 1980s, as we saw in the previous chapter, in response to the economic crisis of the previous decade, liberal economic theories, which had been ignored during the period when Keynesian-inspired economic policies had seemed to succeed, came back in force. Western economies would have suffered from excessive state intervention, and deregulation and privatization seemed necessary.

In the oil exploration and production sector, after the creation of national companies in the 1970s, the trend was reversed at the end of the 20th century. Faced with low oil prices and the difficulties of their national companies in maintaining production, many countries once again opened their borders to international companies with recognized technological expertise and substantial financial capacity. Oil activities are now often managed by associations of national and international companies. Only a few countries in the Middle East (Saudi Arabia, Kuwait, Iran, etc.) maintain almost total control over oil and gas activities through a national company with a monopoly.

This openness has continued since the beginning of the 21st century, although periods of high crude oil prices have led some countries to try to curb it.

State control was also very strong in the refining and marketing sector in many countries, with the notable exception of Western countries. Deregulation took place in the 1980s to increase competition and thus lower prices. It was implemented long ago in the United States, then in Europe and Japan. In France, the last fuel price controls were abolished in 1986, and a new law enacted in 1992 considerably reduced government control over the oil industry.

However, in many countries, fuel prices and consumer gas and electricity prices are still controlled by the government.

4.8. Situation in developing countries

The oil shock of 1973, reinforced by that of 1979–1980 and combined with the economic crisis of the 1970s, put many developing countries in a difficult economic position, typified by budget deficits and endemic external debt. The crisis would force these countries to turn to industrialized nations and international organizations for loans to make up their deficits. This was the start of the "structural adjustment loans", made by international institutions to these countries that could not use capital markets to finance their debt.

However, for the poorest countries, a condition of these loans was that they agreed to transform the way their economies operated. As in industrialized countries, their difficulties were attributed to excessive government intervention: creation of national industrial companies with too large personnel, price freezes to avoid inflation, and frequently, currency exchange rates that were totally disconnected from economic reality.

In many developing countries, deregulation and privatization policies were implemented under the influence of international organizations, like the IMF and the World Bank. The results were mixed. Although Asian countries achieved robust economic growth, sometimes without the help of international organizations, in South America, and particularly in Africa, the difficulties remained.

Guyana, formerly British Guiana, is a member of the Commonwealth located between Suriname, Brazil and Venezuela. It is one of the poorest countries in South America, with high unemployment and a relatively unstable economy.

In May 2015, ExxonMobil discovered offshore oil fields in Guyana: in 2019, nearly 16 fields were discovered on the Stabroek permit and surrounding area. In 2020, production from Liza 1 began and is expected to reach nearly 120,000 barrels per day, while Liza phase 2 is expected to add 220,000 barrels per day to existing production. ExxonMobil estimates that potential oil production will be around 1.2 million barrels per day by 2027.

ExxonMobil holds a 45% interest in the Stabroek permit, which it shares with the US company Hess (30%) and the Chinese company CNOOC (25%).

While these discoveries are extremely promising for Guyana, should it fear a "resource curse"? Guyana will need to look to countries that have made similar discoveries in the past to provide effective governance of the hydrocarbon sector. Guyana has begun to develop relations with other oil-producing countries. A Guyanese delegation met representatives of the Scottish oil industry in Aberdeen in 2018. Air links with the USA have also been established, and Kuwait, the United Arab Emirates and Qatar have opened embassies in Guyana. Guyana is also a member of the United Nations, the World Trade Organization (WTO) and the Organisation of Islamic Cooperation (OIC).

There are, however, certain obstacles to harmonious exploitation. These include territorial disputes with Venezuela, which claims the territory along the Essequibo River, encompassing part of the recently discovered fields. This dispute, which dates back to the late 19th century, has been rekindled by the presence of oil. In 2015, Venezuela issued a presidential decree unilaterally extending its maritime border.

Box 4.3. *The example of Guyana*

4.9. Ethics and energy

The production and use of energy raises many ethical and moral issues. Energy production is a source of pollution, whether it is the exploration or exploitation of oil or gas deposits, the transportation of hydrocarbons or the production and transmission of electricity. It can be a source of corruption. As in all business sectors, energy companies – and oil companies in particular – cannot ignore the social and political context in which they operate. They maintain complex relationships with their environment.

What is the company's responsibility? Is it legitimate for an oil company to seek to ensure the "proper" use of the revenues it distributes to the state in which it operates? Does this fall within its remit? Should it secure its production sites against external attack, contribute to local development by building roads and schools, set up health insurance or pension systems? Should it operate in countries where human rights are not respected? Long criticized for interfering in national politics, companies are sometimes asked to assume some of the responsibilities of the state in the countries where they operate[6]. In Guyana, ExxonMobil has invested 2.5 billion Guyanese dollars in education, environmental and women's emancipation projects.

Companies have a permanent duty of vigilance, while governments have a dual responsibility: to lobby for the implementation of effective international rules and then to monitor their proper application. Civil society can play a crucial supervisory role and act as arbiter of last resort, by exercising its power at the time of elections and its ability to lead economic boycotts.

The management of Norway's sovereign wealth fund is a good example of the increasingly close link between ethical concerns and the energy sector. In 2018, the fund's share of investments in the oil sector was around $37 billion. The fund itself has almost $1.3 trillion in assets in 2024 and is an important asset for any energy company. In 2016, it banned 52 companies whose revenues derived more than 30% from coal mining. In 2020, other groups were also excluded from the fund, including Glencore, Anglo-American, AGL Energy and SASOL. Compliance with ethical standards seems to be an increasingly essential issue for companies in the energy sector today. Choosing not to take them into account means risking retaliation.

In electricity generation, there are a few giant companies and a large number of small producers. In the long term, the European market could be shared between a few large multi-energy companies (EDF, ENGIE, RWE, E.On) and a multitude of smaller operators.

4.10. Other often forgotten players

Apart from the players operating directly on the energy markets, there are others who have an influence on the general environment and thus have the ability to affect the markets' operation.

4.10.1. *International organizations*

The UN, a major forum for discussion and an organization for the resolution of problems between nations, has the right to consider all international issues.

6 For these topics, refer also in particular to the chapter on Africa (Chapter 5, Volume 2), the problems in Nigeria and initiatives such as Publish What You Pay, EITI, etc.

Therefore, it plays a role in armed conflicts (direct intervention or by mandate) and in embargos, for example, the Iraq "Oil for Food" program.

The International Monetary Fund and the World Bank affect the structure of the economies of the many developing countries who have obtained finance from them. These institutions have helped to launch the liberalization and deregulation programs in many parts of the world (see section 4.8).

The International Maritime Organization is responsible for international maritime regulations; the WTO agrees rules of international trade, etc.

4.10.2. *Economic and political interests: lobbies*

When energy prices increase, the consequences are felt throughout the entire industrial sector and so, in the end, on retail prices. In some industries, profitability is directly linked to changes in the price of crude oil, for example the automobile industry, or in the price of coal, for example the steel industry. Where companies today are independent of government authorities, they nevertheless try to guide government decisions in favor of their interests.

Pressure groups representing special interests are therefore organized to be omnipresent in political decision-making centers. The typical actions they take are attempts to make tax rules favorable to them or, inversely, unfavorable or penalizing for competitors; the enactment of regulations that are advantageous for them or disadvantageous for competitors and economic diplomacy (use of political power abroad to obtain major contracts). Indeed, even heads of state on international visits are turned into salesmen for their national industries. Innumerable lobbies are present in the corridors of Brussels. The family of both the Bush American presidents is very close to the powerful Texas petroleum industry, and Dick Cheney, the American Vice President up to 2009, was for a long time the CEO of Halliburton, one of the worldwide leaders in oil and gas services industry.

The view that people take of these practices depends on their culture. In the United States and in much of the European Community, allowing these special interests free expression is thought to be the best means of counteracting them. On the contrary, in other countries, lobbying sometimes takes the form of clandestine power plays that are not subject to democratic oversight.

4.10.3. *Civil society*

Non-governmental organizations (NGOs) such as Greenpeace or Human Rights Watch are players who act against what they see as "collusions of interest between the powerful" and have to be taken seriously. They influence public opinion, particularly because they are seen as independent from political or economic powers. They expose political and environmental scandals: for example, Halliburton was accused of having benefitted from the preferential awarding of contracts in Iraq by American authorities; details of corruption by oil companies in Africa were revealed during the 1980s.

The creation of the Extractive Industries Transparency Initiative (EITI) has led to greater control over oil revenues and their use.

The accident at the Fukushima nuclear power plant in 2011 led to an upsurge in international anti-nuclear movements. Germany has accelerated the closure of its nuclear power plants, and in Italy, in a 2011 referendum, 94% of voters voted to ban the construction of nuclear power plants.

Therefore, public opinion is of increasing importance in the debate. Indeed, the major obstacle to the development of nuclear energy is the public's reluctance to face environmental and health risks associated with nuclear power.

4.10.4. *Research and training institutes*

Independent research institutes develop technology in parallel with the major energy companies' research centers. IFP Energies nouvelles (formerly IFP – Institut français du pétrole) was formed in 1944 to promote the development of French technology during an era when American technology was virtually all that was available. Other institutes (the Institute of Petroleum – now merged into the Energy Institute in London – the American Petroleum Institute, etc.) have the mission of creating links to industry, promoting information exchange, training, improving standards, etc. Another example, the Global Energy Interconnection Research Institute Europe (GEIRI), created in 2014, has brought together Chinese and European researchers while promoting cooperation between companies and universities.

4.10.5. *Criminal movements*

Due to the money it generates and the potential damage it can cause, the energy industry naturally attracts some illegal and even some criminal activities. The Strait of Malacca is, for example, the worst channel in the world for piracy. Fees paid by oil companies can be diverted by powerful mafia groups; the destruction of oil pipelines can be threatened or used to apply political pressure, etc.

We must distinguish between groups whose prime objective is financial (e.g. the mafia), and those who are totally politically motivated. However, the latter do not hesitate to use illegal means to finance their terrorist activities. It was clear from the attacks of September 11 that petrodollars from the Arabian Peninsula can be diverted via various buffer organizations (shell companies, so-called charitable organizations, etc.) to finance terrorist activism. In response, Western countries – led by the United States – froze various financial assets that had come from this region. As a result, a number of financial assets were transferred from the USA to Europe or even Asia or the Middle East.

4.11. Evolving strategies

The origins of the oil industry lay in the simple exploitation of the raw material, and its structure was based on private enterprise. Then, when oil became a source of motor fuels – gasoline, jet fuel, diesel oil, fuel oil for ships – security of supply became paramount, and governments sought to control it. This led to numerous nationalizations. Later, in the interests of economic efficiency, governments agreed to deregulate the industry and allow the market to function as it had in the early days of the industry. The oil market saw the development of spot and futures markets.

The energy and gas sector has undergone profound change over the last 30 years. Monopolies have had to make way for new players. Once again, the benefits of this strategy have yet to be demonstrated.

The energy sector must now take account of the energy transition, ensuring that the energy needs of the world's population are met while limiting the use of fossil fuels.

4.12. Energy policies and security of supplies

Energy plays a fundamental role in economic and social activity, particularly in the transport sector. Two examples illustrate this well:

– During World War II, the availability of crude oil for the manufacture of motor fuels was the priority for German strategic decisions: after seizing the Romanian oil fields, one of Germany's objectives in declaring war on the Soviet Union and invading Russia was control of the oil deposits of Baku and the Volga. In fact, the

German troops were defeated at Stalingrad and so failed to take control of Russian oil. A little later, Rommel headed towards the Middle East where giant oil deposits had just been discovered, but British troops and a lack of gasoline and diesel oil prevented him from reaching his goal. Germany had to resort to coal liquefaction for the manufacture of motor fuels.

– In third-world countries, any shortage of petroleum products makes it more difficult to harvest food supplies and more importantly impossible to transport them to cities and thus feed urban populations. In the 1970s, the higher oil prices had particularly harmful consequences for many African countries: unable to buy oil they had to let the harvests wither because there was no transport available for them.

During the 1973 crisis, the OPEC countries' embargo on oil deliveries to Western countries that supported Israel during the Yom Kippur war led these countries to take drastic measures to reduce their oil consumption. The fact that both the scope and duration of the embargo were limited did not change the fact that, in Western eyes, oil supplies from Arab countries are not secure and other sources must be sought.

To reduce their dependence on OPEC oil, Western governments promoted the development of new oil fields in Alaska, the North Sea and later the Gulf of Mexico, the Gulf of Benin and the Caspian region. Although in 1973 Western countries depended on Gulf countries to make their economies run (up to 70% of energy requirements in some countries were met by oil, mainly imported from the Middle East), the position in the 21st century is quite different. Oil's share in energy consumption has decreased, and OPEC's share of these supplies has also decreased. In addition, although consuming countries still need oil and gas, producing countries also need the revenues they provide.

The control of energy resources has to do with their strategic and military characteristics: oil is essential for waging war. The US Air Force consumes more than 10% of the country's jet fuel. At the same time, the development of more powerful storage batteries is encouraged to support the creation of even more powerful drones.

Security of energy supplies is therefore a priority. However, although 40 years ago it seemed that recourse to military means might be necessary, today the operation of an active and transparent market is seen as an alternative method for having secure supplies.

4.13. Supply security: solutions offered by the market

Starting from the observation that embargos like that of 1973 have never reoccurred, in 2000, John Mitchell (Royal Institute of International Affairs, Chatham House, Great Britain) told a European summit dedicated to the topic that it was now exporting countries and no longer importing countries that were vulnerable to the risk of disruption in supplies for political reasons. In fact, recently, it was exporting countries that were subject to embargos (Libya, Iraq and Iran) and thus to the risk of revenue losses.

Until the second oil shock, most oil was bought and sold under a rigid system of long-term contracts. After 1980, the development of a spot market was made possible by the increasing flexibility of contracts (particularly spot contracts, negotiated for single cargoes on a cargo-by-cargo basis). This now makes it possible to achieve an almost instantaneous balance between supply and demand by changes in the price. The risk has therefore become a financial risk. To meet the risk that arises from possible price changes, increasingly varied and complex financial coverage products have been developed, to the extent that the oil market has now become a financial market. This system enables physical risk to be anticipated and taken into account by financial means.

However, monitoring developments in the market can be difficult because of the lack of data. The availability of better statistics improves supply security. The impact of American statistics on stock levels on market prices is well known.

There is also a trend towards the development of a spot market for gas, particularly for LNG, even though importing countries still use long-term contracts to ensure supply security. The crises of autumn 2021 and 2022 (when prices on the open markets rose sharply as a result of the economic recovery and then the war in Ukraine) demonstrate the value of such contracts for sellers.

4.14. How to improve supply security

The best way to ensure supply security is by controlling consumption, i.e. by improving energy efficiency. An increase in demand makes improving energy efficiency an even more important challenge. It has also meant that diversification of energy and supply sources are more and more indispensable.

4.14.1. *An example: energy efficiency in the European Union*

Since the early 2000s, the European Union has set strong objectives in this area. The "3 × 20" adopted at the time were aimed at:

– a 20% reduction in energy demand by 2020 compared with 2000;

– a 20% share of renewable energies in the energy mix by 2020;

– a 20% reduction in greenhouse gas emissions by 2020 (compared with 1990).

In 2005, the European Union published a "Green Book" on energy efficiency, in which several measures were proposed to reduce waste as much as possible. It was stressed that success cannot be based solely on technological advances; it must also come from increased awareness encouraging citizens to change their behavior as consumers. In 2012, the EU Energy Efficiency Directive established binding measures to make European countries energy efficient.

More drastic measures were then recommended. In 2024, the targets for 2030 are:

– 27% improvement in energy efficiency compared with the trend scenario;

– a 27% share of renewable energies in the energy mix;

– a 55% reduction in greenhouse gas emissions (compared to 1990).

In 2018, the European Parliament adopted a series of non-legislative recommendations drawn up by its Committee on Industry, Research and Energy (ITRE). They recommend education programs to help citizens save more energy, and an increase of at least 50% in funding for energy-saving projects.

4.14.2. *Diversification of energy sources*

The breakdown of total energy consumption into the different forms of energy used varies greatly from country to country. Industrialized countries use varying proportions of oil, natural gas, coal, nuclear energy and renewable energies. Canada's and Norway's electricity generation is mainly hydraulic, while France uses its massive nuclear energy development. Gas meets some 50% of Russia's energy needs, but a much lower proportion in France and Spain. These differences are essentially due to local availability and national policies.

The situation in developing countries is even more diverse. The least advanced countries of course rely overwhelmingly on biomass and, among commercial energies, oil plays a predominant role.

4.14.3. *Geographical diversification of supply sources*

There were two different reactions to the 1973 oil shock:

– the first was a reduction in energy consumption;

– the second was replacing heavy fuel oil as much as possible with nuclear power, gas and coal[7].

The second oil shock in 1979 reinforced this trend and led to a substantial reduction in world oil consumption. Both oil shocks made consuming countries aware of the absolute necessity of avoiding dependence on Arabian/Persian Gulf countries or on any limited number of suppliers. Diversification of oil supplies was made easier by the tenfold increase in the price of oil, which made possible the development of oil fields (Alaska, the North Sea, offshore production in Latin America and Africa, etc.) that had previously been unprofitable.

This supply diversification is now even more necessary as, although OPEC's share of world oil production fell from 50% in 1973 to under 30% in the mid-1980s, it rose again to about 42% in 2023, and the IEA estimates that it will exceed 50% towards 2030. OPEC will therefore regain considerable weight, given the reserves of the Gulf countries (nearly half of the world's proven oil reserves).

Although the diversification of oil supply sources may be considered simple, it is far more difficult for gas. However, the halt in Russian natural gas deliveries to Europe has shown that this is possible, albeit with a longer adaptation period than for oil.

Despite a more balanced distribution of reserves, coal consumption is bound to decrease due to CO_2 emissions. Coal reserves are evenly distributed: 24.1% in North America, 42.7% in the Asia–Pacific region, 17.8% in the CIS and 12.6% in Europe (excluding the CIS). Only the Middle East (0.1%), Africa (1.3%) and Latin America (1.3%) have no significant reserves. Such a distribution offers interesting prospects for diversifying supplies. However, coal remains the main source of CO_2, and its future is limited.

Finally, it is difficult for countries in an unfavorable geographical position to diversify their electricity supplies. In Europe, for example, this is the case for peninsulas such as Spain, Portugal and Italy. Electricity has the advantage that it can

7 Although industrialized countries absorbed the effects of the first oil shock relatively easily, developing countries had far more difficulty. From 1974 to 1975, they simply no longer had the means to pay for the oil they needed. In any event, all countries sought to make energy savings after 1973.

be produced wherever appropriate. However, interconnections are essential to secure supplies and reduce costs. Transmission lines between different countries are therefore essential.

4.15. Means of supply

4.15.1. *Pipelines*

Pipelines are used for two reasons:

– because a pipeline is necessary to transport crude oil from its production site to a refinery or a coastal export terminal;

– for economic reasons, for example to reduce costs and/or to diversify export routes and thus decrease risks.

The risks associated with oil pipelines are twofold:

– if a pipeline is located in a single country, the risk is accidental or terrorist in nature;

– if a field requires the construction of a pipeline crossing another country, the risk is geopolitical.

4.15.1.1. *Alaskan oil*

Oil was discovered in the north of Alaska in the 1960s but production only started in the late 1970s. After considering shipment by icebreaking vessels, the producers decided on a pipeline across Alaska as the solution (see the map in Figure 4.1).

At first, Alaskan oil was not seen as strategically important and opposition to pipeline construction from the environmentalists was sufficient to prevent its construction. One of the grounds for this was that it would interrupt the caribou migrations. The fact that a considerable portion of Alaskan oil was owned by a foreign company (BP) did not help the cause of pipeline construction. However, after the 1973 oil shock and the Arab boycott of oil supplies to the USA, Alaskan oil was recognized as a strategic necessity. Congress, despite the opposition, which was still considerable, passed the necessary legislation. The pipeline was built (and the caribou are still migrating happily).

However, construction was complex: the environment is fragile, and it was essential to ensure that the oil's high temperature did not melt the permafrost (a permanently frozen layer that covers the ground in this region). The pipeline therefore had to be built above the ground. The construction was long and costly and only completed in 1977.

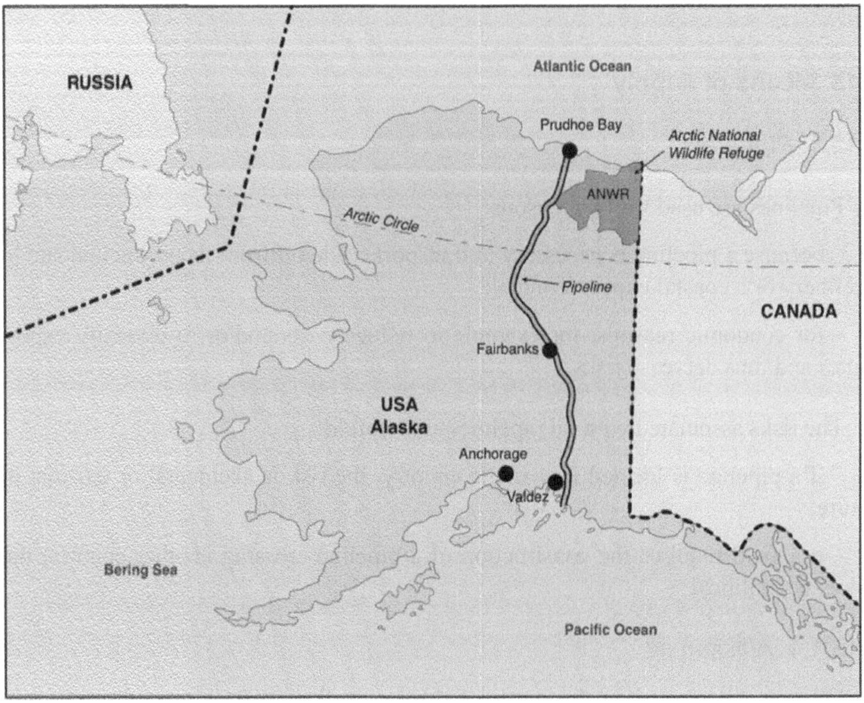

Figure 4.1. *The Trans-Alaska Pipeline*

4.15.1.2. *Exploitation of Russian oil*[8]

Most Russian oil is produced in Western Siberia. The Siberian oil is routed to the West by a network of pipelines delivering to the Baltic Sea at Primorsk and the Black Sea at Novorossiysk and Odessa (Ukraine). Russia now has two problems: first, its loss of influence over its "near abroad" – as shown by the events in Georgia and in Ukraine – and second, the immensity of its territory and remoteness of the oil fields.

Belarus, Ukraine, Poland, Hungary, the Czech Republic and Slovakia are supplied by the *Druzhba* (friendship) pipeline. This pipeline was formerly entirely

8 The geopolitics of the evacuation of hydrocarbons from Russia, and also from Central Asia, is described in further detail in Chapter 4 of Volume 2, dedicated to the CIS.

within the Soviet zone of influence; today it supplies the Leuna refinery in Germany (formerly East Germany) and crosses several EU member states.

4.15.1.3. *Export of oil from the Caspian*

Except for Russia and Iran, the countries bordering the Caspian Sea – Azerbaijan, Kazakhstan and Turkmenistan – are landlocked and are therefore entirely reliant on their neighbors, particularly Russia, for access to the open sea.

For some time, Kazakhstan's hydrocarbon production could only be exported via Russia using a network of oil and gas pipelines from the Soviet era. The network includes the Caspian Petroleum Corporation (CPC) oil pipeline, which can transport 50 million tons of crude oil per year from Tengiz to Novorossiysk. Kazakhstan now exports part of its oil to China.

Oil is exported from Azerbaijan via the BTC pipeline (Baku–Tbilisi–Ceyhan, on the Turkish coast). This pipeline was built on BP's initiative in 2002 and went into operation in 2006. It can transport around 1 Mbpd.

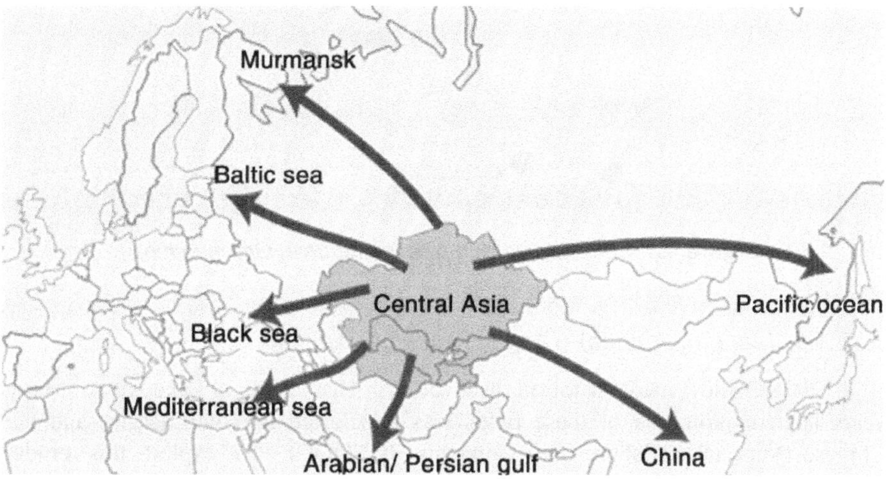

Figure 4.2. *Central Asia's oil export routes*

4.15.1.4. *Chad–Cameroon pipelines*

The exploitation of oil reserves discovered in southern Chad required the construction of a 1,070 km (665 miles) pipeline between the Doba fields and the port of Kribi in Cameroon. The development of this pipeline was the subject of long negotiations between the government, oil companies and NGOs, who were concerned about the consequences of pipeline construction for people (Pygmies, etc.) living near the route and for the ecologically sensitive environment. It was thanks to the World Bank's intervention and their involvement in securing finance for the project that the pipeline could be built.

The agreement stipulated that revenues from the project would be allocated to the health and education budgets and to a fund for future generations. The rise in oil prices from 2002 onwards enabled the government to repay the World Bank loan and free itself from the obligations under the agreement.

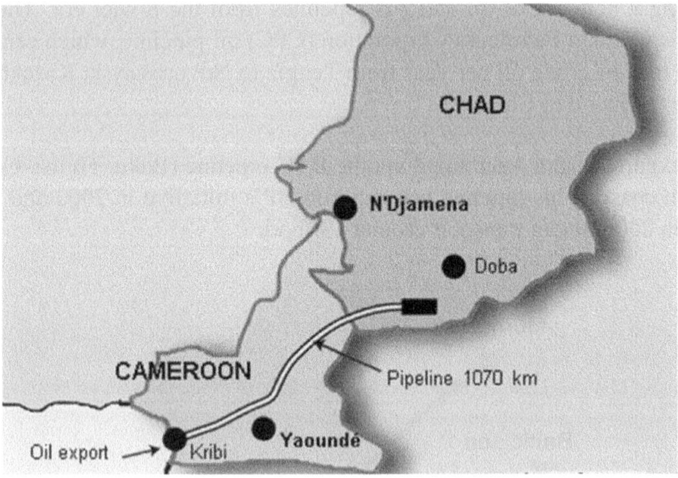

Figure 4.3. *Chad–Cameroon pipeline (source: Greenpeace)*

4.15.1.5. *Tilanga (Uganda)–Tanga (Tanzania) pipeline*

In 2006, Tullöw made major oil discoveries in Uganda along Lake Albert. Many years later, exploitation of these fields was transferred to TotalEnergies and the Chinese National Offshore Oil Company (CNOOC). To exploit this crude, a pipeline of almost 1,440 kilometers has to be built between the fields of the Tilenga and Kingfisher in Uganda and the port of Tanga in Tanzania. This pipeline requires heating, as the crude is heavy and viscous, and could freeze in the pipes.

This project, like the Doba Kribi project 20 years earlier, has given rise to a great deal of criticism, particularly from NGOs: drilling wells in protected areas (Murchison Falls area), the need to evict farmers from their fields to make way for the pipeline and sometimes late compensation payments. Other environmental problems have also been raised.

The cost of the project is estimated at $3.5 billion. It has been financed by investors and loans from Chinese banks, since Western banks have refused to finance the project.

However, both the Ugandan and Tanzanian governments are staunch supporters of the project. Not only will it bring in foreign currency, but it should also give Uganda a degree of self-sufficiency in petroleum products. This is particularly important for a landlocked country which in the 1970s, under the dictator Imin Dada, was deprived of fuel following a war with Tanzania.

4.15.1.6. *Middle East pipelines*

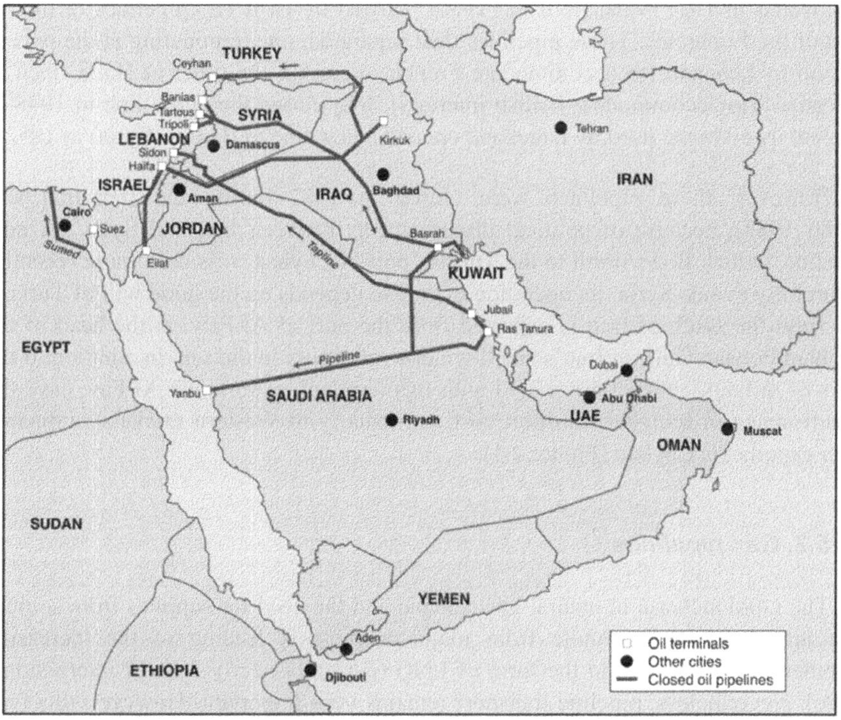

Figure 4.4. *Main pipelines in the Middle East. For a color version of this figure, see www.iste.co.uk/favennec/geopolitics1.zip*

The cost of crude oil transport to Europe or the USA is critical for exports from the Middle East. The lowest-cost route is via pipeline to the Mediterranean, but this involves considerable political risks. The Trans-Arabian Pipeline (TAP) was built in 1950 and transported Saudi Arabian crude oil, via Jordan, to the Lebanese port of Az Zahrani. However, because of political conflicts in the region, it had to be closed by the end of the 1970s and Saudi Arabia now exports its crude oil by tanker from the Arabian/Persian Gulf and the Red Sea. The Petroline pipeline, built in 1981 and connecting the eastern Saudi Arabia oil fields to Yanbu on the Red Sea, can reduce transport costs, provided of course that the Suez Canal is open. Hence, after the canal's closure in 1967, the Sumed pipeline was built (in 1974) between Suez and Alexandria, with a capacity of 120 million tons per year and a length of 330 km (200 miles). Its Mediterranean terminal is at Sidi Kerir, where the crude oil is reloaded and shipped to Europe and America.

The case of Iraq is particularly interesting. Part of Iraqi production comes from two northern regions: Mosul and Kirkuk. Oil produced from the Kirkuk field, discovered in 1927, was, from the 1930s, carried by twin 12" pipelines to the far side of the Euphrates. These pipelines then separated, one terminating at the port of Tripoli in Lebanon (to accommodate French interests), the other at Haifa, then in Palestine (to accommodate British interests). Iraq closed the Haifa line in 1948 to prevent its oil being used by Israel and opened a new line to Banias (Syria) in 1952.

However, these pipelines were closed in 1982 during the Iran–Iraq war (1980–1988), because of political disagreements between Iraq and Syria[9]. A new pipeline, which flows north to the Turkish port of Ceyhan, was built more recently; it carefully avoids Syria. Its operation of course depends on the good will of Turkey. Oil from the south of Iraq is exported from the port of Al-Faw, at the head of the Arabian/Persian Gulf, in Iraq's small window of access to the sea. In addition to the risks of military conflict associated with this terminal, exports via Al-Faw have the disadvantage of a higher transport cost, particularly to Western markets, compared with exports via Ceyhan (Figure 4.4).

4.15.2. *Gas pipelines*[10]

The rapid increase in natural gas demand and the need for supplies from sources that are increasingly remote from major markets is leading to the increasing shipment of natural gas in the form of LNG (currently nearly 30% of international trade). Nevertheless, pipeline transport remains very important. However, this type of transport is inflexible: supplies by pipeline from Russia to Europe cannot be diverted to Asia. The gas pipe lines between Russia and Europe are currently unused due to the conflict between Ukraine and Russia (and because of sabotage of Nordstream 1 and 2). Therefore, for a pipeline to operate successfully, there must be

9 The Kirkuk–Banias pipeline was used again from 2001 by Saddam Hussein in order to breach the oil embargo, until 2003 when it was damaged by US air strikes.

10 This topic is discussed again in Chapter 4 of Volume 2 on the CIS and the periodic crises between Russia and Ukraine concerning the transit of Russian gas through Ukraine.

an ongoing partnership in the project between the producing countries, the consuming countries and the transit countries.

4.15.2.1. *Turkmenistan (and Kazakhstan)*

Turkmenistan, which has a lot of gas but little oil, was hit hard by the collapse of the Soviet Union. Before 1990, it exported large quantities of gas to Russia. This gas was either used for Russian consumption or exported to European countries. Turkmen production fell from 80 billion cubic meters in 1990 (3 Tcf or 72 million toe) to 12 in 1998, as falling consumption in Russia made imports from Turkmenistan unnecessary. Turkmen production has recovered to previous levels over the last few years.

Gradually, Turkmen exports turned towards China. A network of gas pipelines from Turkmenistan, Kazakhstan and Uzbekistan now links Central Asia to China. This network is almost 2,000 km long. Increased demand for gas in China will translate into higher volumes imported from Central Asia.

4.15.2.2. *Nordstream*

As of 2012, a Nordstream 1 gas pipeline linked Russia to Germany via the Baltic Sea. Capable of transporting 55 billion cubic meters of gas a year, it has enabled Russia to reduce its dependence on Ukraine, through which the main gas pipelines linking Russia to Europe transit.

Following the “Maïdan revolution” in Ukraine in 2014 and the conflict in Donbass, Russia was seeking to further reduce its dependence on Ukraine and was developing the Nordstream 2 project. Similar to Nordstream 1, it also crosses the Baltic Sea and links Russia to Germany via Russian, Finnish, Swedish, Danish and German waters over a distance of more than 1,200 km. Like Nordstream 1, it has a transport capacity of around 55 billion cubic meters of gas per year.

Nordstream 2 has been highly controversial. Critics believed it would make EU countries even more dependent on Russian gas, which contradicts Europe’s strategy of an efficient, resilient energy mix. The United States has also taken a dim view of this pipeline project, as it competes with American LNG exports, which are booming as a result of increasing shale gas production. In 2020, however, the European Union condemned Donald Trump’s sanctions against European companies involved in the project, deeming them to be in contradiction with international and EU law. Joe Biden’s administration, initially very reluctant, eventually agreed that the pipeline should be completed.

However, Russia's invasion of the Ukraine on February 24, 2022 led the German authorities to prohibit the commissioning of this pipeline. In September 2022, attacks on both pipelines rendered them unusable.

4.15.2.3. *Tensions in the Eastern Mediterranean: Eastmed*

Since 2009, tensions have been running high between several Eastern Mediterranean countries: Cyprus, Egypt, Israel, Lebanon and Turkey. These countries' natural deposits are not particularly large (only 2% of the world's reserves), but they are located in a strategic region for the countries seeking to exploit them.

In 2017, Cyprus, Greece and Egypt signed an agreement to build an undersea gas pipeline, called Eastmed. With a length of around 2,000 km, it is expected to deliver 9–11 billion cubic meters of natural gas per year to Greece and probably also to Italy. This project is part of Greece's strategy to become one of Europe's leading gas distributors.

However, this project could clash with Turkey's strategy in the region. Tensions between Turkey and Greece are running high. Turkey has carried out several drilling operations in Cyprus's exclusive economic zone. In 2019, Turkish President Recep Tayip Erdogan signed a maritime and military agreement with Libya, further aggravating relations with Greece.

At the European level, Turkey uses its geographical position to avoid excessive sanctions: it plays an important role in controlling migratory flows and occupies an essential strategic position for NATO in terms of security.

Turkey has also signed agreements with Russia. The Turkish Stream gas pipeline (which is a gas pipeline under the Black Sea which can transport 31 billion cubic meters per year, 14 of which are destined for Turkey, the rest for Europe) links Russia to Turkey and is extended to Europe by the Tesla gas pipeline.

4.15.3. *Power networks*

The supply of electric power is more dependent on simple geographical factors – mountains, forests, peninsulas, etc. – than any other source of energy. The example of Italy illustrates these difficulties. The mountains of the north make transmission lines more expensive. As Italy is a peninsula, connecting to the European power grid is complex.

4.15.3.1. *The risks posed by cyberattacks*

With the growing importance of renewable energy technologies, countries will face increasingly critical cyber threats. Indeed, renewable energy infrastructures are highly vulnerable to cyber risk, mainly due to their interconnected networks.

Smart grids, made up of sensors placed along power grids, enable real-time adaptation of electricity generation and transmission to consumer needs. This reduces the risk of blackouts, supply chain interruptions and power losses. However, these networks are highly dependent on the ability of governments to maintain a good flow of information between consumption locations and command and control centers. The interconnected nature of smart grids could make them targets for cyberattacks with far-reaching consequences. Cyberspace is often described by the US military as the "fifth dimension of combat", as it combines a technical layer, a software layer and a psycho-cognitive layer. By its very nature, cyberspace represents a factor of vulnerability for its players: the modern world is increasingly dependent on cyberspace. It is complicated for states to assert themselves as sovereign powers, because cyberattackers always benefit from a surprise effect, and it is difficult to trace the sources of an attack.

There are several types of cyberattack: distributed denial of service (DDoS) using "zombie" computers, advanced persistent threats (APTs), which threatened the Japanese Diet shortly after the 2011 tsunami, and above all cyber-conventional combinations (CCCs), the most worrying cyber-weapons. It is this last type of threat that represents the biggest security problem: in 2010, the Stuxnet virus, probably developed by Israel and the USA, targeted the centrifuges at Iran's Natanz power plant, destroying several hundred of them. It is estimated that Stuxnet delayed the Iranian nuclear program by 18 months to 2 years. The virus was initially designed to infect only the closed circuit of the Natanz power plant, but due to a breach in the closed circuit, it infected several thousand other systems in Iran and abroad. This example illustrates how a cyber-weapon can spread rapidly through a system and infect an entire network, rendering it inoperable. The challenge for countries wishing to achieve an energy transition focused on the development of renewable energies is to develop their resilience capabilities in order to secure their energy supply.

In 2009, France set up a national information systems security authority (ANSSI) to provide technical assistance to companies that find themselves in difficulty or victims of a cyberattack, thanks to the Governmental Center for Monitoring, Alert and Response to Cyberattacks (CERT-FR). While many countries have chosen to set up national cyber defense strategies, there is also cooperation at the international level, such as the NATO Center of Excellence for Cooperative Cyber Defense based in Tallinn, Estonia. The energy transition means being able to protect technical data from industrial espionage at all levels, both in laboratories and in companies. The race to control the 5G networks that are developing is an illustration of this principle, as can be seen, for example, with Finland's Nokia and China's Huawei vying for market share.

4.16. Coal

The main coal producers (China, USA, India, etc.) are also the largest consumers and generally local production satisfies demand. Therefore, the main issues involved in the supply of coal arise at a national level. Inland transport of coal is by road (via truck), rail or inland waterway barges.

The risks involved and the responses that can be made to any supply disruption are the same as for any other product transported under the same conditions. Coal is exported by sea. Increased coal demand and the problems that occurred in China, particularly in 2003 (several mines closed due to accidents), have resulted in a considerable increase in freight rates.

Recently (2021), China has had to shut down power plants and experienced massive blackouts due to the lack of coal, which it has had to import in ever-increasing quantities. Admittedly, China is on the way to transitioning to a lower-carbon energy mix with increasing use of gas and renewable energies, but carbon neutrality is not expected until around 2060.

4.17. Threats to energy supplies: the risk of physical failure of transport networks

Energy supplies are most vulnerable during transport.

4.17.1. *Ground transport infrastructure*

Pipelines are an easy target. In Colombia, the main oil fields, Cano Lemon and Cusiana, are inland. Rebel movements, such as the Revolutionary Armed Forces of Colombia (FARC) and more particularly the National Liberation Army (ELN; Guevarist movement), have often blown up pipelines. However, although sabotaging a pipeline is relatively easy, it can also be repaired quickly: teams from Ecopetrol, the national Columbian company, promptly repaired the damage and interruptions to supply were limited. The situation is normal after the peace agreement that was signed in 2016.

Since 2003, the situation in Iraq has been very similar: movements opposing the new regime regularly blow up the two main pipelines: Kirkuk–Ceyhan and Rumaila–Fao. Each of these attacks causes a reduction in exports for several days, although these pipelines are quickly repaired. Iraq is reported to have lost $12 billion as a result of more than 500 attacks that took place between 2003 and 2008, which would mean their average loss was over 0.5 Mb/d. However, the situation has improved.

The destruction or sabotage of one pipeline in a producing country does not endanger the hydrocarbon supplies to any consuming country. The problem would clearly be more serious if such an attack affected a hub[11] close to a center of consumption, for example, on Slovak territory, through which much of Eastern Europe's gas supplies are transported. Another example is the Saudi oil processing center at Ab Qaïq, in the middle of the country. This processing center is vital to Saudi oil production. It has been the target of several attacks, the consequences of which have been limited because the center is obviously highly protected. The last attack in September 2019 interrupted Saudi exports for a few hours.

The problems of supply security for electricity are quite different from those posed by the supply of hydrocarbons, and they relate to the condition of the national infrastructure rather than international trade.

Electricity demand varies considerably, both throughout the day and throughout the year. Demand at its peak is far greater than the average so high production capacity, most of which remains unused at other than peak times, must always be available. Most cases of power failure, for example in California, Northern USA, Italy, London, etc., are caused by a lack of investment.

Box 4.4. *The case of electricity*

4.17.2. *Strategic geographical channels (straits and canals)*

More than two-thirds of world crude oil production is transported by sea. Ships are most exposed to the risk of terrorist or criminal (piracy) attacks during their passage through straits or canals where they must significantly reduce their speed and mobility. We have already mentioned the problems of piracy in the Strait of Malacca or off the coast of Somalia, for example, which are in the process of being resolved (Figure 4.5).

Almost 90% of oil and gas exports from the Middle East pass through the Strait of Hormuz, representing 20% of global supplies. Its importance confers considerable

11 A depot used for reception, storage and dispatch of supplies.

strategic strength on Iran, which controls it de facto. The closure of the Strait of Hormuz would undoubtedly lead to a lasting disruption in hydrocarbon supplies. This would result in a considerable rise in the price of crude oil. This threat should not be overestimated, however, as Iranian exports pass through this strait.

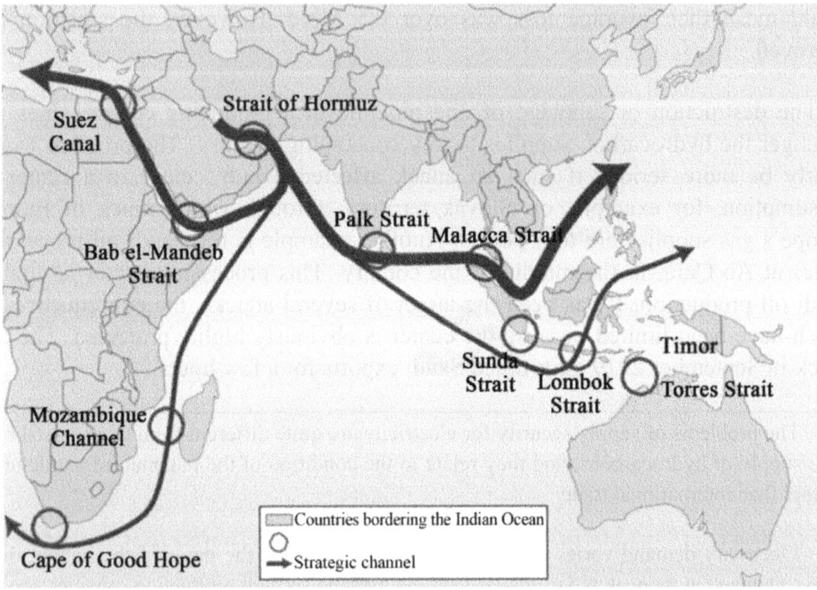

Figure 4.5. *Main strategic channels (source: Le Monde Diplomatique, Philippe Rakacewicz, October 1995). For a color version of this figure, see www.iste.co.uk/favennec/geopolitics1.zip*

Slightly more than 3 Mb/d Arabian/Persian Gulf crude oil pass thorough the Bab el-Mandeb Strait and the Suez Canal heading for Europe. For several years now, terrorist activity has grown along the coasts of Yemen, near the Bal el-Mandeb Strait (bombing of the French oil tanker Limburg in October 2002, attacks in Yemen and in the Horn of Africa, etc.). In response, the USA opened a military training camp with more than 3,000 soldiers in Djibouti, traditionally an exclusively French preserve. At the end of 2023, following the start of the war between Israel and Hamas, the Tehran-backed Houthi rebels, who control part of Yemen, launched numerous attacks on commercial vessels with alleged links to Israel. Several Western states have sent warships to try to put an end to these attacks, which threaten important flows of goods, including hydrocarbons from the Persian Gulf and Chinese products destined for Europe. However, in 2024, a large number of ships will be rerouted to the Cape of Good Hope, lengthening transport times.

Finally, the last of the bottlenecks is the Bosphorus and the Dardanelles Straits. The former is approximately 32 km (20 miles) long and 1.0–2.5 km (0.6–1.5 miles) wide, and bisects the city of Istanbul; the latter is 65 km (40 miles) long and 1.6–6.4 km (1.0–4.0 miles) wide. The terrorist threat appears to be minor, but the Turkish authorities are far more concerned about environmental risks. The Bosphorus is considered hazardous because of its rapid currents that make navigation difficult and, with continuing increases in the passage of oil and methane tankers via these two straits, the probabilities of an accident are growing[12]. Blockage of either of these straits would temporarily halt exports from Ukraine or Russia (cereals, hydrocarbons, etc.). In 1994, a collision between two Cypriot ships, one of which was a tanker, caused the spillage of 20,000 tons of crude oil which resulted in the closure of the strait for a week.

The Suez Canal has been closed on two occasions. The first, of short duration, was in 1956 following Nasser's nationalization of the canal company. Shortly after the nationalization, joint action by British and French troops, supported by the advance of Israeli troops, allowed the two European countries to take back control of the canal. But the United States, not wanting a conflict with the USSR (Nasser's protecting power), forced the British and French to withdraw. The canal re-opened shortly afterward.

On June 5, 1967 at 7:45 a.m., an Israeli air attack destroyed Egypt's air force. The Hebrew state wanted to prevent an attack by Arab countries, which it saw as imminent. In reprisal, Egypt decided to close the Suez Canal.. It did not re-open until 1975. Oil-consuming countries took measures to counter the situation, and the advent of supertankers carrying large quantities of crude oil reduced the costs of the longer voyage via the southern tip of Africa.

In 1974, an oil pipeline, Sumed, was built parallel to the canal so that some tankers could avoid the voyage around Africa.

Today, Egypt is further dredging to enable the largest tankers to use the Suez Canal.

Box 4.5. *Closing of the Suez Canal*

The Turkish Government therefore wants measures to be taken in order to limit these risks as far as possible, including a reduction in traffic and the largest ships being required to use a pilot when passing through the straits.

12 Every year, nearly 50,000 ships cross through this zone with more than 100 million tons of oil and other hazardous materials.

4.17.3. *Growing competition in the Arctic*

The Arctic could be home to a significant proportion of the world's oil and gas reserves and is the object of much interest.

In 2021, the Russian Federation took over the chairmanship of the Arctic Council. It wanted to reassert its power along its northern borders, in order to secure transport lines. In 2007, it sent bombers to patrol near NATO's borders and has reopened 14 air bases since 2014 (Mered 2019).

This area holds great economic promise for the development of energy resources. Russia is already exploiting LNG in the Russian Arctic. Yamal LNG started operations by 2017 and can produce 16 million tons of LNG every year. Additional large export projects (Artic 1, 2 3…) are underway but Western sanctions limit the access of Russian companies to the necessary technology.

China is investing more and more in Yamal, in cooperation with Russia. It wants to secure its access to northern routes, which are safer than the Straits of Malacca or Hormuz. Due to global warming, the icy Arctic Ocean is frozen for a shorter period each year, opening up new trade routes that are 40% faster than through the Suez Canal. Millions of tons of goods now transit the Polar Silk Roads along northern Siberia.

However, exploitation of the Arctic raises other issues: it could lead to massive melting of permafrost and damage to industrial and urban structures. If all projects go ahead, the cost of potential damage is estimated at hundreds of billions of euros by 2050.

4.18. Securing hydrocarbon supplies militarily

Faced with all types of threats (terrorism, rebellion, etc.) at both the international and national levels, it would seem that military force is necessary to ensure the world's continued hydrocarbon supplies. The USA, thanks to its large military capacity, is virtually alone in taking on the task of securing supplies.

4.18.1. *The American military monopoly*

Today, only the United States has the military power to send troops and equipment several thousands of miles from its own territory to operate in several theaters of action simultaneously.

The USA has signed a number of bilateral agreements with other countries, in all corners of the globe, giving them the right to set up military bases. They are present in Kuwait (around 20,000 troops) and Qatar (around 8,000 troops). Bahrain, Oman and the United Arab Emirates are also home to smaller numbers of American troops. US forces, previously numbering some 7,000, were withdrawn from Saudi Arabia in 2003 because it was no longer necessary to enforce the no-fly zone over Iraq. All of this is in addition to the 150,000 soldiers deployed in Iraq in 2003.

Another region that is crucially strategic for the USA is that stretching from the Caspian Sea to the Dardanelles Straits. To secure hydrocarbon exports from the Caspian Sea, and from the Russian port of Novorossiysk, the USA has signed agreements with several Black Sea coastal countries (Bulgaria, Georgia and Romania) to set up bases or provide military training. The USA has also had a military base in Turkey (Incirlik) for several years.

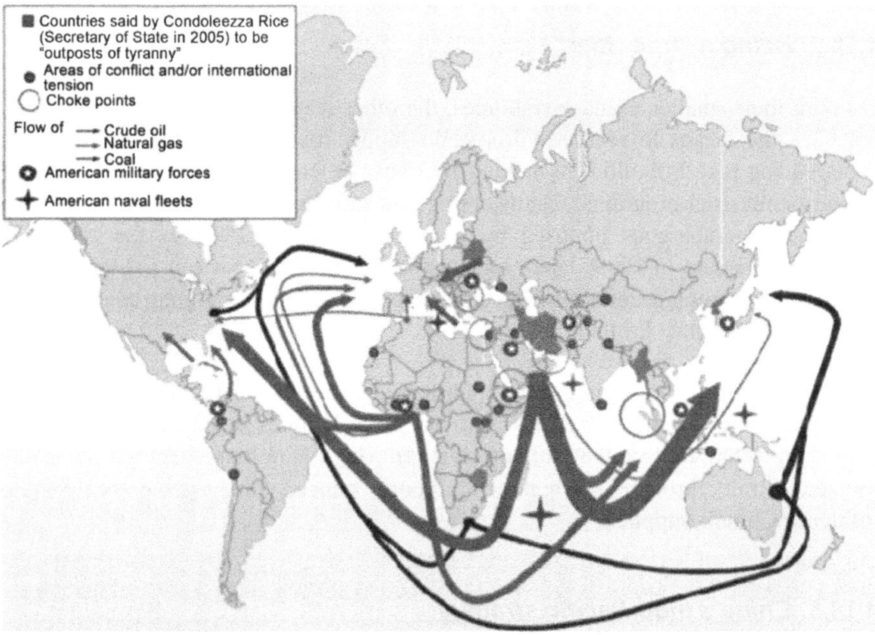

Figure 4.6. *The military security of the world's fossil fuel supply. For a color version of this figure, see www.iste.co.uk/favennec/geopolitics1.zip*

The US navy is present on all oceans and seas throughout the world and can be used to secure the marine transport of hydrocarbons, particularly in coastal regions and in the strategic channels where it is most vulnerable. Therefore, the 6th American fleet is present in the Eastern Mediterranean (close to the Black Sea, the

Bosporus and the Dardanelles Straits and the Suez Canal) and the 5th fleet in the Arabian/Persian Gulf with its command center in Bahrain and the Diego Garcia base in the Indian Ocean.

Finally, the USA has opened a naval base in the Philippines to secure the Malacca Strait against piracy and the growth of radical Islamist groups (Abu Sayyaf, GAM, Jemaah Islamiyah, etc.) in this region.

The USA also intervenes indirectly. The Islamic Republic of Iran advocates a division of the Caspian Sea that is rejected by the other littoral nations, and it therefore disputes Azerbaijan's ownership of several oil fields. Iranian naval forces have therefore launched sorties to intimidate Azeri ships and foreign oil companies working in the sector. As a result, the United States decided to finance Azeri naval forces (Figure 4.6).

4.18.2. *Being a "free rider"*

With their smaller military resources, the other major oil-consuming nations do not have the means to secure hydrocarbon supply routes. The European Union is experiencing real difficulties in making European defense viable; despite interesting military–industrial programs, results are not yet satisfactory. China is still restricted by weapons embargoes imposed by the EU and the USA after the events in Tiananmen Square in 1989. Japan remains dependent on American military forces. The other consuming countries, developing countries and emerging countries can only provide security for their own territory.

This situation is worrying. Even traditional European spheres of influence have been taken over by the Americans (military base facilities in former French areas, for example Djibouti or the Gulf of Guinea). The US military deployment in the Malacca Strait, through which no US imports transit, could enable the USA to influence China's supplies.

4.18.3. *China's Indo-Pacific strategy*

China is aware of its vulnerability in terms of oil and gas supplies. China is trying to protect its hydrocarbons imports from the Middle East by controlling maritime routes, particularly in the South China Sea. China is also claiming sovereignty over the Paracels Islands in the South China Sea, as a means of achieving this (and perhaps tapping into potential oil resources). Finally, good relations between the Chinese government and Myanmar's military junta give China a military base at the entrance to the Malacca Strait.

Since the early 2000s, China has been implementing a "string of pearls" strategy in the Indo-Pacific region (see chapter on China in Volume 2, Chapter 6). They have set up Chinese military bases and ports to control the Indian and Pacific oceans, where a large proportion of China's energy imports transit. China is trying to compete with the American presence in the region. In addition, India has gradually become one of China's rival powers and has been developing its maritime power since the early 2000s. However, the strategies adopted by the various players in the region are very diverse: while the United States is relatively aggressive on the subject, many Asian countries prefer to defuse tensions in the Indo-Pacific, as they often have relations with both China and the United States.

The military solution may appear to be the last resort for dealing with supply disruptions, but there is another way of managing a sudden drop in the supply of hydrocarbons, and oil in particular: stockpiling.

4.19. Strategic stocks

4.19.1. *The role of strategic stocks*

After World War I, several European countries established reserve stocks of petroleum products. These were intended first and foremost to meet the army's fuel requirements in the case of an emergency. Now stocks are no longer set up just to ensure military supplies, but rather for protection against a sudden and sustained drop in supplies from exporting countries.

With its strategic petroleum reserve (SPR), the United States has the largest reserves in the world. The SPR's storage capacity is 714 million barrels, and at the end of 2023, the inventory was 350 million barrels, compared with 620 million barrels in September 2021. This drop was caused by the war in Ukraine and the desire to put more crude oil on the market to cope with a reduction in Russian supplies (which was in fact very limited) and to drive prices down. Although strategic stocks must be sufficient to make up for a shortage of crude oil imports for a certain period (the length of which varies), they cannot, however, compensate for a total disruption of supplies.

Nevertheless, holding these stocks is a crucial and strategic part of the defense policy of the countries that do so. No major oil importer can neglect the need to hold strategic reserves. China, the world's second-largest oil consumer, has significant storage capacity similar to that of Western countries. These stocks are held at four sites: Zenhai, Daishan, Huangdao and Xingang.

Japan is reported to have a capacity of around 600 million barrels.

There are three principal systems for holding strategic stocks:

– First, there are private stocks, held by private companies that are each responsible for managing their obligation, using either their own reserves or by "leasing" reserves under a contract with other operators.

– Next, there are national stocks for which the government is entirely responsible. This is the system used in the USA and Japan.

– Finally, there are agency stocks, i.e. stocks managed by either a public or a private body, with operators paying the agent a fee in proportion to the obligation that the agent meets for them.

These three systems are not incompatible, and some countries use all of them.

4.19.2. *International Energy Agency and European Union compulsory stock obligations*

Following the establishment of the International Energy Agency, the Agency prepared an international energy program including rules for minimum levels of strategic stocks .

Each member state is required to hold oil reserves equivalent to 90 days (originally it was 60 days) of net oil imports. In addition, each participating country must "at all times have ready a program of contingent oil demand restraint measures enabling it to reduce its rate of final consumption" (Article 5, Chapter II).

When a group of member states suffers or is threatened with a reduction in oil supplies equal to 7% of final consumption over the last four quarters for which data are available, each country must reduce its demand by 7% and oil taken from the reserves is allocated among the countries affected.

When the reduction in supplies amounts to 12% of final consumption, the countries are only required to reduce their consumption by 10%.

IEA stocks amount to roughly 4 billion barrels, two-thirds of which are held by the oil industry. These stocks are made up of 58% crude oil and 42% petroleum products.

4.19.3. *European Union compulsory stock obligation*

European strategic stocks were first established in 1968, prior to the first oil shock. Three directives govern the regulation of oil reserves.

These require member states to maintain stocks equivalent to 90 days (65 days until 1972) of average internal consumption during the previous calendar year for each category of petroleum products (automotive gasoline, diesel fuel, kerosene, jet fuel, etc.). Two comments are relevant in comparing this to the IEA system discussed above: first, the 90 days obligation relates to consumption, not just imports, and second, the directives clearly specify that the requirement applies to crude oil as well as several petroleum products – intermediate or end-products – designated by name.

The directives also specify various ways in which these stocks may be held, for example by an agency, and that a country may, through intergovernmental contracts, set up stocks on behalf of companies, organizations or agencies located in another member state. Such stocks are entirely at the disposition of the government that owns them and the "host" country cannot prevent that government from transferring all or any part of them.

Finally, regarding the use of these stocks, the European directives are less precise than those of the IEA and simply stipulate that if there is a supply problem, the Commission will organize a meeting. Member states do not have the right to draw down their stocks without holding such a meeting. In addition, the EU has recently proposed that reserve levels be increased to 120 days consumption. This is still being debated but it does not have the support of private oil companies.

4.19.4. *France's strategic stocks*

As a member of both the EU and the IEA, France is subject to the strategic storage regulations of both organizations: 90 days of internal consumption and 90 days of imports. In fact, France's strategic reserves represent 95 days of internal consumption.

These requirements were introduced by a law of December 31, 1992, which applies to "registered operators", i.e. companies selling petroleum products. The law requires them to hold stocks equivalent to a quarter of the products they sold in the previous year. Operators can meet this obligation in several ways. They can either physically store the products or pay a fee to the Professional Committee for Strategic Petroleum Stocks (Comité professionnel des stocks stratégiques pétroliers (CPSSP)). The CPSSP itself has stocks held by the Société anonyme de gestion des stocks de sécurité (SAGESS). SAGESS was created in 1988, and its shareholders are registered oil operators. Its role is to purchase and hold stocks of crude oil and petroleum products on behalf of the CPSSP.

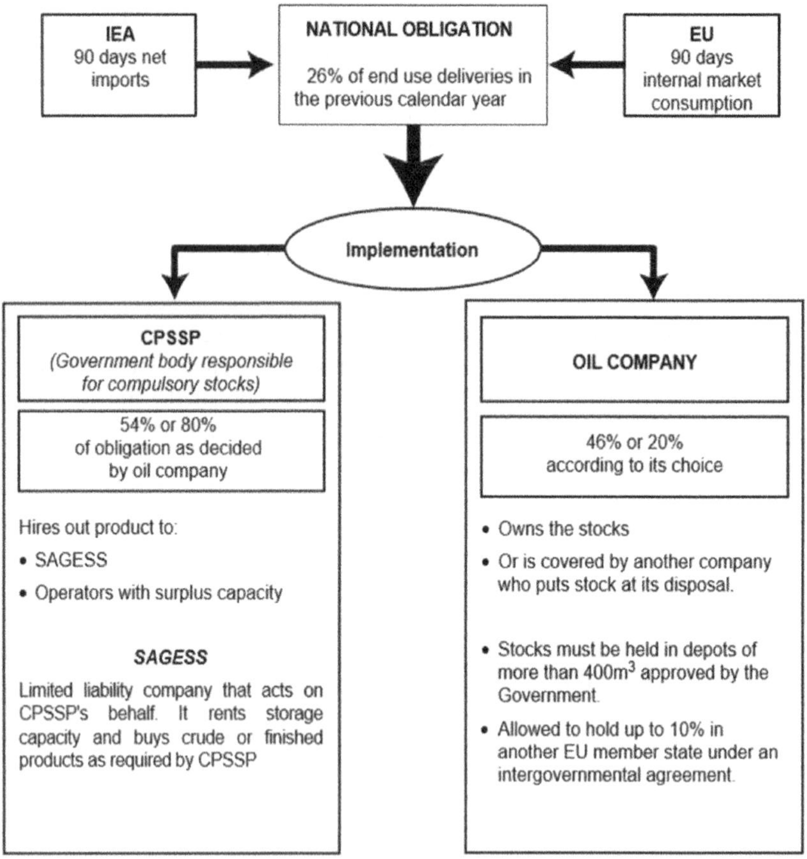

CPSSP: *Comité professionnel des stockages stratégiques pétroliers*

SAGESS: *Société anonyme de gestion des stocks pétroliers*

Figure 4.7. *Strategic stocks in France*

These stocks are constantly monitored by the government. Each operator is required to provide the head of the Department of Energy and Mineral Resources (Direction des Ressources Energétiques et Minérales (DIREM)) with a monthly report detailing the level of stocks held. Any operator failing to meet these obligations is liable to a fine.

4.19.5. *The special case of the American Strategic Petroleum Reserve (SPR)*

During the 1970s, following the first oil shock, President Gerald Ford signed the *Energy Policy and Conservation Act* (December 22, 1975) and authorized the creation of the SPR already described above. Its storage capacity (714 million barrels as already stated) consists of artificial caverns in salt domes along the coast of the Gulf of Mexico. It is the world's largest oil reserve, and it holds a significant part of American strategic stocks.

The SPR has a major role in American policy. Its strength comes from the fact that drawdowns from this stock are rare. It was established to deal with a supply disruption, or the threat of disruption, which is basically the same thing, but it can also be used to lower prices. The American President announced the recourse to SPR oil in 1991 during the first Gulf War to contend with the disappearance of Iraqi and Kuwaiti production from the market. In September 2005, Hurricane Katrina destroyed a significant portion of production capacity in the Gulf of Mexico. The increase in crude oil prices was limited by the announcement of the – and the actual – sale of oil withdrawn from this reserve. In November 2001, the withdrawal of 50 million barrels of stocks was announced to bring down the price of oil after the attacks on the World Trade Center. Similar measures were taken at the same time in most OECD countries.

The value of the SPR is limited in two important ways:

– First, the concentration of storage on the coast of the Gulf of Mexico could pose a problem should massive recourse to it be necessary in an emergency.

– Second, the SPR only contains crude oil. However, when there is a serious crisis what matters immediately is the rapid shortage of petroleum products that occurs.

The hurricanes of September 2005 destroyed both oil production capacity and refineries in the Gulf of Mexico. Although the announcement of recourse to SPR stocks strongly limited the increase in crude oil prices, the lack of product stocks meant that nothing could be done to limit the very strong increase in the price of products, particularly the spike in the price of gasoline, which increased by 30% in a few days.

Strategic stocks can therefore provide a solution to the risks of disruption in energy supplies. However, this solution only works for a crisis of limited duration.

4.20. The energy transition and its strategic challenges

There are strategic issues specific to the energy transition.

Several aspects of the transition may prove crucial for governments. These include the use of critical or rare materials or the use of specific technologies subject to intellectual property rules.

The energy transition has different implications in different countries. In emerging countries, it is most often a question of meeting rising energy needs and promoting economic growth while if possible limiting CO_2 emissions. In the United States, for example, it means freeing itself from the Middle East's need for hydrocarbons, as we have seen with the development of shale gas exploitation. China, in contrast, has developed its use of coal as an energy source and is promoting innovation in the solar and photovoltaic sectors. The European Union, for its part, is promoting an efficient energy mix rich in renewable energies.

4.20.1. *Rare and critical materials*

The energy transition calls for the proper management of critical and rare materials, which are essential to the exploitation of renewable energies such as wind power. These critical materials are also essential for the defense industry and low-carbon technologies.

Criticality is defined as the sum of risks arising from the production, use and recycling of raw materials. These risks can be of various kinds and are intrinsically linked to the interests of the states concerned, their geographical, commercial and political situation and their technological development. For example, the European Union considers lithium to be a critical material, while China does not, and NATO has drawn up a plan to reduce its dependence on China in this area. If the transition is to promote greater energy independence for states from hydrocarbon-producing countries, for instance, then it is essential not to fall back into energy mixes that would accentuate dependence in terms of technology or resources.

Rare materials are a sub-category of the so-called critical materials. They exist only in small quantities, which makes their exploitation complicated and costly. For example, lithium production requires a lot of water, and production is concentrated in a small number of countries, such as Australia, Chile and China (the largest reserves of lithium are in South America). Over the last 10 years, the market for rare earths has varied between 120,000 and 160,000 tons. For example, a wind turbine can contain up to 180 kilograms of elements whose manufacture requires the use of rare earths. The difficulty of recycling this type of material must be emphasized. For instance, tantalum and germanium, often used in high-tech appliances, are recycled at a rate of less than 1%.

There are geopolitical, economic and environmental risks. It is therefore essential to find solutions for the proper management of rare and critical materials. Finland, for example, is developing a lithium extraction project at Kleber, which should enable it to position itself as a producer within the European Union. However, China, which produces over 85% of rare earths, is pursuing a low-price policy that makes it difficult for new competitors to enter this market.

4.20.2. *Technology*

The energy transition relies above all on the development of low-carbon technologies, which will enable a new model of energy system to be devised. The development of new technologies goes through several phases: innovation, which provides a solution to a given problem, and then the commercialization of the proposed new technology. Innovation carries with it the promise of commercial benefits. However, new risks must also be taken into account.

Mastering these technologies can lead to dependency for less developed countries in this field. While Europe, the United States and Japan remain the innovation leaders in low-carbon technologies, there is growing rivalry between countries in this field. According to the International Renewable Energy Agency (IRENA), China holds 29% of patents filed in the renewable energy sector and has over 90% of the world's rare-earth mining capacity. It is seeking to establish itself as a benchmark power in renewable energy storage and production technologies and accounts for 66% of global battery production.

In the same vein, many Asian countries, notably China and South Korea, are asserting themselves as leaders in renewable energies and anticipating the future importance of intellectual property rights over these technologies. For example, the State Grid Corporation of China, 100% owned by the Chinese state, has been buying up assets all over the world.

Similarly, several German companies have been taken over by foreign investors. One example is WindMW GmbH, a wind power company acquired in 2016 by the Chinese company CTG (Chinese Three Gorges, which operates the Three Gorges Dam). Many countries, such as the USA in 2018, have tightened their legislation on foreign investment in anticipation of a growing number of such takeovers.

4.21. Conclusion

Supply security is a political, economic, strategic and military issue. There are two different approaches to the problem. The first is that of the USA, which gives priority to supply and, as a result, to the stability of producing areas, particularly the Middle East. The main objective is to ensure that there are plenty of supplies for the American market, with environmental issues being given second place. The USA is sufficiently powerful to resist calls from the international community, which is more sensitive to pollution problems.

The European Union's approach goes in a different direction; it is based on the need to reduce energy demand. The advantage of this policy is that it complements policies that respond to environmental risks. However, it seems that the European Union has abandoned the task of ensuring the physical security of supplies to the USA.

Above all, the energy transition brings with it new security challenges that governments will have to learn to manage.

References

Agence Internationale de l'Énergie (2020). World Energy Outlook. Report, Agence Internationale de l'Énergie.

Barré, B. and Mérenne-Schoumaker, B. (2015). *Atlas des énergies mondiales*. Autrement, Paris.

Bauquis, P.-R. and Bauquis, E. (2004). *Pétrole et gaz naturel*. Éditions Hirlé, Paris.

Blain, C. and Jancovici, J.-M. (2021). *Le monde sans fin*. Dargaud, Paris.

Bonnet, C. (2019). Négociations climatiques : les enjeux du transfert de technologie. *Revue internationale et stratégique*, 113(1), 187–197.

Boy de la Tour, X. (2004). *Le pétrole, au-delà du mythe*. Technip, Paris.

Bret-Rouzaut, N. and Favennec, J.-P. (eds) (2011). *Oil and Gas Exploration and Production*. Technip, Paris.

Chaliand, G. and Jafalian, A. (2005). *La dépendance pétrolière*. Universalis, Boulogne.

Charlez, P. (2017). *Croissance, energie, climat*. De Boek Supérieur, Louvain.

Charlez, P. (2021). *L'utopie de la croissance verte*. Jean-Marie Laffont, Paris.

Chevalier, J.-M. (2004). *Les grandes batailles de l'énergie*. Folio, Paris.

Darmois, G. and Favennec, J.-P. (2012). *Les marchés de l'énergie*. Technip, Paris.

Eyl-Mazzega, M.-A. and Mathieu, C. (2020). Transition énergétique : Chine, États-Unis et Union européenne. Les technologies bas carbones à l'épreuve de la géopolitique. *Futuribles*, 436(3), 55–66.

Favennec, J.-P. (2009). *Géopolitique de l'énergie*. Technip, Paris.

Favennec, J.-P. and Mathieu, Y. (2016). *Atlas mondial des énergies*. Autrement, Paris.

Fraukel, P. and Cass, F. (1946). *Essentials of Petroleum*. Routledge, London.

Furfari, S. (2012). *Politique et géopolitique de l'énergie*. Technip, Paris.

Ganguly, S. (2011). Overview of various modes of transportation of oil and gas. In *Workshop on 'Transportation of OIL & GAS through Pipelines'*. Petroleum Federation of India, Patna, 15–18 June [Online]. Available at: http://petrofed.winwinhosting.net/upload/15-18June11/1/ppt.

Giraud, A. and Boy de la Tour, X. (1987). *Géopolitique du pétrole et du gaz*. Technip, Paris.

Hansen J.-P. and Percebois, J. (2017). *Transition(s) électrique(s)*. Odile Jacob, Paris.

Harel, X. (2006). *Afrique, pillage à huis clos*. Fayard, Paris.

Jancovici, J.-M. (2011). *Transition énergétique pour tous*. Odile Jacob, Paris.

Jancovici, J.-M. (2015). *Dormez tranquille jusqu'en 2100*. Odile Jacob, Paris.

Jancovici, J.-M. and Grandjean, A. (2011). *Le Plein, s'il vous plait*. Le Seuil, Paris.

Laroche, J.-C. (2006). *Le défi énergétique*. Éditions de Paris, Paris.

Laurent, É. (2006). *La face cachée du pétrole*. Plon, Paris.

de Lestrange, C., Paillard, C.-A., Zelenko, P. (2005). *Géopolitique du pétrole*. Technip, Paris.

Mabro, R. and Horsnell, P. (1994). *Oil Markets and Prices*. Oxford University Press, Oxford.

Mered, M. (2019). *The Arctic: Critical Metals, Hydrogen and Wind Power for the Energy Transition*. Édito Energie, Ifri.

Mitchell, J. (2000). *The New Geopolitics of Energy*. The Royal Institute of International Affairs, London.

Mitchell, J. (2001). *The New Economy of Oil*. Earthscan, London.

Noreng, O. (2006). *Crude Power Politics and the Oil Market*. I.B. Tauris, London.

Pauwels, J.-P. (1997). *Géopolitique de l'approvisionnement énergétique de l'Union Européenne au XXI*[e] *siècle*. Bruylant, Brussels.

Pitron, G. (2018). *La guerre des métaux rares*. Les Liens qui Libèrent, Paris.

Pitron, G. (2021). *La guerre des métaux rares*. Les Liens qui Libèrent, Paris.

Sadek, B., Pauwels, J.-P, Locatelli, C., Swartenbroekx, C. (2006). *Le défi pétrolier*. Vuibert, Paris.

Sealan, J. (2019). La Chine et les terres rares. Son rôle critique dans la nouvelle économie. Notes de l'Ifri.

Tellenne, C. (2021). *Géopolitique des énergies*. La Découverte, Paris.

Terzian, P. (1983). *L'étonnante histoire de l'OPEP*. Les Éditions Jeunes Afrique, Paris.

Wingert, J.-L. (2005). *La vie après le pétrole*. Autrement, Paris.

Yergin, D. (1991). *Les hommes du pétrole*. Plon, Paris.

Yergin, D. (2011). *The Quest*. Penguin Books, London.

Websites

Department of Energy, Energy Information Administration: https://www.eia.gov/.

International Energy Agency (IEA): https://www.iea.org/.

Organization of the Petroleum Exporting Countries (OPEC): https://www.opec.org/opec_web/en/.

Planète énergie: www.planete-energies.com.

United Nations Conference on Trade and Development (UNCTAD): https://unctad.org.

Index

I, J

K, L

M, N

O, P

Q, R

Other titles from

ISTE

in

Energy

2024

BENALLOU Abdelhanine
Heat Exchangers: Design and Sizing Algorithms
(Energy Engineering Set – Volume 6)

MORY Mathieu
Mechanical Energy Conversion: Exercises for Scaling Renewable Energy Systems

2023

ALVAREZ-HERAULT Marie-Cécile, GOUIN Victor, CHARDIN-SEGUI Trinidad, MALOT Alain, COIGNARD Jonathan, RAISON Bertrand, COULET Jérôme
Distribution System Planning: Evolution of Methodologies and Digital Tools for Energy Transition

BEN KHADER BOUZID Monia, CHAMPENOIS Gérard
Electrical and Mechanical Fault Diagnosis in Wind Energy Conversion Systems

JANNOT Yves, MOYNE Christian, DEGIOVANNI Alain
Heat Transfer 1: Conduction and Convection
Heat Transfer 2: Radiation and Exchangers

ROBYNS Benoît, LENGLET Claude, BARRY Hervé, BOZZO-REY Malik
Smart Users for Energy and Societal Transition

2022

ABOUELATTA Mohamed, SHAKER Ahmed, GONTRAND Christian
Smart Power Integration

BOUTAUD Benoit
Energy Autonomy: From the Notion to the Concepts

GONTRAND Christian
Electromagnetism: Links to Special Relativity

2021

ROBYNS Benoît, DAVIGNY Arnaud, FRANÇOIS Bruno, HENNETON Antoine, SPROOTEN Jonathan
Electricity Production from Renewable Energies (2nd edition)

2020

BOISGIBAULT Louis, AL KABBANI Fahad
Energy Transition in Metropolises, Rural Areas and Deserts

SOUALHI Abdenour, RAZIK Hubert
Electrical Systems 1: From Diagnosis to Prognosis
Electrical Systems 2: From Diagnosis to Prognosis

2019

BENALLOU Abdelhanine
Energy Transfers by Convection
(Energy Engineering Set – Volume 3)
Energy Transfers by Radiation
(Energy Engineering Set – Volume 4)
Mass Transfers and Physical Data Estimation
(Energy Engineering Set – Volume 5)

LACHAL Bernard
Energy Transition

2018

BENALLOU Abdelhanine
Energy and Mass Transfers: Balance Sheet Approach and Basic Concepts (Energy Engineering Set – Volume 1)
Energy Transfers by Conduction (Energy Engineering Set – Volume 2)

JEMEÏ Samir
Hybridization, Diagnostic and Prognostic of Proton Exchange Membrane Fuel Cells: Durability and Reliability

RUFFINE Livio, BROSETA Daniel, DESMEDT Arnaud
Gas Hydrates 2: Geoscience Issues and Potential Industrial Applications

VIALLET Virginie, FLEUTOT Benoit
Inorganic Massive Batteries (Energy Storage – Batteries and Supercapacitors Set – Volume 4)

2017

BROSETA Daniel, RUFFINE Livio, DESMEDT Arnaud
Gas Hydrates 1: Fundamentals, Characterization and Modeling

LA SCALA Massimo
From Smart Grids to Smart Cities: New Challenges in Optimizing Energy Grids (Advanced Smart Grids Set – Volume 2)

MOLINA Géraldine, MUSY Marjorie, LEFRANC Margot
Building Professionals Facing the Energy Efficiency Challenge

SIMON Patrice, BROUSSE Thierry, FAVIER Frédéric
Supercapacitors Based on Carbon or Pseudocapacitive Materials (Energy Storage – Batteries and Supercapacitors Set – Volume 3)

2016

ALLARD Bruno
Power Systems-on-Chip: Practical Aspects of Design

ANDRÉ Michel, SAMARAS Zissis
Energy and Environment
(Research for Innovative Transports Set – Volume 1)

DUFOUR Anthony
Thermochemical Conversion of Biomass for the Production of Energy and Chemicals

SOUSTELLE Michel
Phase Transformations
(Chemical Thermodynamics Set – Volume 5)
Thermodynamics of Surfaces and Capillary Systems
(Chemical Thermodynamics Set – Volume 7)

2015

MONCONDUIT Laure, CROGUENNEC Laurence, DEDRYVÈRE Rémi
Electrodes for Li-ion Batteries: Materials, Mechanisms and Performance
(Energy Storage – Batteries and Supercapacitors Set – Volume 2)

ROBYNS Benoît, FRANÇOIS Bruno, DELILLE Gauthier, SAUDEMONT Christophe
Energy Storage in Electric Power Grids

ROSSI Carole
Al-based Energetic Nanomaterials: Design, Manufacturing, Properties and Applications
(Nanotechnologies for Energy Recovery Set – Volume 2)

TARASCON Jean-Marie, SIMON Patrice
Electrochemical Energy Storage
(Energy Storage – Batteries and Supercapacitors Set – Volume 1)

SOUSTELLE Michel
Phases Modeling Tools: Application to Gases
(Chemical Thermodynamics Set – Volume 1)
Modeling of Liquid Phases
(Chemical Thermodynamics Set – Volume 2)
Thermodynamic Modeling of Solid Phases
(Chemical Thermodynamics Set – Volume 3)
Chemical Equilibria
(Chemical Thermodynamics Set – Volume 4)
Ionic and Electrochemical Equilibria
(Chemical Thermodynamics Set – Volume 6)

2014

DE LARMINAT Philippe
Climate Change: Identification and Projections

2012

BECKERS Benoit
Solar Energy at Urban Scale

FOULADGER Javad
Electrothermics

2011

GAO Fei, BLUNIER Benjamin, MIRAOUI Abdellatif
Proton Exchange Membrane Fuel Cell Modeling

MONMASSON Eric
Power Electronic Converters: PWM Strategies and Current Control Techniques

MULTON Bernard
Marine Renewable Energy Handbook

RAZIK Hubert
Handbook of Asynchronous Machine with Variable Speed

2010

BRUNET Yves
Energy Storage

JUFER Marcel
Electric Drives: Design Methodology

2009

SABONNADIÈRE Jean-Claude
Low Emission Power Generation Technologies and Energy Management
Renewable Energy Technologies

2008

MEUNIER Gérard
The Finite Element Method for Electromagnetic Modeling

Printed and bound by CPI Group (UK) Ltd, Croydon, CR0 4YY
28/07/2026
14931341-0001